.

Symposium on Chinese Historical Geography

中国历史地理论集

侯仁之 著

外语教学与研究出版社
FOREIGN LANGUAGE TEACHING AND RESEARCH PRESS
北京 BEIJING

图书在版编目 (CIP) 数据

中国历史地理论集：英汉对照 ／ 侯仁之著. — 北京：外语教学与研究出版社，2015.5
(2022.4 重印)

ISBN 978-7-5135-6033-7

I. ①中… II. ①侯… III. ①历史地理－中国－文集－英、汉 IV. ①K928.6-53

中国版本图书馆 CIP 数据核字 (2015) 第 108482 号

地图审图号：GS (2013) 433

出 版 人 王 芳
系列策划 吴 浩
责任编辑 易 璐 蒲 瑶
装帧设计 视觉共振设计工作室
出版发行 外语教学与研究出版社
社 址 北京市西三环北路 19 号（100089）
网 址 http://www.fltrp.com
印 刷 中农印务有限公司
开 本 650×980 1/16
印 张 20.5
版 次 2015 年 6 月第 1 版 2022 年 4 月第 4 次印刷
书 号 ISBN 978-7-5135-6033-7
定 价 49.00 元

购书咨询：（010）88819926 电子邮箱：club@fltrp.com
外研书店：https://waiyants.tmall.com
凡印刷、装订质量问题，请联系我社印制部
联系电话：（010）61207896 电子邮箱：zhijian@fltrp.com
凡侵权、盗版书籍线索，请联系我社法律事务部
举报电话：（010）88817519 电子邮箱：banquan@fltrp.com
物料号：260330001

记载人类文明
沟通世界文化
www.fltrp.com

"博雅双语名家名作"出版说明

　　1840 年鸦片战争以降，在深重的民族危机面前，中华民族精英"放眼看世界"，向世界寻求古老中国走向现代、走向世界的灵丹妙药，涌现出一大批中国主题的经典著述。我们今天阅读这些中文著述的时候，仍然深为字里行间所蕴藏的缜密的考据、深刻的学理、世界的视野和济世的情怀所感动，但往往会忽略：这些著述最初是用英文写就，我们耳熟能详的中文文本是原初英文文本的译本，这些英文作品在海外学术界和文化界同样享有崇高的声誉。

　　比如，林语堂的 *My Country and My People*（《吾国与吾民》）以幽默风趣的笔调和睿智流畅的语言，将中国人的道德精神、生活情趣和中国社会文化的方方面面娓娓道来，在美国引起巨大反响——林语堂也以其中国主题系列作品赢得世界文坛的尊重，并获得诺贝尔文学奖的提名。再比如，梁思成在抗战的烽火中写就的英文版《图像中国建筑史》文稿（*A Pictorial History of Chinese Architecture*），经其挚友费慰梅女士（Wilma C. Fairbank）等人多年的奔走和努力，于 1984 年由麻省理工学院出版社（MIT Press）出版，并获得美国出版联合会颁发的"专业暨学术书籍金奖"。又比如，1939 年，费孝通在伦敦政治经济学院的博士论文以 *Peasant Life in China—A Field Study of Country Life in the Yangtze Valley* 为名在英国劳特利奇书局（Routledge）出版，后以《江村经济》作为中译本书名——《江村经济》使得靠桑蚕为生的"开弦弓村"获得了世界性的声誉，成为国际社会学界研究中国农村的首选之地。

　　此外，一些中国主题的经典人文社科作品经海外汉学家和中国学者的如椽译笔，在英语世界也深受读者喜爱。比如，艾恺（Guy S. Alitto）将他1980 年用中文访问梁漱溟的《这个世界会好吗——梁漱溟晚年口述》一书译成英文（*Has Man a Future? —Dialogues with the Last Confucian*），备受海内外读者关注；

此类作品还有徐中约英译的梁启超著作《清代学术概论》（*Intellectual Trends in the Ch'ing Period*）、狄百瑞（W. T. de Bary）英译的黄宗羲著作《明夷待访录》（*Waiting for the Dawn: A Plan for the Prince*），等等。

有鉴于此，外语教学与研究出版社推出"博雅双语名家名作"系列。

博雅，乃是该系列的出版立意。博雅教育（Liberal Education）早在古希腊时代就得以提倡，旨在培养具有广博知识和优雅气质的人，提高人文素质，培养健康人格，中国儒家六艺"礼、乐、射、御、书、数"亦有此功用。

双语，乃是该系列的出版形式。英汉双语对照的形式，既同时满足了英语学习者和汉语学习者通过阅读中国主题博雅读物提高英语和汉语能力的需求，又以中英双语思维、构架和写作的形式予后世学人以启迪——维特根斯坦有云："语言的边界，乃是世界的边界"，诚哉斯言。

名家，乃是该系列的作者群体。涵盖文学、史学、哲学、政治学、经济学、考古学、人类学、建筑学等领域，皆海内外名家一时之选。

名作，乃是该系列的入选标准。系列中的各部作品都是经过时间的积淀、市场的检验和读者的鉴别而呈现的经典，正如卡尔维诺对"经典"的定义：经典并非你正在读的书，而是你正在重读的书。

胡适在《新思潮的意义》（1919 年 12 月 1 日，《新青年》第 7 卷第 1 号）一文中提出了"研究问题、输入学理、整理国故、再造文明"的范式。秉着"记载人类文明、沟通世界文化"的出版理念，我们推出"博雅双语名家名作"系列，既希望能够在中国人创作的和以中国为主题的博雅英文文献领域"整理国故"，亦希望在和平发展、改革开放的新时代为"再造文明"、为"向世界说明中国"略尽绵薄之力。

外语教学与研究出版社

人文社科出版分社

❶ BEIJING: ITS CHARACTERISTICS OF HISTORICAL DEVELOPMENT AND TRANSFORMATION*

Introductory Remarks

Mr. President of the University of British Columbia,

First or all, allow me to express my deep gratitude to you, and to Mr. Chairman and to all members of the Committee of the Cecil H. and Ida Green Visiting Professorships. Thanks to all of you. It's my great honor to visit your beautiful country. And I feel especially happy to be here, for Canada is the fatherland of the great internationalist, Dr. Norman Bethune, of whom we Chinese people will always deeply cherish the memory. Just forty years ago, Dr. Norman Bethune gave his whole life to the cause of the liberation of the Chinese people. He made himself an important bridge linking China and Canada, which has become the symbol of the ever-lasting friendship between our two peoples. The cause to which he had dedicated his own life has turned out to be victorious in China; and the ideal for which he had worked hard has come to be brought to fruition on the land where he had fought bravely. A new China is forging ahead on a new long march towards her modernization, in spite of all the interferences and obstacles from both inside and outside. To attain our goal, we must learn from the West with modesty all their advanced things. Of course, in this respect, there is quite a lot for us to learn from your country. On the other hand, we must also conserve all the valuable and useful items of the cultural legacy left to us by our own ancestors. Thus in the course of forming our new socialist culture, learning from our own past has been found even more significant and complicated.

On this issue, I want to give a simple but concrete example. That is how we are to build up our people's capital in the new socialist era on the basis of the ancient city of Beijing.

Today I am going to deal with my first topic: "The City of Beijing—A

Historical Perspective".

Next time I'll come to my second topic: "The New Metropolitan Planning of the City of Beijing".

The City of Beijing—A Historical Perspective

The city of Beijing has been the capital of the People's Republic of China for only thirty years. But her history can be traced back to remote antiquity.

壹 北京城：历史发展的特点及其改造*

我深感荣幸有此机会来到你们美丽的国家，这是我国人民所难以忘怀的伟大的国际主义战士诺尔曼·白求恩的祖国。整整四十年前，白求恩大夫为中国人民的解放事业，献出了自己宝贵的生命。他是把中加两国连接在一起的重要桥梁，是中加两国人民友谊长存的象征。当初他为之献身的事业，在我国已经取得了伟大的胜利；他的理想，在他战斗过的土地上已经开花结实。一个新中国在不断排除来自内部和外部的一切干扰和破坏，正在一个新长征的道路上，向着现代化的目标努力前进。为此我们就需要向西方虚心学习一切先进的科学技术——在这方面，贵国就有许多值得我们很好学习的地方；另一方面，我们还需要从自己的历史文化遗产中吸取一切有价值的部分，而这一点，在我们建设社会主义新文化的过程中，乃是更为重要和更为复杂的一个问题。

对于这个问题，我希望能用一个显而易见的例子，作个简要的说明，这就是如何在古老的北京城的基础上，建设社会主义新时代的人民首都的问题。为了充分说明这个问题，概括地回顾一下北京城历史发展的过程及其特点，还是必要的。

北京城作为中华人民共和国的首都，刚刚度过了三十周年，然而它的历史却可以追溯到悠久的过去。

● **Part One: The Pioneers Who Opened Up Beijing Area**

As early as half a million years ago, in the place now called Zhou-koudian District, which is located in the southwestern suburbs of Beijing, there lived Chinese ape-men, who are now well-known as "Beijing Man".

In the caves inhabited by Beijing Man were excavated fossils of the skulls and bones of primitive ape-men. Simple tools used by the primitive ape-men and animal fossils were also found out there. These discoveries have provided very important scientific basis for the study of the origin and evolution of mankind. They are not only gems of China's ancient cultural legacy, but also rarities in the treasure-house of the world's culture.

Among these discoveries there are traces of fire used by Beijing Man. In that vast and wild world, Beijing Man succeeded in starting a fire and burning it into raging flames, and learned how to keep fire, thus proclaiming the coming of the age when man would be free from darkness and begin his early cultivation.

Beijing Man made its appearance at the initial stage of primitive society and lived a gregarious life then. With the simplest tools made of sticks and stone, they engaged themselves in fruit-gathering and hunting, so as to keep themselves alive and breed and bring up their offspring. For this purpose, they had to carry on arduous and tenacious struggles against nature.

Hundreds of thousands of years passed and primitive society evolved into its last stage. About 4,000 years ago, it happened that a few tiny dwelling places began to emerge on the plain near the present-day city of Beijing. This is one of the places where those practicing farming and hunting first settled down. They no longer moved round in search of fruit and wild animals as food. Having settled down there, they started to farm and raise livestock as their chief means of life. These earliest settlers were pioneers who opened up the Beijing Area.

With the rise of productivity, the quantitative increase of surplus products, and the division of labour, there appeared private ownership and a few exploiters who lived on other people's labour. Then primitive society began to disintegrate. At the same time slave society which was the first society with class oppression in human history gradually came into being.

The appearance of the earliest cities marked the formation of slave society.

一、北京地区开发的先驱

远在五十万年前，北京西南郊的周口店地区，已经有中国猿人生活在那里，这就是举世闻名的"北京人"。

在"北京人"住过的山麓洞穴里，发现了埋藏的丰富的原始人类的化石和他们使用过的工具以及动物化石，这些发现为研究人类起源和发展提供了非常重要的科学依据。这不但是中国远古文化遗产的瑰宝，也是世界文化宝库中的奇珍。

在这些发现中，还有"北京人"用火的遗迹。"北京人"在洪荒的世界里，燃起了熊熊的火焰，宣告了人类黎明时代的来临。

"北京人"处在原始社会的初期，过着群居的生活。他们用木棒和石头所制造的最原始的工具，从事采集和狩猎，以维持自己的生存和抚育后代，为此他们不得不和自然界进行着艰苦顽强的斗争。

经过了几十万年的漫长岁月，一直到原始社会末期，也就是大约四千年前，在北京近郊的平原上，开始出现了一些最初形成的小居民点，这是最早的农民和牧民集居的地方；他们已经从迁移不定的采集和狩猎生活过渡到以农牧为主的定居生活。这些最早的农民和牧民，正是开发北京地区的先驱。

随着生产力的发展和剩余产品的增加，以及社会劳动的分工，开始出现了私有制和极少数不劳而食的剥削者。原始社会开始解体，人类历史上第一个阶级压迫的社会即奴隶制社会逐渐形成。

最初城市的出现，正是奴隶社会形成的标志。

- **Part Two: Beijing's Primitive Settlement—Ji & the Geographical Features of the City of Ji**

Over 3,000 years ago, when China was still in her early days of slave society, Beijing's primitive settlement came into existence. At that time, China was basically dominated by the emperors of the Shang Dynasty. In that period, written symbols were invented to keep a record of events. The territory under the rule of the Shang Dynasty covered the area which is now the central part of the North China Plain. The great plain was made up of the alluvial soil left mainly by the Yellow River and some other smaller rivers. So it is also called the Yellow River Alluvial Plain. The central part of the great plain has generally been called "Zhongyuan" (which means "The Central Plain") in history. The Shang rulers founded their capital on the Central Plain, and the primitive settlement in Beijing was located far in a remote place to its north. But the Shang culture which was chiefly characterized by fine bronze wares and was broadly disseminated also found its way to this far-away place.

At the beginning of the eleventh century B.C., the rulers of the Zhou Dynasty which first started in the highland areas of the middle reaches of the Yellow River and later expanded towards the east, eventually conquered the Shang Dynasty on the great plain. As a result, a more developed country with slave-owning system was established. Beijing's primitive settlement was then becoming larger and larger at a high speed, which was to turn into a famous principality called "Ji". And "Ji" is the earliest name of Beijing found in historical records.

Records of the Grand Historian says that Zhouwuwang, the founder of the Zhou Dynasty, for the first time enfeoffed the duke Zhaogong with the "Ji" area, and this realm was known as "Yan Princedom". Soon the realm Yan became one of the most important states in the north under the rule of the Zhou Dynasty. This state continued for more than 800 years.

Here arises a question we must pay special attention to, that is, how the site of the city of Ji was selected. Or, let's put it in more exact words: what geographical features enabled the primitive settlement of Beijing to expand rapidly and remain prosperous for such a long time without declining.

This is a very interesting question, which has long attracted the attention of both Chinese and foreign geographers. There was scholarly guessing as to the reasons why this spot was chosen and all these can be ignored because we are now fortunate enough to have access to new source material unearthed recently.

Here I cannot but refer to a world-famous scholar who is well-known to the older generation of Canadian geographers. He is none other than Professor Griffith Taylor, who was engaged in teaching at Toronto University for some time.

二、北京的原始聚落：蓟及其城址的地理条件

还在三千多年以前，也就是中国奴隶社会的前期，北京的原始聚落已经存在。那时中国的主要统治者，是已经发明了文字记事的商朝。商朝统治的地区，集中在华北大平原的中部，历史上泛称"中原"。对于建都在"中原"的商朝统治者来说，北京的原始聚落还远在北方，可是以青铜器为重要标志的商朝文化，已经传布到这里。

公元前十一世纪初，兴起于黄河中游高原地区的周朝，向东发展，终于征服了大平原上的商朝，继而建立了一个更加发展了的奴隶制国家。北京的原始聚落也就在这时迅速成长起来，这就是日后闻名的蓟城。蓟也就是北京最早见于文字记载的名称。

史书称蓟原是周初在北方的重要封国之一，在蓟的西南方不远、傍近太行山东麓，还有另一个重要封国叫做燕。后来燕国吞并了蓟国，并迁都到蓟城。

在这里有一个需要特别注意的问题，那就是：蓟的城址是怎样选择的？或者更确切地说：究竟有哪些地理上的因素，使得蓟城的原始聚落得以发展起来，历久而不衰？

这是一个饶有趣味的问题，早已为中外地理学家所注意，而且到今天还仍然是一个值得深入探索的问题。

为了说明这一点，不能不提到加拿大地理学家所熟知的一位负有国际声望的学者，这就是曾在多伦多大学任教的澳洲人 G. 泰勒教授。

Before he came to Canada, Professor Taylor had taught at Chicago University for a period of time. And he was elected President of the Association of American Geographers in 1941. In his presidential address delivered to the Association of American Geographers, Professor Taylor talked about the selection of the earlier site of the city of Beijing, on the basis of the result of his personal on-the-spot investigations and research in Beijing. The main content of his presidential address made to the Association of American Geographers was included into a book written by him, which was entitled *Urban Geography*, one of his books dealing with the study of site, evolution, pattern and classification in villages, towns and cities. He devoted several pages to the discussion of the geography of Beijing and paid special attention to the study of the origin and evolution of the city.

On page 26 of the book (2nd ed., 5th imp., 1968), he says,

> Pekin offers a fair example of a large city which has developed under temperate conditions in a gigantic plain.... It is difficult to point to any environmental factor which has led to Pekin's dominance over most of the towns in the deltaic deposits of the Huang-ho.... One would have expected the chief northern city to have developed either in the centre of the plain, or near the main river, or possibly at a good harbour on the coast. Pekin fulfils none of these conditions.

In the following two pages, he raised his point of view:

> It seems clear that a considerable 'human' element is involved in the choice of the site of Pekin. In early days necromancers ascribed to the site a peculiarly fortunate character.... The magical and political factors (briefly referred to earlier) led to the city's birth, perhaps as far back as 723 B.C. At this time 'Chi' was the capital of the Yen kingdom, according to the Encyclopedia Sinica. Given this start, no other city seems to have arisen to compete with it... (pp. 27, 28)

Finally, he came to the conclusion:

It must be admitted that the choice of the site of Pekin is not due to any marked environmental factors.... We may perhaps grant that Pekin—situated in a vast region of *uniform* environment—is a good example to suggest that the possibility theory does, under such conditions, explain the facts of geographical distribution. (p. 29)

泰勒教授在到加拿大之前，曾任教于美国芝加哥大学，并于1941年当选为美国地理学家协会主席。正是在这一次当选时的就职演讲中泰勒教授根据他实地考察和研究的结果，讲到了关于北京早期城址选择的问题。这次讲稿的主要内容又编入了他所写的《城市地理学》一书中。现在我就从他这本书中引用几段，以说明他对于北京城址问题的看法。

在这部书的第26页上他写道：

要指明北京所以凌驾于黄河冲积平原的绝大部分城市之上的任何环境因素，是困难的。本来可以期待北方的主要城市，或者是在大平原的中心、或者是靠近主要的河流、或者是在沿海的一个良好港口上发展起来。但是这样的条件，北京都不具备。

在以下两页中，他提出了自己的一种看法：

看来在北京城址的选择上，显示包含有许多"人"的因素。在古代，巫师们认为这一城址是特别吉利的。

大约早在公元前723年，由于巫术上和政治上的原因，导致了这个城市的诞生。当时蓟是燕国的首都。以此为起点，似乎再没有其他城市相与颉颃。

最后，他的结论是：

必须承认，北京城址的选择，不是由于任何明显的环境上的因素，……我们或许可以认为北京——位于一个具有同一环境的辽阔地区——是一个很好的例子，暗示在这样的情况下，偶然性的理论说明了地理分布的事实。（第29页）

9

Forty years have since passed. Over this period, especially since the founding of the People's Republic of China, there have frequently been new archaeological finds and new results in scientific research, which are of great help to the study of the original site of the city of Beijing. It is a pity that Professor Taylor, a scholar so enthusiastic about the study of the geography of the city of Beijing had passed away before he could personally read these new materials. It would be unfair if we should make a criticism of some of Professor Taylor's theses by basing ourselves on the newly-discovered materials. What we need to do is to make full use of all the new concerning materials we have so far grasped, and to make further investigations on the origin of the city of Ji and its characteristics.

For this purpose, it is necessary to make some essential explanations about the location of the city of Ji and its geographical features.

Firstly, the grounds of argument found in the special writings about the exact location of the site of Ji City, written either in Chinese or in other languages, were mostly insufficient and even unreliable. On the basis of the new materials hitherto grasped, the original site of Ji City can be located in the southwestern corner of the present-day Beijing city proper, that is, in the vicinity of the present-day Kwang'an Gate (The Gate of Extensive Peace).

Secondly, this original site is also situated in the southwestern corner of a vast stretch of flat land, which is called the Beijing Plain. To the west, north and northeast of the plain, there are continuous encircling mountains, which remind people of a bay. Seeing this topographical feature, people also name this plain "Beijing Bay". This plain was principally washed by two rivers, the Yongding River on the west, the Chaobai River on the east, which had cut through the hills and found their ways into the bay. Like the Yellow River, these two rivers are well-known for their carrying large quantities of silt. The sand and mud carried along by the two rivers gradually silted up the ancient bay and turned it into flat land, which extended southward, linking itself with the alluvial plain formed by the Yellow River.

Thirdly, talking about the conditions for communications, we must take note of the relationship between the Beijing Plain and the great North China Plain. Over the last three thousand years, great changes have taken place geographically in this area. If we fail to see this, we won't be able to really understand the reason why the ancient city of Ji should have developed here.

　　四十年的时间过去了，在这期间——特别是从新中国建立以来，在研究北京城城址起源的问题上，不断有新的考古发现和新的研究成果可供参考。可惜的是泰勒教授未能来得及看到这些新材料就离开了我们。如果根据这些新发现的材料来批评泰勒教授的某些论断，是不公平的。现在极需要做的是利用到目前为止我们所能掌握的新材料，对蓟城的起源和城址的特点，再作些进一步的探讨。

　　为此，就需要对蓟城的地理位置及其特征，再作些必要的说明。

　　第一，过去关于蓟城城址的确切地点，无论是在中文或外文的研究著作中，论证多不可靠。到目前为止，根据所掌握的新材料，可以确定蓟城的故址，就在今日北京市区的西南隅，相当于现在广安门附近的一带地方。

　　第二，这一城址的位置，也正好处于附近一个小平原的西南隅。这个小平原，可以称之为"北京小平原"。从地形的特征来看，也有人叫它做"北京湾"。因为这个小平原的西、北和东北三面，有丛山环抱，其形势有如海湾。二三百万年前，这里也确曾是一个海湾，海湾的东西两侧，各有一条大河，切开山岭，注入海湾。东边的一条河，现在叫做潮白河，其下游曾是旧日南北大运河的一段。西侧的一条河，现在叫做永定河，也和黄河一样以携带泥沙之多而闻名。这两河所携带的泥沙，逐渐把这个古代的海湾淤为平地，向南与黄河冲积平原连成一片。

　　第三，这个北京小平原和华北大平原的关系，从交通条件来看，是特别值得注意的一个问题。因为三千年来这里的地理情况，已经发生了巨大的变化。看不到这一点，就不能真正理解古代蓟城之所以在这里发展起来的原因。

Now, from the viewpoint of the geographical conditions, it is very easy to go from the North China Plain northward to the Beijing Plain, and vice versa. But at the time when the city of Ji first rose over three thousand years ago, it was difficult for access. At that time, to the south and southeast of Ji City, there were lakes, ponds, swamps and marshes spreading all over, which isolated the city from the south. It was only thanks to the careful cultivation of the hard-working peasants from generation to generation that vast reaches of wet low land in this area were turned into fertile cultivated fields. This is one of the greatest geographical changes the last three thousand years have ever witnessed here. It is a pity that I have no time to elaborate on that point in this talk.

Over three thousand years ago, there was only one way leading from the North China Plain to the Beijing Plain. One had to walk northward along a path to the west of the North China Plain and to the east of the Taihang Mountains. The path was gradually trodden along a narrow belt between the plains and the mountains. The Taihang Mountains mark the east edge of the Shanxi Loess Plateau, from which numerous rivers run eastward, and cutting through the Taihang Mountains, surge over into the North China Plain, where they converge into several bigger rivers and flow into the sea. The rivers which ran through the mountains into the plains formed many alluvial fans, big or small, and then provided many good points of crossing for the long path on the east side of the Taihang Mountains. One could then walk northward along this long road, get over one crossing site after another, and finally come to the most difficult point for crossing which was situated on a large river. This is the exact place of the ancient ferry-place on the Yongding River. Crossing the river at this point, one would set foot into the Beijing Plain. So this point of crossing was actually the gateway to the Beijing Plain. When he reached the north end of the plain, one would encounter a range of mountains lying to the north and northeast of the plain, which hindered him from going further northward into the mountainous regions.

As a Chinese old saying goes, "there is always a way for people in great straits." In the mountains situated to both the northwest and the northeast of the Beijing Plain there were two passes. The one located to the northwest is called the Nankou Pass (South Mouth Pass). If one entered the mountains by way of the Nankou Pass and went through a long valley, he would come to a place called the Badaling Hill, a part of the Great Wall which is near to Beijing and now frequently visited by tourists. If one got over the gently sloping Badaling Hill and went further northwestward, he would pass through a vast basin area among the mountains and finally get to the Inner Mongolian Plateau.

　　根据现在的地理情况来看，从华北大平原北上进入北京小平原，或者是从北京小平原南下华北大平原，无处不可通行。但是在三千年前，当蓟城开始兴起的时候，情况就大不一样了。那时蓟城的南面和东南一带，湖泊沼泽，星罗棋布，阻隔了一切南北来往的道路。只是在世世代代勤劳的农民长期经营之下，大片湖沼低地才被改造为肥沃的良田，这是三千年来地理景观上的一大变化，只是在这里无暇细讲了。

　　且说在三千年前，假如有人从华北大平原北上进入北京小平原，就只有一条道路可以畅行无阻，那就是沿着华北大平原的西侧和太行山的东麓，步行北上。这条道路是沿着高山与平原之间的一条狭长地带逐渐发展起来的。太行山标志了山西高原的东部边缘，高原上的无数河流，大体都是自西而东，切穿了太行山，奔腾而下，注入大平原，然后汇集入海。河流出山之后，形成了或大或小的冲积扇，为太行山东麓的南北大道，提供了良好的渡口。沿着这条大道北上，越过一个又一个的渡口，最后来到最大河流上的一个最难越过的渡口，这就是永定河上的古代渡口。越过这个渡口之后，就进入了北京小平原。因此这个渡口就等于是小平原的门户。一旦进入小平原之后，如果还要继续前进，越过崛起于小平原北面和东北面的崇山峻岭，以到达遥远的山后地区，那就必须在有天然峡谷提供了南北通道的地方，才有可能。

　　正如乐观的中国劳动人民一个谚语所说的那样，"天无绝人之路"。在北京小平原的西北隅和东北隅，各有一处山峡缺口。在西北隅的一个叫做南口，从南入山，穿过一段峡谷，翻过平缓的八达岭——也就是离北京最近的一段"万里长城"所在的地方——转向西北，经过一带宽阔的山间盆地，可以直上内蒙古大高原。

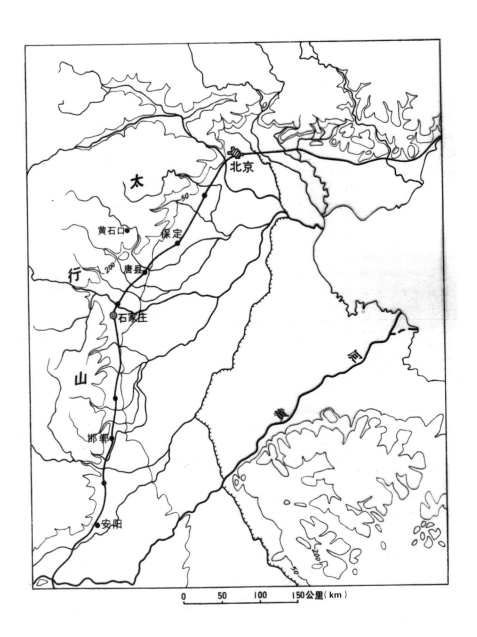

1-1 East side of the Taihang Mountains 太行山东麓地形略图

Beijing 北京　　　　Taihang Mountains 太行山　　　　Yellow River 黄河

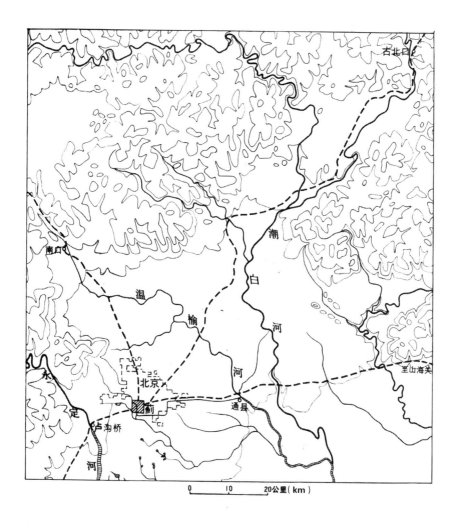

1-2 Ancient way on the Beijing Plain　北京小平原古代大道示意图

Beijing 北京	Ji City 蓟城	
Nankou pass 南口	Gubeikou Pass 古北口	Shanhaiguan Pass 山海关
Lugou Bridge 卢沟桥	Yongding River 永定河	Chaobai River 潮白河

The entrance to the northeastern mountains is called Gubeikou Pass. Starting from Gubeikou Pass and going northeastward in the mountains, one would cross a chain of hills in undulation and finally reach the Northeast China Plain.

Besides, there is another way leading to Northeast China. If one started from the Beijing Plain and went onward in an eastern direction along the southern edge of the Yan Mountains, he would come to the juncture of the mountain and the sea, which is now well-known as Shanhaiguan Pass (Mountain-Sea Pass). Getting out of Shanhaiguan Pass and walking northeastward along the coastal corridor, one could come to the plain located in the lower reaches of the Liao River.

From the above-mentioned facts, we can see that when one got across the ancient ferry on the Yongding River in the old times, he could take three different ways onward. Then here arises a very interesting question: Where was the actual juncture of this ancient road?

Under normal circumstances, the juncture of this road should be at this crossing site itself. As a ferry-place, the point of crossing was in effect a hub of communications. With the development of social economy and the ever-increasing exchange of commodities, such kind of the crossing site would provide favourable conditions for the growth and expansion of cities. This is not rare in the history concerning the development of cities in the world. One of the typical examples is the growth of the city of London which was built on the basis of an ancient crossing place on the Thames. If such an inference was reasonable, then the ancient city of Beijing should have first risen on the basis of the ancient ferry-place on the Yongding River. But it was not the case. The ancient city of Beijing did not first start there. Instead of a city, a big stone bridge made its appearance there in 1192. In some Western historical documents, this big stone bridge was called "Marco Polo Bridge", for Marco Polo, the famous traveller from Venice was the first well-known guest from the West who had ever crossed the bridge. This eleven-arched bridge is 266.5 metres in length. This bridge is noted for its magnificent structure, graceful ornament and delicate carving. Marco Polo made detailed descriptions of it in his famous travelling notes. As a result, it became known to the West.

In Chinese, this big stone bridge is called "Lugou Bridge", which was after the original name of the Yongding River. Now the name of the river itself has long been changed, but the bridge across the river as well as its old name has always remained unchanged, and well-preserved.

在东北隅的一个叫做古北口，从古北口入山，偏向东北，穿过连绵不断的丘陵山地，就进入了东北大平原。

此外，还有一条大道，从北京小平原一直向东，沿着燕山南麓前进，直到山与海相接的地方，便是现在有名的山海关。出山海关，沿滨海走廊向东北，直达辽河下游平原。

在说明了上述情况之后，这里就出现了一个饶有趣味的问题，即从华北大平原沿太行山东麓北上的大道，在渡过永定河的古代渡口之后，随即分歧为三，继续前进，那么这个大道的分歧点，应该在哪里？

在一般的情况下，这个大道的分歧点，应该就在渡口上。作为这样的一个渡口，实际上也就是来往交通的枢纽。随着社会经济的发展，交换关系日趋频繁，这样的一个渡口，也就为一个城市的成长，提供了有利的条件。这种情况，在世界城市的发展史上是不乏其例的。例如从泰晤士河的古代渡口上发展起来的伦敦城，就是一个典型的例子。如果这一推断是合理的，那么北京城本来就应该从永定河的古代渡口上成长起来，然而事实并不如此。北京城并没有在这里成长，代替了一个城市而在这里出现的，是公元 1192 年才在这里建造起来的一座大石桥，去今也已七百多年。这座大石桥在某些西方文献中也叫做"马可·波罗桥"，因为威尼斯的旅行家马可·波罗（1254—1324）是第一个从这座大桥上经过的享有盛名的西方客人。这座长达 266.5 米、共有十一孔的大石桥，造型壮丽，雕饰精美，马可·波罗在他那部著名的旅行记里，曾有详细的描述，因而传名于西方。

在中国，这座大石桥叫做卢沟桥。"卢沟"乃是建桥时永定河原有的名称，现在河流本身的名称虽然改变了，可是河上的石桥却以其原有名称，十分完好地保存到今天。

Here I'd like to mention one thing in passing. It is at "Lugou Bridge" that the Japanese imperialists launched their aggressive war against the Chinese people on July 7, 1937. That is the famous "Lugou Bridge Incident".

The ancient ferry-place on the Yongding River, running under the present "Lugou Bridge", provided favourable conditions for the development of a city. However, it had its disadvantages to the growth of a city at this very point as well. That was the threatening floods of the Yongding River. This is the reason why people altered the name of the river into "Yongding", whose literal meaning is "Tranquility Forever", showing the hope that the river would always remain tranquil and never overflow its banks.

The Yongding River, as a big river, had an unsteady rate of flow. In the rainy season, the Yongding River rose higher and higher, swelled by the water running from the mountainous areas which were to the northwest of the Beijing Plain. Such ancient ferry-place as the crossing site where the present Lugou Bridge is situated stood in the way of the seething and rolling waters. The floods formed a constant menace and an incessant danger to the crossing point in the old times. The ancient people decided that they shouldn't build their city in such a place. They should have their city built up in a place which was close to the crossing site and free from the threat of floods. The place they found was the site of the original settlement which later turned into the city of Ji. As it was located at a hub of communications linking the north and the south, this place had more favourable conditions than its neighbouring settlements. That is why it could develop into a city at a greater speed.

Besides, the original settlement of Ji also had its own local and regional favourable conditions which enabled it to grow up smoothly in its early stage. For instance, it was positioned on a ridge of the alluvial fan formed by the ancient Yongding River. Moreover, it was situated to the east of a belt of overflowing phreatic water near the alluvial fan. In this area, there were rich sources of water underground. To the west of the city of Ji there was a lake formed by the overflowing phreatic water. It was called the West Lake in the past and is now called the Lotus Pond. The lake led to a stream which ran through the southwest part of Ji City. The small river provided a good source of surface water for the early development of the city of Ji.

在这里特别值得一提的，是 1937 年 7 月 7 日，日本帝国主义者，捏造了一个借口，从卢沟桥畔发动了对中国人民的侵略战争，这就是举世周知的"卢沟桥事变"。以此为起点，中国人民在中国共产党的领导下，进行了八年之久的抗日战争[1]，并且取得了最后的胜利。就是在这次战争的初期，白求恩大夫就在离卢沟桥西南只有一百六十多公里的太行山中的一个小农村——黄石口村，为中国人民献出了他宝贵的生命。

卢沟桥所代表的永定河上的古代渡口，虽然为一个城市的成长提供了有利的条件，但是也还有一个不利的因素，排斥一个城市在这里成长，这就是永定河的洪水威胁。

永定河虽然是一条大河，但是它的流量极不稳定，每当雨季，特别是遇到暴雨在北京西北山区集中下降的时候，永定河的洪水猛涨，从出山之口，一泻而下，卢沟桥所代表的古代渡口，首当其冲。正是由于这种不可避免的洪水威胁，就把原来是应该在古代渡口上成长起来的城市，排斥到过河之后去渡口最近而又开始不受洪水威胁的地方，这个地方就是蓟城的原始聚落所在处，而这里也就成为古代南北交通的枢纽。正是因为这个枢纽地位，蓟城才能超越附近其他居民点而迅速地发展起来。

其次，也要看到蓟城的原始聚落，还有一些局部的有利条件，使它在早期的发展中得以顺利成长。例如它不仅位于古代永定河冲积扇的背脊上，而且还靠近冲积扇上一条潜水溢出带的东侧，这里既有丰富的地下水源，便于凿井汲取，同时在城市的西郊还有一个清澈的小湖，古称西湖，现在叫做莲花池。这个小湖就是潜水溢出所形成的，它的下游是一条小河，正好流经蓟城西南侧，又为蓟城的早期发展，提供了良好的地表水源。

From the analysis made above, we can see that the rise of Ji City depended not only on the decisive factors for the social and economic development, but also on the favourable geographical conditions of its own. As these geographical conditions existed objectively, their analysis is possible. If we ignored these geographical conditions, we would find it difficult to explain why the original settlement of Ji should have risen up in this very place.

- **Part Three: The Moving Away of the Original Site of the City and the Construction of Dadu City in the Yuan Dynasty**

In this part, I'll talk about the historical development of the city at its later stages.

During the long years before the third century B.C. a small enfeoffed princedom called Yan had the city of Ji as its political centre. In the later part of the third century B.C. the State of Yan and all the other states which had been enfeoffed by the Zhou Dynasty were conquered successively by the newly-rising Qin. At this time China evolved into the early stage of feudal society. The first emperor of the Qin Dynasty Qinshihuang founded the first centralized and unified feudal empire with many nationalities living together in China's history.[2]

Feudal society in China, starting from the Qin Dynasty, lasted over 2,100 years in which one dynasty was replaced by another. It was not until 1911 that the last feudal dynasty—the Qing Dynasty—was overthrown. Over these long years, China became split up politically from time to time. That is to say, two or more independent empires co-existed on this territory for some time and vied with one another. But for most of the time in this long period, China was in a state of unification, which promoted the economic and cultural development of the country.

The political centre of the whole country altered several times in the long history. Two out of the cities which acted as capitals were much more important. Chang'an which is known as Xi'an now, used to be the major political centre of the country in the earlier period of feudal society. Only much later did Beijing become the major political centre of the whole country.

Though Chang'an served as the major political centre of the country, Beijing also played an important political role for it occupied a key position to link the Central Plain and the remote regions of the Northeast China. During this period, the dynasties which ruled the Central Plain were mostly established by members of the Han Nationality. As they

　　根据以上的讨论，可以说明：蓟城的兴起，除去社会经济发展的决定因素外，它还具备了必要的地理条件。这些地理条件，都是客观存在的，因此也是可以分析的。忽略了这些地理条件，就难以说明北京的原始聚落之所以在这里成长的原因。

　　以上是在讨论北京城的历史发展时所必须交代清楚的一个问题，如果有不妥之处，还希望得到同行们的批评和指教。

三、原始城址的迁移和元朝大都城的兴建

　　在分析了蓟城——也就是北京原始城址的地理条件之后，我们再来继续探索这个城市的历史发展。

　　公元前三世纪晚期，以蓟城为统治中心的燕国，和其他一些为周朝所分封的同一性质的侯国，都先后为新兴的秦所征服。这时中国已经进入封建社会的初期。秦朝的统治者秦始皇，在中国历史上创建了第一个中央集权的、多民族的、统一的封建国家。

　　从秦朝开始，封建王朝相继更迭，一直延续了二千一百多年，到本世纪初，也就是 1911 年，最后一个封建王朝——清朝才被推翻。在这期间，中国的政局有时陷于分裂，也就是说有两个或两个以上的王朝同时并存、互争雄长。但大部分时间还是统一的。这种统一时期，是中国的社会经济与文化发展的重要时期。

　　全国统一时期的政治中心，前后也有过几次迁移，但是真正称得上是全国最大、最重要的政治中心的，只有两个，在前期是长安，也就是现在的西安，在后期就是北京。

　　当长安作为全国最大的政治中心的时候，北京以其地理位置的关系，在中原与东北的边远地区之间，起着非常重要的作用。特别是因为在这期间统治中原地区的大都是汉族所建立的王朝，农业是

took agriculture as their chief means of production, they came to a rather advanced stage in social economy and culture. In the meantime, the outlying areas of Northeast China were distributed with several national minorities who were still leading a nomadic life. They were under-developed in production, as they were in a developing stage of slave society. So within China there existed simultaneously two social structures which were in different stages of development and thus often in opposition to each other. Such contradictions could by no means be solved under the old social system. The valiant horsemen of the nomadic tribes, led by their militant and bellicose chieftains, often rode southward over to the Central Plain, forming a threat to the inhabitants who engaged in farming in these areas. Their intrusion threatened to overthrow the rulers of the areas of the Central Plain. Consequently, the rulers of the Central Plain, when powerful, would often send expeditionary forces against the nomadic tribes inhabiting the remote areas in the North. But they would more often act on the defensive rather than take the offensive. Hundreds of thousands of labourers were driven into the mountains in North China and were forced to build a long-distance bulwark in the mountainous areas for the sake of defence. This is the famous Great Wall. In fact the Great Wall is a witness to one of the most important national contradictions that ever existed in history. And this colossal and magnificent Great Wall built by the ancient labouring people with their own hands has turned into a well-known interesting place which is frequently visited by numerous Chinese and foreign tourists with astonishment, admiration and joyfulness.

From the third century B.C. to the ninth century A.D., the rulers of different dynasties from the Central Plain, when they were powerful, would take the city of Ji as their springboard on their punitive expeditions against the nomadic tribes in the north and northeast. But when the imperial empires in the Central Plain were on the decline or in a state of disintegration, the nomadic tribes from the north and northeast would seize the chance to go all the way downward and ride roughshod over the Central Plain, robbing the people there of their property and even capturing many of them as slaves. In such cases, the rulers of the Central Plain would turn the city of Ji into a defence place of strategic importance. But once the chieftains of the nomadic tribes from the north succeeded in capturing the city of Ji, they would certainly, in their turn, make it a base for advancing onward to the south.

主要的生产手段，社会经济和文化都比较先进。东北的边远地区则是以游牧为主的少数民族分布的地方，还处在奴隶社会的发展阶段，生产比较落后。在一个国家内这两种不同发展阶段的社会结构之间，经常处于相互矛盾的对立状态，而这种矛盾在旧的社会制度下，又是无法解决的。停留在奴隶社会发展阶段的游牧部族是剽悍的骑手，在雄杰好战的首领统治下，就会纵马南下，对中原地区的农业居民造成威胁，并且有颠覆中原统治者的危险。因此中原的统治者在势力强大的时候，也常常组织兵力，主动进攻，向北方的游牧部族进行征讨。但更多的时候，是采取防御手段，役使千千万万的劳动人民，沿着北方的高山峻岭，修建万里长城，以事防御。因此，有名的万里长城实际上就是这种矛盾存在的历史见证。而在今天，这个由古代劳动人民用双手所建筑的庞大而雄伟的建筑物，却已成为中外无数旅游者，怀着无限惊讶与赞叹的心情，兴高采烈地攀登和纵情眺望的一处名胜古迹了。

现在，让我们从驰骋于万里长城的返想中，再回到我们现实的话题上来吧。

简单地说，从公元前三世纪到公元后九世纪的一千多年之间，每当中原统治者势力强大的时候，就常常要以蓟城为前进的基地，对东北游牧部族进行征讨。反之，当中原统治者势力衰微或陷于分裂的时候，东北游牧部族的统治者，又常常乘机南下，掠夺中原地区的财富，甚至俘虏人民充当奴隶，而这时的蓟城又成为中原统治者一个军事防守的重镇。到了防守无效，游牧部族的统治者入侵成功之后，就一定要以蓟城作为进一步南下的据点。

Of course, for most part of this millennium, people lived in peace without any wars. In the time of peace and settlement, the city of Ji acted as an important trade centre to link the north and the south, and also played an active part in promoting the cultural exchange between the Central Plain and the remote areas in the north and northeast part of China.

From the tenth century A.D. on, the national minorities living in Northeast China began to rise up one after another and got stronger and stronger. Soon the leaders of the Qidan Nationality (the Khitans) commanded their troops on a southward expedition and occupied the city of Ji. They changed the name of the city into Nanjing (South Capital) or Yanjing and proclaimed it their "accompanying capital" (the second important political centre) and also took it as a military base for their further southward advancement. This took place in a period called the Liao Dynasty (916-1125) in China's history. At the beginning of the twelfth century, another national minority living in the northeast—the Nuzhen Nationality—sprang up. Before long, they defeated the Qidan rulers and conquered the city of Nanjing of the Liao Dynasty. Then the Nuzhen rulers officially moved their capital to the city of Nanjing and changed its name into Zhongdu (Central Capital). This historical period was called the Jin Dynasty (1115-1234).

The city of Zhongdu of the Jin Dynasty was the last and the biggest city which had ever been built on the original site of the city of Ji. The palatial buildings in the city were luxurious and magnificent. But this new city had a history of less than one hundred years only. Meanwhile, the Mongolian Nationality, a national minority living on the northern plateau, got stronger and stronger, with an outstanding brave man called Genghis Khan as their leader. In 1215, a large group of cavalrymen under Genghis Khan broke through the natural barrier at Nankou Pass and rode all the way to the city of Zhongdu. After fierce battle with the garrison troops of the Jin Dynasty, they forced their way into the city. The town was thrown into confusion and the huge and splendid palaces were burned down to the ground.

In 1260, Genghis Khan's grandson called Kublai Khan who was the founder of the Yuan Dynasty in China's history, came to the city of Zhongdu and chose to make it the capital of his dynasty. After careful considering, the emperor took the advice of a Han scholar named Liu Bing-zhong and decided not to build his imperial palace here. As a learned man with rich knowledge of and practical experience in city construction and with a mastery of many other branches of science and technology, Liu Bing-zhong suggested that a new city should be built on a new place selected in the northeastern suburbs of the original site of the city of Zhongdu. Another brilliant scientist called Guo Shou-jing also took an active part in the planning and building of the new city.

自然在这期间，主要的还是和平安定的局面时间最长，在这种局面下，蓟城也就成为一个重要的南北贸易的中心，并促进了中原与东北地区之间的文化交流。

但是，从十世纪开始，东北少数民族的势力，逐渐兴起，首先是契丹族的统治者拥兵南下，占据了蓟城，以蓟城为陪都（第二政治中心），作为继续向南方推进的据点，并改称蓟城为南京（或叫燕京），这是中国历史上的辽朝（916—1125）。十二世纪初，又一个东北少数民族——女真族，继而兴起，占据了辽朝的南京城后，就正式迁都到这里，并扩建了南京城，改名中都，这就是金朝（1115—1234）。

金朝的中都城，乃是在蓟城的旧址上发展起来的最后也是最大的一个大城。城中的宫殿建筑尤其豪华。可是这座大城兴建之后不到百年，又一个来自北方高原上的少数民族——蒙古族，在它的杰出领袖成吉思汗的领导下，迅速强大起来。公元1215年，成吉思汗部下的一支骑兵，突破南口一带的天险，直捣中都，经过一场激烈的战斗，杀进城中。在混乱的情况下，城内的豪华宫殿，竟被放火焚烧，化为一片废墟。

此后又过了四十五年，也就是公元1260年，成吉思汗的孙子忽必烈——中国历史上元朝的创建人，来到中都城，并决定在这里建都。经过一番考虑之后，接受了当时对城市建筑和科学技术具有丰富学识和实践经验的汉族学者刘秉忠的建议，决定放弃中都旧城，另在东北郊外，选择新址，建设新城。积极参加新城的规划和建设的，还有一位杰出的科学家郭守敬。

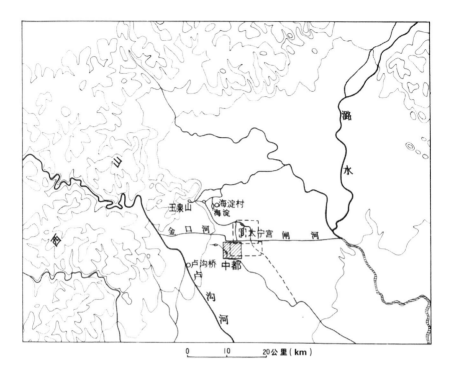

1-3 Watercourses in the adjacent areas of Zhongdu City of the Jin Dynasty
金中都城近郊河渠水道略图

Zhongdu City 中都	Taining Palace 太宁宫	Lugou Bride 卢沟桥
West Mountains 西山	Yuquan Hills 玉泉山	Lugou River 卢沟河

When Guo Shou-jing was young, he used to be a student of Liu Bing-zhong. As a scientist, Guo Shou-jing was not only good at astronomy and the science of calendar, but also specialized in surveying and water conservancy. Guo Shou-jing and his teacher Liu Bing-zhong cooperated very well with each other and formed a core of leadership in the city construction. They also invited many skilled masons whose ancestors had engaged in masonry for generations from the Taihang Mountains to participate in the construction of the new city. Among these stonemasons, there were two noted folk artisans of stonework by the names of Yang Qiong and Yang Hao. Besides, assisting in the building of the city were some foreign craftsmen who were from Middle Asia. The construction of the new city started in 1267. The new city was named Dadu

(Grand Capital), out of which the present city of Beijing grew.

Here I'd like to raise the following two questions, whose answers may help us to have a better understanding of the development of the present city of Beijing.

1. What made them decide to give up the old town of Zhongdu and build the new city of Dadu instead?

2. How was the site of the new city of Dadu selected? How was the planning of the new city made?

Let us discuss the first question now.

Obviously, the reason why they gave up the old town was that the original palaces had been burned down to the ground. They would rather build a new city with new palaces than to rebuild them on the ruins of the old town. But there was an even more important factor which made them build a new city in a new place. That was the need of new water sources.

郭守敬自幼从学于刘秉忠，精通天文历法，又长于测量，也是一位水利学家。刘、郭师生合作，形成了一个专家领导的核心。他们还招来了太行山中一些世代从事石工而且富有艺术才能的匠人，参加新城的建设，其中最有名的就是民间出身的石雕艺术家杨琼和杨浩。此外，还有来自中亚的外籍工匠，也参加了筑城的工事。人才济济，盛极一时。新城的建设，于1267年开始动工，这就是历史上赫赫有名的大都城，也就是现在北京城的前身。

这里有两个值得注意的问题：

第一，当时为什么要放弃中都旧城，另建大都新城？

第二，大都新城的城址是怎样选择的？又是怎样规划的？

我们必须回答这两个问题，因为这和了解现在的北京城是有直接关系的。

现在分别讨论如下。

关于第一个问题：

当时放弃中都旧城，有一个明显的原因，那就是旧城的宫阙已被焚毁，与其在一片废墟上重行修建，还不如另筑新宫，营造新城。但实际上，还有一个更为重要的原因，导致了城址的最后迁移，这就是对于开辟新水源的要求。

When the city of Ji was in its early stage of development, its need for the sources of surface water was limited, as its size and population were not big. The West Lake located near the city and the small river running by the city could quite satisfy the city's demand for water. But great changes took place after the Jin Dynasty founded its capital in this place. To keep up China's ancient tradition, the emperors would have imperial gardens built in connection with the building of the imperial palaces in their feudal capitals. An important factor of building imperial gardens was that they must be embellished with streams, lakes, hills and mounds. If there weren't any natural hills or waters, then artificial lakes would be made by digging into the ground and artificial hills would be piled up with the earth dug out from the lakes. So the lakes and ponds in the imperial gardens were given a fixed name: "the Heavenly Water Pond", which meant that the water of the imperial lakes came directly from the Heaven and that this elemental force was the origin of life. To build imperial gardens, large quantities of water were needed. Thus larger and richer sources of surface water were required. Besides, for the construction of canals leading to the capital sources with plenty of surface water were also needed. The man-made rivers were important channels by which grain collected from the peasants and other articles of daily necessity provided for the royal families, the central governmental institutions and the garrison troops were transported to the capital.

When the rulers of the Jin Dynasty expanded their capital of Zhongdu, they enclosed the river running into the lower part of the West Lake within the city. And they also built their imperial gardens in the west of the imperial palaces. The West Lake as a water source could supply enough water to fill in the imperial lakes. However, it was far from being able to provide the canals with sufficient water. The rulers of the Jin Dynasty did open up a canal linking the city of Zhongdu eastward to a river called the Chaobai River. Their original plan was to direct water from the Yongding River located to the west of the city. Dams and dykes were built to keep back water. Ditches were dug up to direct the controlled water running to the east. But because of the unsteady flow rate of the Yongding River and the limitation of the low-level technology then, they didn't achieve their desired results with these projects. All the attempts they had made to direct water into the canal all turned out to be unsuccessful. This was the most important reason why the Yuan rulers decided to give up the old town and build a new one.

　　按蓟城早期的发展，城市性质比较单纯，规模也不很大，因此对于地表水源的要求是有限的。近在城郊的西湖和流经城侧的小河，完全可以满足城市用水的需要。可是，到了金朝在这里正式建都之后，情形就大不相同了。按照中国的传统，作为一个封建王朝的都城，照例要结合宫阙的修建开辟皇家园林。园林之中又照例要有河湖岗阜作为点缀，这是造园的重要因素，即使没有天然山水，也要用人工凿地为湖，堆土成山。因此宫苑中的湖泊，也就取得了一个固定的名称，叫做"太液池"。这个名称象征着宫苑里的湖水，直接来自天上，也含有水是生命本源的意思。为了开辟皇家园林，就要大量用水，从而大大增加了对于地表水源的需求。特别重要的是，为了供应皇家以及庞大的中央官僚机构与驻防军队的需要，每年还必须把大量从民间征收的食粮，通过水上运输，送到都城，在中国封建王朝的历史上，这也形成了一种制度，叫做"漕运"。中国有名的大运河，就是因此而开凿起来的。因此，为了运河的开凿，就需要更加丰沛的地表水源。

　　金朝扩建中都城时，已经把西湖下游的小河，圈入城中，并在宫城的西侧，开辟了皇家园林。西湖的水源虽然满足了宫苑用水的需要，却远远不足以供应运河的用水。金朝的统治者曾经开凿了一条郊区运河，从中都城下顺自然地势，引水东流，直接潮白河。它的上源主要是从城西永定河上，筑坝拦水，凿渠东下。这本来是个很好的计划，只是由于永定河流量极不稳定，当时的工程技术也有一定限制，未能达到预期的效果。其他引水的尝试，也都未能奏效。这一情况是参加新城规划的郭守敬所十分清楚的。放弃中都旧址，另建新城，郭守敬应该是最有关系的一个人。

Now let's come to the second question about the selection of the site of the new city and its planning.

Here I'd like to mention something interesting in passing. When Khublai first came to Zhongdu in 1260, he had no place to live in, as the palatial residence had been burned down to the ground. He had to live in a place not far from the ruined city. This fact was definitely recorded then. (Later the fact was recorded again in the "Biography of Khublai" contained in *The History of the Yuan Dynasty*.) But the exact place where he lived was intentionally ignored for the sake of his security. Now over 700 years have since passed. Over this period, people had no idea where Khublai lived when he first came to Zhongdu. Now having made careful investigations, we discovered that he lived in a summer palace originally built for the emperors of the Jin Dynasty and their royal families, which was built on an expanse of waters on the northeastern outskirt of the capital. This palatial residence during the Jin Dynasty was called Taining Palace (Great Tranquility Palace) whose main building stood on an island in the middle of the lake. The building was named the Lunar Hall, which referred to the mythical palace on the moon. This name also suggested the scenery here which was as beautiful as on a fairy land. Fortunately, this temporary palatial residence outside the capital remained untouched when the Mongolian horsemen forced into the city of Zhongdu and set fire to the imperial palace inside the city in 1215. The construction of the city of Dadu started in 1267. According to the city planning, the lake around Taining Palace was taken as the centre of the plane designing. This lake was given the name of "the Heavenly Water Pond".

那么新城的城址又是怎样选择和怎样规划的呢？这就是必须回答的第二个问题。

在这里顺便提到一个有趣的插话，或许还是必要的。公元 1260 年，忽必烈初到中都，由于城中宫殿已成废墟，无处可以安身，他只好住到城外一个离城不远的地方，这在当时的记录中是有明确记

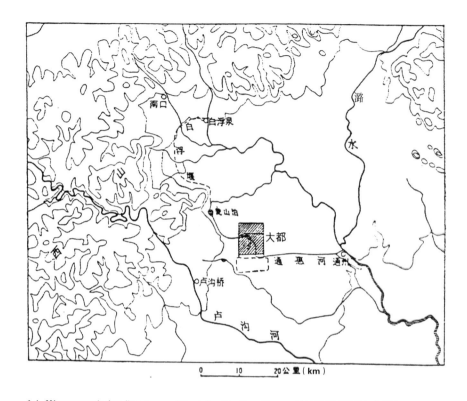

1-4 Watercourses in the adjacent areas of Khanbaliq of the Yuan Dynasty 元大都城近郊河渠水道略图

Dadu City 大都　　　　　　　Tonghui River 通惠河　　　　　　Lugou Bridge 卢沟桥
Lugou River 卢沟河　　　　　Nankou Pass 南口　　　　　　　West Mountains 西山

载的, 以后又被转载在重要的《元史》忽必烈的本纪中, 但是他所居住的确切地点, 都被有意识地避而不记, 这大约也是为了他本身的安全而有意保密的缘故吧? 现在, 七百多年的时间过去了, 我们还是经过一番细心的侦察才弄清楚, 原来忽必烈初到中都时所居住的地方, 就是金朝统治者在东北郊外一片天然湖泊上所兴建的一座离宫, 名叫太宁宫。这座离宫的主要殿宇, 就建筑在湖泊当中的一个岛上, 名叫广寒殿, 取名于中国神话中所构想的月亮上的宫殿, 同时也暗示了这里风景幽美, 有如仙境。

　　需要指出的是: 当 1215 年蒙古骑兵攻占中都城并使城中宫阙化为灰烬的时候, 东北郊外这座离宫却幸得保全。相继发生的事实说明: 1267 年开始营建大都城, 正是利用太宁宫的湖泊作为平面设计的中心而进行规划的, 从此这片湖泊也就获得了 "太液池" 的名称。

From the planning of Dadu City, we can see clearly that on the east bank of the Heavenly Water Pond was built the emperor's palace while on its west bank stood two groups of palatial buildings facing each other, which were respectively inhabited by the empress dowager and the crown prince. A small round island situated in the middle of the lake served as the link of the three palaces. A wooden bridge was put up to connect the east end of the island and the east bank of the lake, while another wooden bridge was built to link the west end of the island with the west bank of the lake. To the north of the small island, a stone bridge was built to span the water between the small island and the big island on which stood the main building of the old temporary palatial residence—the Lunar Hall. This big island was called "Jade Flower Island", which was suggestive of a place where there were richly decorated jade palaces and beautiful flowers in blossom. The buildings around the lake were well-distributed, around which was put up a square bulwark encircling these imperial palaces. The bulwark actually formed the imperial city wall.

To the north of the imperial city, there was a larger lake then called Jishuitan (the Water Storing Pond), which had previously interlinked with the Heavenly Water Pond in the imperial city. The construction of the imperial city cut the two lakes apart. A new canal was dug up to supply water for the Heavenly Water Pond. This canal was named the Golden Water River in keeping with the ancient tradition.

The water of the Water Storing Pond was originally from a natural river called the Gaoliang River. Its former course in the lower reaches supplying water for the Water Storing Pond was perhaps filled up or turned into an underground river, in the construction of the city of Dadu. So a new canal was opened up, which ran along the east wall of the imperial city and flew out of the city of Dadu. This new canal was the last part of the Grand Canal, through which the ships and boats carrying grain collected from South China sailed into the city of Dadu and anchored in the Water Storing Pond. The ships and boats also transported goods from the south. So the place on the northeastern bank of the Water Storing Pond and its nearby streets became the most busy market-place in the city of Dadu.

Now we can see that superficially, the summer palace of the Jin Dynasty led to the construction of the city of Dadu in this area. But in fact, the new source of water from the Gaoliang River formed the decisive factor of the selection of city site in this very place.

　　从大都城的平面图上，可以明显地看到，太液池的东岸建有皇帝的宫城，西岸建有两组宫殿，南北对峙，分别为皇太子和皇太后所居。三宫之间，乃是以太液池中的一个圆形小岛作为相互联系的中心。小岛的东西两侧，各架一座木桥，分别与东西两岸相连接。小岛的北侧另建一座石桥，通向旧日离宫的主体建筑广寒殿所在的大岛上。这个大岛叫做琼华岛，意思是说这里是琼楼玉柱百花争艳的地方，如实地反映了这里已成为太液池上的风景中心。环绕太液池的整个平面布局，构成了一幅匀称的图案，在它的周围修筑了近似正方形的宫墙，就是皇城的城墙。

　　皇城北侧，有更大的一片湖泊，当时叫做积水潭，原与皇城内的太液池相连。由于皇城的修建，就把这两处湖泊截分为二，并为太液池另外开凿了一条供水渠道，也是根据古代的传统，命名为金水河。

　　积水潭原为一条天然河流——高梁河所灌注。积水潭下游的高梁河故道，在大都城的规划过程中，可能是已被改为暗渠，或被填埋，因此另开一条新渠道，经由皇城的东墙外，流出大都城。后来郭守敬又利用这条改造后的新渠道，作为南北大运河的最北一段，把来自江南的漕船，一直引进大都城，停泊在积水潭里。随漕船北来的还有南方的百货，因此积水潭东北岸及其附近一带，就成了大都城内最繁华的市场所在。

　　从以上的讨论中可以看出，从表面现象来说，金朝的离宫似乎是导致兴建大都城的原因，但实际上高梁河的新水源，才是选建大都城城址的重要因素。

Here is a thing we must pay special attention to, that is, the determination of the central axis of the city which was of the first importance in the plane designing of the city of Dadu. This central axis went along the east bank of the Water Storing Pond. And the centre of the emperor's palace was fixed on the central axis of the whole city and it occupied the most important position. The apex of the central axis was at the northeastern bank of the Water Storing Pond. This point was taken as the geometric centre of the plane designing of the whole city. Here at this very point was erected a designating building which was called "the Central Pavilion". On the right side of the pavilion was set up a stone tablet on which were inscribed four Chinese characters, meaning "the Central Platform". This shows that when the planning and designing of the whole of the new city were made, a precise plane survey was also made.

To the west of the Central Platform was put up the "Drum Tower". And to the north of the "Drum Tower" was built the "Bell Tower". The drum and the bell were instruments to give the standard time in old days. So the two towers became centres telling the time for the whole city. The fact was also clearly recorded in *Marco Polo's Travelling Notes*.

Once the geometric centre of the whole city was determined, the position of the outer walls of the city was also decided. The construction of the city was basically carried out according to the original planning. Only the east wall slightly drew in for the purpose of avoiding some topographical disadvantages.

The east, west and south walls of the city had three gates each. Its north wall had only two gates. Inside each gate there was a straight main road. These roads in the city formed a criss-cross network of communications which resembled a chessboard. The middle gate of the south wall was fixed on the central axis of the whole city. The gate was on the central trunk line, which led northward to the emperor's palace. Inside the emperor's palace, only the main halls which were symbolic of the imperial power, were arranged on the central axis, while those less important buildings were symmetrically arranged on either side of the central axis.

Outside the imperial city were arranged many horizontal streets and lanes parallel with each other in between meeting these vertical main roads at right angles. These districts were chiefly living quarters of the local inhabitants. These areas were dotted with many central and local government offices and institutions, temples, warehouses and other public buildings. Only two groups of important buildings were laid out in a planned way. The first group of edifices was positioned inside the south gate of the east wall of the big city.

　　这里需要特别注意的是在大都城平面设计中具有头等重要意义的全城中轴线的确定。这条中轴线恰好选定在积水潭的东岸，而皇帝宫城中的中心点，也就正好布置在这条全城的中轴线上，而且占据了最重要的位置。中轴线的顶点，止于积水潭的东北岸，同时把这一点也就定为全城平面设计的几何中心，并在这里建立了一座指示性的建筑物，就叫做"中心阁"。中心阁的右侧，特意立了一块石碑，刻有"中心之台"四个大字，这就说明在全城进行规划设计的同时，是进行了精密的平面测量的。

　　中心阁以西建立了鼓楼，鼓楼之北又建钟楼。钟鼓楼是全城报时的中心。这一点在《马可·波罗游记》中是有明确记载的。

　　全城的几何中心确定之后，大都城最外围四面城墙的位置，也就相应地确定下来。只是在动工过程中，东面城墙可能是为了避开不利的地形，又向内稍有收缩。这一措施对于全城的平面规划，是无关紧要的。

　　大都城东、西、南三面城墙，各设三门，北面城墙只设二门。各城门内都有笔直的干道，纵横交错，略成棋盘状。南面城墙的正中一门，也正好设在全城的中轴线上，是中心干道所经，由此北上，直入宫城。宫城之内，也只有代表皇权统治中心的主要大殿，被布置在这条中轴线上，其他次要建筑物，都采取严格对称的形式，排列在中轴线的左右两边。

　　在皇城以外的南北干道之间，开辟了众多东西平行排列的街巷，主要是居民住宅分布的地区。中央和地方官署以及寺庙、仓库等公用建筑错列其间。只有两组有重要意义的建筑群，是按计划布局的。一组设在大城东墙的南门以内，叫做"太庙"，是皇帝祭祀祖先的地方。

This group of edifices was called the Imperial Ancestral Temple, a place where the emperors offered sacrifices to their ancestors. The other group of buildings was situated inside the south gate of the west wall of the big city. It was called the Altar of Land and Grain, a place where the emperors offered sacrifices to the God of Land and the God of Grain.

This plane arrangement of the city of Dadu was similar to a kind of ideal designing of imperial capitals in the ancient time. This ideal designing was first seen in a book entitled "A Study of Engineering" which came out in the fifth century B.C. This book exclusively dealt with engineering and also referred to the designing of imperial capitals. According to *A Study of Engineering*, the imperial city walls in the four directions must form a square. The wall on each side had three gates. Inside each gate there were three main roads parallel to each other. So the main roads and streets in the city formed a criss-cross network of communications. The imperial city was supposed to face the south. In front of the central point of the imperial city (in the south direction) were located the imperial courts. At the back of the imperial city (in the north direction) were concentrated the market-places. To the left of the imperial courts (in the east direction) was located the Imperial Ancestral Temple. To the right of the imperial city (in the west direction) was situated the Altar of Land and Grain. It is clear that the planning of Dadu City was made on the basis of this ancient ideal designing and also in the light of the specific conditions of the distribution of lakes and waterways on the spot.

一组设在大城西墙的南门以内，叫做"社稷坛"，是皇帝祭祀土地之神与五谷之神的地方。

这里需要指出的是，大都城的这一平面布局，和古代关于帝王都城的一种理想设计，极相近似。这一理想设计，见于大约成书在公元前五世纪时的一部著作，叫做《考工记》，是专门讲工程技术与器物制作的。其中提到帝王都城的设计，四面城墙应作正方形，每面各开三门，门内各有三轨平行的干道，纵横相交。城内中央的前方（南方）是朝廷，后方（北方）是市场，左方（东方）是太庙，右方（西方）是社稷坛。简单地说，就是面朝、后市、左祖、右社。大都城显然是参考了这一古代理想的设计，又结合了地方湖泊水道分布的特点而后进行规划的，它具有特殊的历史意义，就在于此。

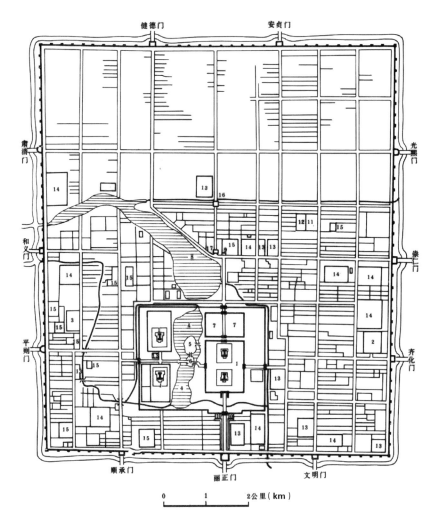

1-5 Plan of Khanbaliq of the Yuan Dynasty 元大都城平面图

1. Palaces 宫殿
2. Imperial Ancestral Temple 太庙
3. Altar of Land and Grain 社稷坛
4. Heavenly Water Pond 太液池
5. Jade Flower Island 琼华岛（万寿山、万岁山）
6. Round City 圆坻（瀛洲）
7. Imperial Garden 御园
8. Jishuitan (Water Storing Pond) 积水潭
9. Central Platform 中心之台
10. Corridor of a Thousand Steps 千步廊
11. Confucian Temple 文庙
12. Imperial College 国子监
13. Yamuns 衙门
14. Barns 仓库
15. Temples 寺观、庙宇
16. Bell Tower 钟楼
17. Drum Tower 鼓楼

（Reproduced on the basis of Xu Pingfang's *Atlas of Dadu* 根据徐苹芳《元大都城图》原稿复制）

This plane arrangement was aimed at placing the imperial palaces on the most important position of the whole city. This designing embodied the absolute power of feudal emperors.

Eight years after the construction of the large-scale well-planned city of Dadu started, Marco Polo came here. He was thought highly of by Khublai and appointed as a high official in the imperial courts of the Yuan Dynasty. In his famous travelling notes, he made a detailed description of the city of Dadu. He called it "Khanbaliq", which meant "the city of the great Khan". His book was read by many people in the West. It is well-known that in the fifteenth century, Christopher Columbus himself hadn't made up his mind to make a voyage to China until he read *Marco Polo's Travelling Notes*. Columbus believed that the earth was round, and thought that he would certainly reach China by sailing westward in a ship, since Marco Polo could succeed in getting to China through going eastward by land. Of course he failed to get to China. But the determination of this brave and talented man led to an unexpected discovery—the discovery of the New Continent.

- **Part Four: The City of Beijing in the Ming and Qing Dynasties— A Remarkable Example of the Imperial Capitals for Its Excellent Planning and Designing**

The domination of the Yuan Dynasty lasted less than one hundred years only. It was replaced by the Ming Dynasty founded by the Han Nationality. The Ming rulers rose up in the lower reaches of the Yangzi River and made Nanjing their first capital. Then they began their northern expedition. In 1368 they captured the city of Dadu, and changed its name into Peiping (North Pacification). When the third emperor of the Ming Dynasty came to the throne, he decided to move his capital northward to Beijing (North Capital). This is the first time to use the name of Beijing. At this time a large-scale reconstruction of the city was carried out. In 1420 the rebuilding of the city was basically completed.

When the Ming troops first conquered Dadu City, they leveled down the Yuan imperial palaces to the ground. For the sake of defence, they built up a new bulwark on the bottle-neck of the Water Storing Pond, which was positioned 2.5 kilometres inside the original northern city wall.

The reconstruction work consisted of the following items:

1. The emperor's palace was rebuilt, with the original central axis as the central line. The new emperor's palace moved a bit southward, which was later called the Purple Forbidden City (which is now well-preserved and opened up as the Palace Museum). In the Forbidden City, the

这一平面布局的主要目的，就是要把帝王的宫殿摆在全城最重要的位置上，它所力求表达的主题思想，就是封建帝王的"唯我独尊"。

这座规模宏伟、规划整齐的大都城开始兴建后八年，马可·波罗就来到这里。他深受忽必烈赏识，并且出仕元朝。后来在他那部游记里，他对大都城作了详细的描述。他称大都城为 Khanbaliq，也就是"大汗之城"的意思。这部游记的英译本流传甚广，这里就不引述了。但是应该指明的一点，即到了十五世纪，哥伦布正是在读了《马可·波罗游记》之后，才决定要远航中国，由于他相信地球是圆的，如果马可·波罗从陆路东行可以到达中国，那么他从海路西航，也同样可以到达中国。他的这一天才的判断，导致了一个伟大的"发现"，这也是众所周知的事，这里也就无须饶舌了。

四、明清北京城：规划设计的特征

元朝的统治也不到一百年，就被汉族建立的明朝所代替。明朝的统治者兴起于长江下游，首先建都在南京，然后北伐，于 1368 年攻下大都城，改称北平。到了它的第三个皇帝即位之后，又决定迁都北平，并把北平改称北京。北京的名称就是从这时开始的。与此同时，还进行了大规模的城市改建工作，到 1420 年基本完工。

明兵最初攻下大都城时，为了便于防守，曾在原来的北城墙内约 2.5 公里的地方，跨过积水潭上最窄狭之处，另建新墙。同时还平毁了元朝的宫殿。

决定从南京迁都到这里之后，又进行了下列主要的改建工程。

一、重建宫城：仍在原来中轴线的旧址上，只是稍向南移，建造了新宫城，这就是保留到现在的紫禁城（今为"故宫博物院"）。紫禁城内

six great halls symbolic of the imperial power ranged from south to north on the central axis of the whole city. The other buildings were as usual arranged on either side of the six great halls in strict symmetry.

2. With the southward moving of the emperor's palace, the south wall of the imperial city and the south wall of the city of Beijing proper were also moved southward. And as a result, the imperial city and the big city got larger space each. A new Imperial Ancestral Temple and a new Altar of Land and Grain were respectively put up in the increased space on the two sides of the central trunk line in front of the Forbidden City. The two groups of buildings which were erected in keeping with the old tradition, were more closely connected with the emperor's palace. With these two groups of new buildings, the position of the central trunk line became more conspicuous from the viewpoint of the plane arrangement.

Besides, in the very front of the imperial city was opened up a new T-shape court square, out of which the present Tian An Men Square grew. On the two sides of the court square, many central governmental offices and organs were concentrated symmetrically.

3. As a result of the southward moving of the south wall of the imperial city, there appeared an expanse of open land to the south end of the Heavenly Water Pond. So a new artificial lake was dug out in this place, which linked the Heavenly Water Pond and made it much larger. The original parts of the lake were called the Middle Sea and the North Sea while the expanded part of the lake was called the South Sea. Just to the north of the Forbidden City, a new man-made hill was piled up with the earth dug out from the South Sea and from the moat around the Forbidden City. This hill was named the Jing Hill or the Coal Hill. The middle peak of the Jing Hill is 47 metres in height. It formed a remarkable point of the central axis of the whole city and became the new geometric centre of the rebuilt city.

4. On the old site of the geometric centre of the former Dadu City, a new Drum Tower and a new Bell Tower were put up. The two buildings

marked the apex of the central axis of the whole of the new city.

5. While the city was reconstructed, two groups of buildings were put up just to the south of the city. The two groups of buildings stood side by side. The one on the east side was called the Temple of Heaven, a place where the emperors offered sacrifices to the Heaven and prayed for good harvests. The one on the west side was called the Altar of Mountain and River, a place where the emperors offered sacrifices to the God of Mountain and the God of River. Between the two groups of buildings,

象征皇权统治中心的六座大殿，自南而北，依次奠基在全城的中轴线上。其他一切建筑，照例是严格对称地排列在六座大殿的东西两侧。

二、由于紫禁城南移的结果，旧日皇城的南墙与大城的南墙，也都依次南移，中间的空间距离也都各有增加。在紫禁城前方中心干道左右两侧扩大了的空间里，新建了太庙和社稷坛，既加强了这两组重要建筑与宫城之间的联系，又仍旧保持着左祖右社的传统，同时在平面布局上还进一步突出了中心干道的位置。

其次，在皇城的正前方，开辟了一个新的"T"字形的宫廷广场，这就是现在天安门广场的前身。当时在广场的东西两侧，还集中布置了中央衙署，同样也是左右对称排列的形式。

三、旧日皇城南墙向南迁移的结果，原来太液池的南端，也出现了大片空地，于是就在这片空地上加凿了一个新的湖泊，从而扩大了太液池的面积，这扩大的部分也叫南海，原有的部分则分别叫做中海与北海。开凿南海时挖起的泥土，再加上开凿紫禁城护城河时挖起的泥土，都用来在紫禁城的正北方，堆筑了一座土山，俗称煤山，后来正式命名为景山。景山中峰高达 47 米，也恰好标志了全城中轴线所在的地方，同时也是经过改造后的全城几何中心。

四、在原来大都城几何中心的旧址上，新建了鼓楼与钟楼。这两座建筑物又标志了全城中轴线的顶点。

五、在城市改建的同时，又在大城正南方修建了两组大建筑，东西并列。在东边的叫做天坛，是皇帝祭天和祈祷五谷丰登的地方。在西边的叫做山川坛，是皇帝祭祀山河之神的地方。这两大建筑群之间，

there was a central trunk line which led northward straight to the middle south gate of the big city. This entrance was called Zhengyang Gate or Front Gate. In 1553, an outer city wall was built to reinforce the defence of the imperial capital. This newly-built outer city enveloped the Temple of Heaven and the Altar of Mountain and River (which was later called the Xiannong Altar). The old city in the north was called "the Inner City" while the newly-built city in the south was called "the Outer City". The combination of the two cities formed an outline which resembles a Chinese character "凸" meaning "protruding".

With the Outer City built, the central axis of the Inner City extended southward to the due south gate of the Outer City. The new central axis was as long as nearly eight kilometres. The new central line became even more outstanding in the plane arrangement of the old city of Beijing.

With the Outer City built, the construction of the old city of Beijing was fundamentally completed. In 1644, the Qing Dynasty—the last feudal dynasty in China's history—was founded.[3] The rulers of the Qing Dynasty also took Beijing as their capital. They didn't make any more changes in the construction of the city. The city remained as it had been until the liberation of Beijing City in 1949. This is now what we call the old city of Beijing.

也有一条中心干道，向北直达大城的正南门，叫做正阳门（俗称前门）。到了 1553 年，为了加强城防，又在城南加筑了一个外罗城，正好把天坛与山川坛（后改称先农坛）包入城中，从而形成了北京城所特有的凸字形的城市轮廓。北部的旧城，也叫"内城"；新筑的外罗城，也叫"外城"。

由于外罗城的修建，原来内城的中轴线，又向南延伸到外城的正南门，总长近八公里，这在整个北京旧城的平面布局上，显得最为突出。

历史上北京城的建设，到此基本完成。1644 年建立的中国历史上最后一个封建王朝——清朝[3]，完全继承了明朝的北京城作为都城，没有更多的改变，这就是完整地保留到 1949 年解放前夕的北京城，现在我们叫它做北京旧城。

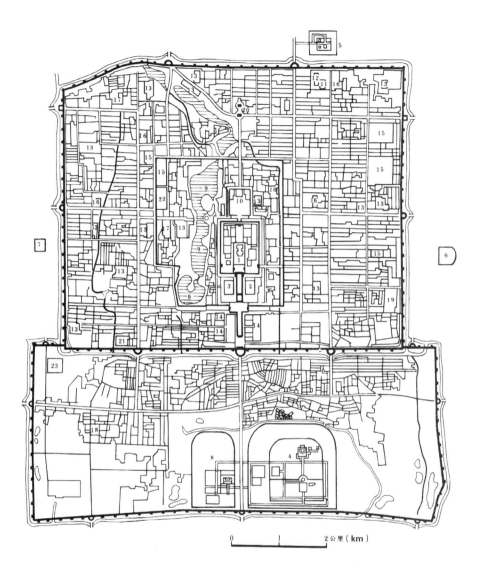

1-6 Plan of old Beijing City 旧北京城平面图

1. Palaces 宫殿
2. Imperial Ancestral Temple 太庙
3. Altar of Land and Grain 社稷坛
4. Altar of Heaven 天坛
5. Altar of Earth 地坛
6. Altar of Sun 日坛
7. Altar of Moon 月坛
8. Xiannong Altar 先农坛
9. Western Garden 西苑
10. Jing Hill 景山
11. Confucian Temple 文庙
12. Imperial College 国子监
13. Residences of princes and princesses 诸王府、公主府
14. Yamuns 衙门
15. Barns 仓库
16. Buddhist temples 佛寺
17. Taoist temples 道观
18. Islamic mosque 伊斯兰教礼拜寺
19. Examination Hall 贡院
20. Bell and Drum Towers 钟鼓楼
21. Elephants stall 象房
22. Catholic church 天主教堂
23. Barrack 营房

（From *A Brief History of Chinese Architecture*, Vol.1, pp.183–184 采自《中国建筑简史》第一册，页一八三——一八四）

This old city of Beijing which was developed on the basis of Dadu City of the Yuan Dynasty, has been considered an excellent example of the construction of feudal capitals in China's history. It embodied all the better the absolute power of feudal emperors.

But as a Chinese saying goes, "things will develop in the opposite direction when they become extreme." The planning and designing of the old city of Beijing demonstrated that the autocratic feudalism in Chinese history had gone to its extreme. And this extreme autocracy led to its own collapse.

In 1911, the democratic revolution led by Dr. Sun Yat-sen broke out. It put an end to the domination of feudal dynasties which had lasted over two thousand years in China.

In 1919, the May Fourth Movement broke out in the old city of Beijing. It marked the prelude to China's new democratic revolution.

After 30 years' hard and bitter struggles, the Chinese people succeeded in achieving their liberation in 1949. During the most arduous struggles, many people, including the great internationalist Dr. Norman Bethune, sacrificed their lives.

On October 1, 1949, Comrade Mao Tse-tung solemnly proclaimed the birth of the People's Republic of China, on the rostrum of Tian An Men Gate (Heavenly Peace Gate). The old city of Beijing became the capital of the People's Republic of China.

We were confronted then with a new question: How should we transform the old capital planned and designed in the interest of the feudal emperors into a new capital of the people who live in the new era of socialism?

We know very well that the guiding principle of the planning and designing of the old city of Beijing was to extol the absolute power or autocratic monarch. Now what should be the guiding principle of the overall planning of the new city of Beijing which serves as the people's capital in the new socialist era?

I'll deal with this question in my next talk.

Thank you very much for your attention.

A Discussion on the New City Plan of Beijing

The transformation of the old city of Beijing started as soon as it was made the capital of the People's Republic of China, to meet the needs of a new era. In addition to the establishment of a special city-planning institution, three guiding principles have been formulated: it must serve first, proletarian politics, second, industrial and agricultural production, and third, the labouring people.

这个从元朝大都城的基础上发展起来的北京旧城，被认为是中国封建时代都城建设的最杰出的典型，它进一步发展了大都城的平面布局，更加突出地表达了封建帝王"唯我独尊"的主题思想。

但是，正如中国的谚语所说的那样："物极必反"——事物发展到极端，就要转向它的反面。

北京旧城的规划设计，乃是中国历史上封建专制主义发展到极端的一种表现，同时这也就导致了它最后的崩溃。

1911 年由孙中山先生所领导的资产阶级民主革命，结束了在中国长达两千多年的封建王朝的统治。

1919 年在北京旧城里爆发的五四运动，又揭开了新民主主义革命的序幕。

经过整整三十年艰苦卓绝的流血牺牲——其中包括以白求恩大夫为代表的伟大的国际主义战士的流血牺牲——中国人民才终于获得了解放。

1949 年 10 月 1 日中华人民共和国宣告成立。历史悠久的北京旧城，又被定为新中国的人民首都，从而迎来了城市建设的一个新起点。

五、改造北京旧城的新起点

中华人民共和国建都北京之后，为了适应新时代的要求，立即着手于北京旧城的改造。

To serve proletarian politics means to turn the old city, which was constructed in the past to satisfy the political needs of the feudal emperors, into a new one which will best suit the political demands of a people's capital in the new era of socialism.

To serve industrial and agricultural production means to turn the old city which used to be the largest consumer centre in the country, into a base for modernised industrial production and centre of well-developed suburban agriculture.

To serve the labouring people means to completely reform the slummy districts swarming with working people in the past, and on an overall scale, give preference in our city planning to those projects of urban construction which will satisfy the immediate needs in their lives. Under guidance of these three principles, great achievements have been made in both the city planning and the construction of Beijing and profound changes have been brought about in its functions and appearance during the last thirty years. There are experiences of success as well as lessons of disappointment in the process. However, to comment on them at length here would be both unnecessary and beyond my power. As a scholar of the historical geography, the question I would like to put forth for discussion is exactly the one which I posed at the conclusion of my last lecture. I shall repeat it here.

How do we transform an imperial capital which was once planned and designed for the benefit of feudal emperors in the past into a people's capital of the socialist new era? Or rather, in contrast with the theme of glorifying the supremacy of feudal monarchs as illustrated in the city planning of the old Beijing, what new theme should we adopt for the city planning of today's Beijing serving as a people's capital and how can such a theme be effectually materialised?

This problem is not merely one of engineering technology, but above all, one of great significance to the development of history and culture. In China today, with the transformation of social system, the values of an age-old tradition are also undergoing unprecedented changes. We could never imagine that a new socialist culture would drop from the sky, nor could it be transplanted from a certain foreign land. It can only grow up out of its native soil. For instance, isn't the Renaissance, which had its root in ancient Greek and Roman culture, and which, in turn, with a completely new mental outlook, created a great new epoch in European culture of the Middle Ages, such a shining precedent?

In China today, people have also been discussing and looking forward to the advent of a great new era of renaissance, sprouting out of its native soil. Consequently, how to regard one's own historical and cultural heritage becomes a problem of considerable importance.

　　三十年来，北京的城市面貌已经发生了巨大的变化。在这一改造过程中，既有成功的经验，也有失败的教训。在这里一一加以评述，既非必要，也不是我所能胜任的。我作为一个城市历史地理的学者所愿意提出来讨论的一个问题，就是：我们怎么样才能把一个过去为封建帝王规划设计的城市，改造为一个体现社会主义新时代的人民首都？或者更确切地说：和北京旧城城市规划中所表达的那种歌颂封建帝王"唯我独尊"的主题思想相对比，在今天，作为人民首都的北京城，在它的城市规划中所应该表达的主题思想又是什么？

　　这个问题不是一个单纯的工程技术问题，而首先是一个涉及历史文化发展的大问题。今天在中国，随着社会制度的变革，具有悠久传统的历史文化，也正在经历着前所未有的大变化。我们绝不能设想一个社会主义的新文化会从天上掉下来，或者是从某一个外国移植进来，它只能从自己固有的土壤里发育成长起来。例如：植根在希腊罗马的古文化里、而又以崭新的精神面貌为欧洲中世纪的文化开创了一个伟大的新时代的"文艺复兴"，不就是这样一个光辉的先例么？

　　今天，在中国，人们也在议论着、期待着一个植根在自己土壤里的伟大的社会主义"文艺复兴"新时代的到来。因此，在这一情况下，如何正确对待自己的历史文化遗产，就成了一个极为重要的问题。

Our basic principle is critical inheritance. During the long period of feudal society, the Chinese people have created a magnificent ancient culture, which, however, also contains some feudal dregs. It is wrong to accept ancient culture without discrimination, and equally wrong to reject it altogether; the only correct attitude, of course, is to assimilate its essence and discard its dregs, to make the past serve the present and weed through the old to bring forth the new, so as to create a new culture characteristic of the epoch, on the basis formed in the course of history. Naturally, during this process of creating a new culture, it is necessary for us to endeavour to absorb all that is advanced from other countries to serve our own purpose, to use a catch-phrase, "to make foreign things serve China".

So far, we have only touched upon abstract principles. But I've already digressed too far from the point in question. So let us return to it now.

In fact, the old city of Beijing which has been kept intact all through is part of China's historical and cultural legacy. The reconstruction of the city shall also be carried on under the guidance of the principle of critical inheritance. First of all, we should keep one thing in mind; that is, as a people's capital of the socialist new era, it must adopt a theme for its city planning in praise of the people, of their strength, their dignity, of the truth: "The people, and the people alone, are the motive force in the creation of the world." It should not only demonstrate the great creations of the people in the past, but also embody the stark reality that the people have become masters of their country. The fulfillment of this new theme shall serve as a thorough criticism of the old theme centred upon the eulogy of the supremacy of the feudal monarchy.

How to bring about the fulfillment of this new theme is a problem of vital importance in the new city planning of Beijing.

It seems to be a very difficult problem, but actually many valuable experiences have been gathered during the transformation of the old city of Beijing since liberation, and need to be summed up and brought up to a theoretical height so that they may give further guidance to the city planning and construction of Beijing later on. I shall cite only one example here, the reconstruction of the Tian An Men Square for illustration.

Tian An Men Square is closer to the centre of the city now than in the past.

我们的基本原则，就是要批判地继承。

在我国长期的封建社会里，曾经创造过灿烂的古代文化，但是其中也还存在着封建的糟粕。对于古代文化无条件地兼收并蓄是错误的；一律予以排斥，也是错误的。唯一正确的态度，就是吸其精华，弃其糟粕，古为今用，推陈出新，从而在历史形成的基础上，创造出一个富有时代特征的新文化来。当然，在这一创造过程中，去努力吸收外国一切先进的东西，为我所用，也是完全必要的。用我们惯用的一个名词来说，这就是"洋为中用"。

以上所讲，还只是一些抽象的原则，或许已经离题太远了。现在急需回到我们所讨论的具体问题上来。

实际上，被完整地保留下来的北京旧城，也就是中国历史文化遗产的一部分。对于这个城市的改造，也必须遵循批判继承的原则。这里首先必须明确的一点，就是今天作为社会主义新时代的人民首都，它在城市规划上的主题思想，就应该是歌颂人民——歌颂人民的力量、人民的尊严，歌颂"人民，只有人民，才是创造世界历史的动力"。它既要显示出历史上劳动人民的伟大创造，又要体现出当前人民当家做主的现实。如果做到这一点，这也就是对北京旧城的城市规划上所集中表现的那种封建帝王"唯我独尊"的主题思想，进行了彻底的批判。

怎样才能在北京旧城的改造中，具体实现这一新的主题思想，乃是新的城市规划中一个最为重要的问题。

看起来这是一个十分困难的问题，实际上在解放以来改造北京旧城的过程中，已经创造出一些可贵的经验，需要加以总结，并提升到理论的高度上来，以进一步指导今后北京城的城市规划和城市建设的实践。这里只提出一个例子作为说明，这就是天安门广场的改造。

天安门广场现在比过去更加接近于全城的中心位置了。

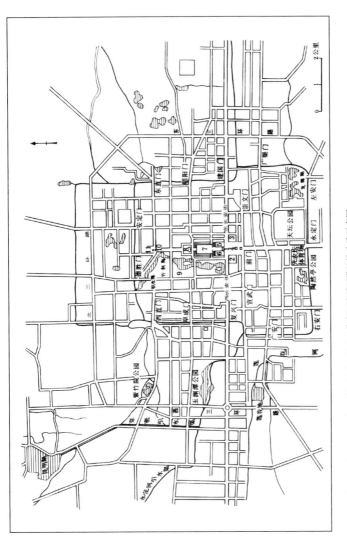

1-7 Sketch map of reconstruction of Beijing's old city 北京旧城平面设计的改造示意图

1. Tian An Men Gate 天安门　　　　　　　　　2. People's Conference Hall 人民大会堂

3. Museum of Chinese Revolution and Museum of Chinese History 中国革命博物馆、中国历史博物馆

4. Monument of the People's Heroes 人民英雄纪念碑　　5. Working People's Palace of Culture 劳动人民文化宫　　6. Sun Yat-sen Park 中山公园

7. Palace Museum 故宫博物院　　　　　　　　8. Jing Hill Park 景山公园　　　　　　　　9. North Sea Park 北海公园

10. Drum Tower 鼓楼　　　　　　　　　　　　11. Bell Tower 钟楼

(Redrawn according to Urban Traffic Map in *Beijing Tourism Atlas*, simplified version, 2nd edition, 1972

根据地图出版社《北京市游览图》1972 年第 2 版中的《市区交通图》缩简改绘）

It was decided in the city planning of an earlier stage after liberation that the reconstruction and extension of Beijing should centre around the old city. Today Beijing's new urban districts have broken the bounds of the former city walls and expanded in every direction. The limit of extension was roughly set at the third suburban ring road which is now under construction. Within this limit, the layout of the streets was to retain, on the whole, the traditional pattern. Beyond it, the main lines of communication were to radiate in all directions. The plane design of the city preserved the traditional character of balance and symmetry, thus enhancing the outstanding position of the Tian An Men Square which used to be a court square in front of Tian An Men, the south gate of the old imperial city. It was nominally a "gate", but in reality, an imperial palace built on a purple terrace. The artisans who undertook the construction of Tian An Men have bestowed upon it such majestic beauty as to illustrate fully the characteristic of ancient Chinese architecture. The feudal emperors' aim in building such an enormous structure on this spot was not merely for the sake of fortification, but also to display the dignity of their kingly abode. According to the tradition of feudal dynasties, here was the so-called "outer court" where receptions of distinguished foreign guests and celebrations of grand occasions took place.

早在解放初期的城市规划中，就已决定北京城的改建，应以旧城为中心，在此基础上进行改建和扩建。现在北京城的新市区，已经突破旧日的城圈，向四外扩展。扩展的范围，大体以正在兴建中的郊区环路（即三环路）作为界限。在此界限以内，街道的布局基本上保持着旧城以内的传统格局。在此界限以外，重要交通干线，呈辐射状、通向四面八方。整个城市的平面设计，继续保持着平衡匀称的特点，因而使天安门广场的位置显得更加明显、更加突出。这个广场原是天安门前的一个宫廷广场，天安门也就是旧日皇城的正南门。它名义上是一座门，实际上是建筑在红色台基上的一座殿堂。当初经手建造天安门的工匠，赋予它以如此庄严壮丽的形象，充分体现了我国古代建筑艺术的特色。封建帝王要求在这里建筑这样一座巨大的建筑物，除去了为了加强对宫城的保卫外，更重要的还是为了显示帝王之居的尊严与华贵。按照封建王朝的传统，这里就是所谓"外朝"。"外朝"原来是皇帝接见外国宾客的地方，也在这里举行其他盛大节日的庆典。

The last feudal dynasty, the Qing Dynasty, also used this "outer court" to celebrate the issuing of the imperial edict on the coronation day, that is, to publicise the coronation of a new emperor to the subjects of the kingdom. The imperial edict was placed on a tray carved in the shape of cloud and carried to Tian An Men from the Forbidden City in a miniature "Dragon Pavilion". Then, jubilant music was played on Tian An Men, whose square was strewn with prostrate civil and military officials and "elders" chosen and dispatched here to represent the common people. After the edict was read by the Edict Reader on Tian An Men, it was placed in the beak of a carved golden phoenix and lowered slowly down along the middle of the gate where it was put back into the "Dragon Pavilion" again and carried to the "Ministry of Rites" to the east of the square, where fair copies of it were made in yellow paper and distributed to the whole kingdom. The sole purpose of this ritual performance was to show that the divine rights of monarchs came directly from the Heaven. This is only an illustration of how feudal emperors used this court square to make a display of themselves and fool the people.

The square was somewhat T-shaped and closely confined by red walls all around, leaving only one entrance on every side for passage. These entrances, however, were strictly forbidden to the common people.

But the dialectics of history is relentless. When the Qing Dynasty was overthrown in 1911, it was this square which had been so strictly forbidden to the ordinary people that became the rallying centre of the revolutionary masses for patriotic demonstrations. And it was here, some sixty years ago, that the May Fourth Movement, which set the new democratic revolution ablaze, broke out. Again, it was here that the last mass movement was launched on the eve of the nation's liberation, against Chiang Kai-shek's attempt to unleash a civil war and his persecution of young students.

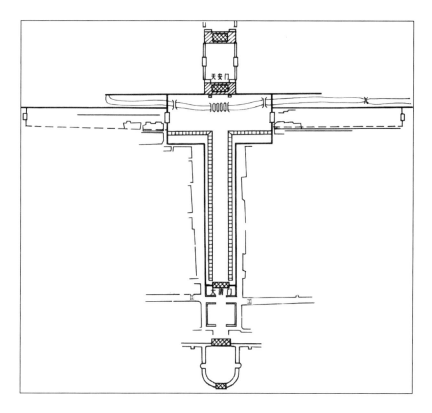

1-8 The Qing Dynasty's T-shaped imperial square 清乾隆扩建后的天安门宫廷广场

到了最后一个封建王朝——清朝，还利用这个"外朝"，为皇帝的登基，举行"颁诏"大典，也就是用"诏书"把皇帝即位的事，宣告全国。诏书被放在一只像一朵云彩一样的盘子里，然后用"龙亭"从紫禁城里抬到天安门上。这时天安门上奏起了欢庆的乐章，天安门前的广场上则跪满了文武百官和被选派来代表老百姓的"耆老"。宣诏官在天安门城楼上宣读诏书之后，随即用一个雕制的金色凤凰，口衔诏书，从城楼的正中，徐徐系下，放进"龙亭"里，抬送到天安门广场东面的"礼部"衙门，然后用黄纸誊写，传送全国各地。扮演这套仪式的用意，不外是说"君权神授"、"命自天降"。这仅仅是一个例子，用以说明封建皇帝是如何利用这个宫廷广场，来炫耀自己和愚弄人民的。

这个"T"字形的宫廷广场，周围用红墙严格封闭起来，只留有东、西、南三个大门可以行走，但是人民群众是绝对不准涉足的。

然而历史的辩证法是无情的。在清王朝 1911 年被推翻之后，也正是这个过去严禁老百姓涉足的广场，却成了革命群众集合起来举行爱国示威游行的中心。整整六十年前点燃了新民主主义革命的熊熊火焰的五四运动，就是从这里开始的。解放前夕最后一次反对蒋介石进行内战和迫害青年学生的群众运动，也是在这里开始的。

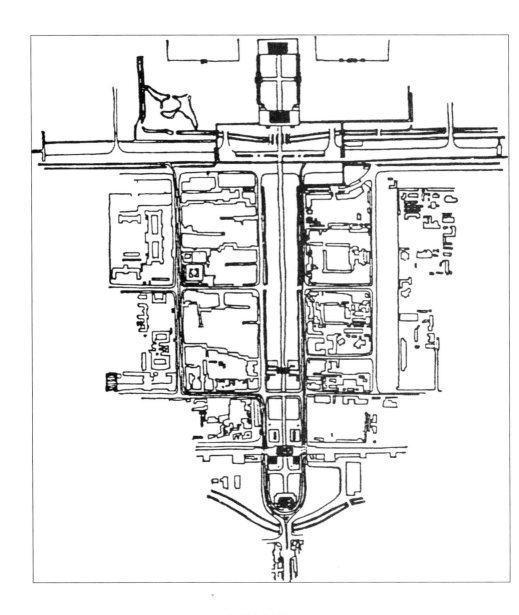

1-9 Tian An Men Square before redevelopment 改建前天安门广场图

Due to this glorious revolutionary tradition, the Tian An Men Square was chosen to be the site for the grand founding ceremony of the People's Republic of China on October 1, 1949. Subsequently Tian An Men, the magnificent structure erected by labouring people in ancient times, was engraved on the national emblem of the republic to symbolize the renaissance of an ancient culture. The square has been transformed from a feudal court square into a people's square in the new socialist epoch. It has now become the centre of the country's political life, cherished by people of all nationalities.

But, at the time when the founding ceremony was being celebrated, the square was still confined on all sides by walls which seriously hindered popular activities by obstructing their sight and compressing their hilarious atmosphere within the square. As we look at it today, Tian An Men represents the essence of ancient Chinese architecture whereas those walls represent the dregs of feudalism. We must preserve the essence part and, according to the principle of making the past serve the present and weeding through the old to bring forth the new, weave it into the urban life of the present day, so that it may better serve the people. As to the feudal dregs, we must discard them in order to clear the way for our advance towards a new life.

正是由于北京古城里的这一光荣的革命传统，1949 年 10 月 1 日中华人民共和国的开国大典，也就选择在这里隆重举行。从此，天安门这座古代劳动人民一手创造的庄严壮丽的形象，终于出现在中华人民共和国的国徽上，象征着一个古老的文明，从此获得了新生。这样，天安门广场也就从一个封建时代的宫廷广场，转化成为一个社会主义新时代的人民广场，在我国的政治生活里，它已成为各族人民共同向往的中心。

但是，在开国大典举行的时候，这个广场还被包围在东、西、南三面围墙之内。这三面围墙严重地限制了广大群众的活动，阻碍了他们的视野，封锁了他们在广场上的热烈欢腾的气氛。现在看来，如果说天安门所代表的乃是古代建筑的精华，那么广场上的围墙所代表的却是封建性的糟粕。精华的部分，我们一定要保留，并且本着古为今用、推陈出新的原则，把它组织到现代的城市生活中来，使它有更好的条件，为人民服务。封建的糟粕，我们一定要排除，从而扫清我们向新生活迈进的道路。

On October 1, 1959, when we celebrated the tenth anniversary of the founding of the republic, the first transformation project of the Tian An Men Square was brought to a successful termination in accordance with the new city planning programme. After the reconstruction, the old walls on the three sides had disappeared and an entirely new square, many folds larger than the old one, presented itself to the public. It remains on the same premises, but has taken on a brand new appearance. Its magnificent, solemn, spacious and shining physiognomy is the embodiment of the ocean-like mind and overwhelming power of the people. The Monument of the People's Heroes towering in the centre of the square, had been completed a year before. With the People's Conference Hall that represents the centre of popular power on its west side and the Museum of Chinese Revolution and the Museum of Chinese History which serve to praise the people as the motive force in history-making, the square has become the heart of the political life of China's various nationalities, whence were spread abroad the aspirations of the Chinese people.

During the reconstruction of the square, its two wings, the East and West Chang An Streets, were extended accordingly. Thus, the great smooth boulevard now forms a new thoroughfare threading the whole city from east to west. By contrast, it has definitely belittled the traditional thoroughfare which runs across the old city from south to north. This is as good as thoroughly negating the theme in the design of the old city, thus giving prominence to the unique position of the people's square in the plane layout of the whole city. The Forbidden City, which perched imposingly in the centre of the city during the old days, is now but a "backyard" of the people's square where only in spare time do people come and enjoy themselves in appreciation of the magnificent palaces built by the labouring people of ancient times and the gems of art in store there.

When Chairman Mao's Memorial Hall was completed in July 1977, the people's square was further expanded and endowed with new significance, adding to the serenity and tranquility of the south end. The lofty antique building of Qian Men (or Zheng Yang Men) has been preserved as well as the majestic Tian An Men. But these two age-old gates have now lost their former function as vanguards of the Forbidden City. They now serve with their artistic features as boundary marks of the new people's square on its south and north borders respectively. Once the thoroughfare—South Qian Men Street—from Qian Men to Yong Ding Men is expanded, the prominence of the Tian An Men Square as the centre of the whole city of Beijing will be further enhanced.

1959 年 10 月 1 日，在庆祝建国十周年的时候，根据新的城市规划的要求，第一次改建天安门广场的工程，胜利完成。改建之后，不仅是旧日的三面围墙不见了，而且是一个崭新的广场，以数倍于过去的面积，出现在人们面前。它的基础依旧，而面貌一新。它以宏伟、壮丽、广阔、明朗的景象，象征着人民群众海洋般的胸襟，排山倒海的力量。早一年建成的是矗立于广场中央的人民英雄纪念碑。这时又在广场的西侧建成了人民大会堂，在东侧建成了中国革命和中国历史博物馆。随着这两座现代大建筑物的落成，天安门广场已经形成为全国各族人民政治生活的心脏，从这里传播出中国人民最强烈的心声。

在广场改造的同时，又把作为广场两翼的东西长安街，加以扩建。于是一条宽阔平直的林荫大道，实际上就形成为从东到西横贯全城的新轴线。对比之下，它使得那条传统的自南而北、纵贯旧城的中轴线，相形见绌，这就等于是彻底否定了北京旧城在规划设计上的主题思想，从而突出了人民广场在全城平面布局中独一无二的重要地位。而旧日雄踞全城中心的紫禁城，如今也只能算是人民广场的一个"后院"了。只有在工作之余，人们才到这里来，欣赏古代劳动人民用自己的双手所创造出来的雄伟瑰丽的建筑物，和收藏在这里的世间罕见的艺术珍品。

1977 年 7 月毛主席纪念堂建成之后，又进一步扩建了人民广场，并赋予它以新的意义，增加了南半部肃穆宁静的气氛。正阳门这座巍峨屹立的古老建筑，和庄严壮丽的天安门，同样被保留下来，但是这两座旧的城门，作为紫禁城前门的功能，不复存在。相反的，它们却以其固有的艺术造型，为新出现的人民广场，标志了它的南北界限。将来从正阳门到永定门的干道——前门南大街——展宽之后，就会更加突出天安门广场在北京全城的中心位置。

The square, which is now still undergoing further planning, is only an example to illustrate that if we persist in critical inheritance on the basis formed in the course of history and in accordance with the principles of making the past serve the present and weeding through the old to bring forth the new, a court square whose theme it was to extol feudal emperors can certainly be transformed into a people's square whose theme it is to praise the strength of the people. By analogy, the city of Beijing whose theme it was to extol feudal emperors, can likewise be transformed into a people's capital whose theme it is to praise the strength of the people.

But we must also acknowledge that there did arise controversies in regard to certain measures taken during the transformation of the old city. Although the demolition of the outer red walls enclosing Tian An Men Square did not give rise to any dissent, it was not the case with that of the old city walls. When the question of removing the old city walls was first taken into consideration in the new city planning, opinions varied. Now that the city walls have already been removed, we have come to realize through the test of practice that whether it was absolutely necessary to get rid of them is indeed a question worth investigation, especially when part of the city moat has been turned into an undercurrent with their removal, thus reducing the water area in the city, which has proved detrimental to the improvement of its environment. It was particularly true with the moat outside Qian Men which runs through the middle of the city from west to east. If it had been preserved, it would not only have added to the natural beauty of the city, but also promoted its climate conditioning and helped to provide the city with fresh air, which would be extremely advantageous to the improvement of the city's environment and would supply its residents with excellent recreation ground.

It ought to be mentioned here that before the Cultural Revolution, there was a certain project in a district planning for the transformation of Tian An Men Square to bring a section of the moat outside Qian Men into the new plan of the Tian An Men Square. As a result, there would appear in the south of the square, a wooded garden abounding in natural views. If this proposal had been adopted, it would have added to the serenity and tranquility in the southern part of Tian An Men Square by setting off the green lawns around Chairman Mao's Memorial Hall with a riverside park outside Qian Men. But all this has proved to be something irremediable now.

　　目前仍在规划和改建中的天安门广场，只是一个例子，足以说明在历史形成的基础上，坚持批判的继承，根据古为今用、推陈出新的原则，原来一个以歌颂封建帝王为主题思想的宫廷广场，是完全可以改造为一个以歌颂人民力量为主题思想的人民广场的！以此类推，原来一个以歌颂封建帝王为主题思想的北京旧城，也是完全可以改造为一个以歌颂人民力量为主题思想的人民首都的。

　　但是，也要看到，在改造北京旧城的过程中，也有一些措施，是存在着争议的。如果说拆除围绕天安门广场的三面红墙，没有引起任何异议，而拆除围绕北京旧城的城墙，却不是这样。在新的城市规划中，最初考虑要拆除旧城城墙的时候，就曾有过不同的争论。现在在拆除城墙之后，经过实践的检验，使我们进一步认识到，旧日城墙的完全拆除，是否绝对必要，这个问题确是值得讨论的。尤其是随着城墙的拆除，部分护城河也被改造为地下暗渠，这样就减少了城市中的水面积，是不利于环境条件的改善的。特别是正阳门外的护城河，自西而东正好穿过城市的中心地带，如果保留下来，注满清澈的河水，同时沿河两岸进行绿化，既增加了市容的自然景色，又有利于调节城市气候和向城市中心输送新鲜空气，这是大大有利于城市环境的改善的，同时也就为市民提供了良好的游憩场所。

　　应该提到，在"文化大革命"的十年动乱之前，在改造天安门广场的小区规划中，曾有一种方案，就是要把正阳门外的一段护城河，纳入天安门广场的规划之中。这样，在广场的南部，就出现了一区富有自然风光的园林。如果当初采纳了这一方案，那么1977年修建毛主席纪念堂之后，除去紧傍纪念堂周围的绿地之外，还有正阳门外的滨河公园作为陪衬，那就会增加天安门广场南部的肃穆宁静的气氛。但这一切都已是不可挽救的事实了。

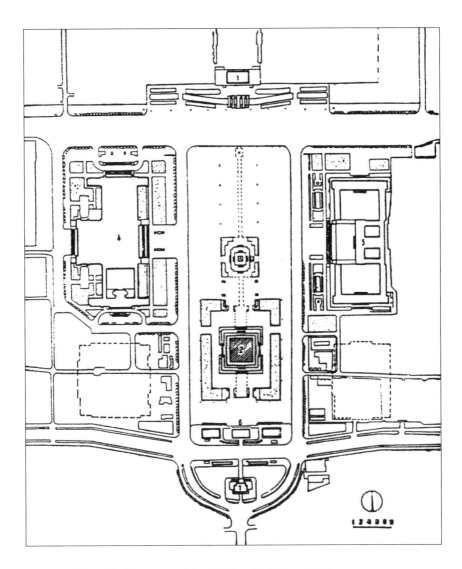

1-10 Plan of Tian An Men Square on completion of Chairman Mao's Memorial Hall

毛主席纪念堂建成时的天安门广场总平面图

1. Tian An Men 天安门

2. Chairman Mao's Memorial Hall 毛主席纪念堂

3. Monument of the People's Heroes 人民英雄纪念碑

4. People's Conference Hall 人民大会堂

5. Museum of Chinese Revolution, Museum of Chinese History 中国革命博物馆、中国历史博物馆

6. Zheng Yang Men (Qian Men) 正阳门（前门）

7. Archery Tower 箭楼

(From *Journal of Architecture*, 1977, No. 4 采自《建筑学报》1977：4)

This is an example which illustrates that during the transformation of the old city of Beijing, there did exist setbacks in our experience which need to be summed up for future reference when we revise the city plan of Beijing. Of course, this is only my personal view on the matter which may not be correct after all. The heartening thing is that we are free to carry on liberal discussions on controversial issues now. A correct conclusion is sure to be brought about through practice as to the truth and falsehood of an issue. There was a time in the past when academic discussion was confused with political problems, which impeded free discussion and brought about harmful results. For instance, when the question of preserving or demolishing the city walls of Beijing was being discussed, those who favoured its preservation were inclined to be labelled as "conservative", "retrograde" or even "reactionary", thus forcing people to refrain from speaking their mind. Consequently, many valuable opinions were stifled, which proved detrimental to our work. This state of affairs was allowed to develop to an incredible degree during the ten years when the "Gang of Four" was in power, especially in the sphere of culture and learning where "ten thousand horses stood mute".

借此一例用以说明,在我们改造北京旧城的工作中,也还有不少经验教训,需要加以总结,以便在修订新的城市规划时,作为借鉴。当然这也只是我个人的一点看法,并不一定完全正确。可喜的是,现在我们在一些有争议的问题上,是可以充分展开自由讨论了。何是何非,通过实践是会得出正确的结论的。过去有一个时期,在讨论问题的时候,确实有把学术问题和政治问题混在一起的情况,这样就会阻挠自由讨论,以致造成不良的后果。例如,过去在讨论北京城墙存废的问题上,主张保留城墙的人,就容易被扣上"保守"、"复旧"等等帽子,这样就不能使人畅所欲言,因此有些好意见就会被埋没,并使工作遭受损失。这种情况,在"四人帮"掌权的十年间(1966—1976),竟然发展到令人难以置信的程度。尤其是在文化学术领域里,更是"万马齐喑"的局面。

It is most encouraging to see that during the last two years there has emerged once more the flourishing scene of allowing a hundred flowers to blossom and a hundred schools to contend. Emancipation of the mind and free airing of views are considered to be vital conditions of accelerating the realisation of the modernisation.

As has been proved by experience, as far as critical inheritance of history and culture is concerned, it is not always so easy to distinguish the essense from the dregs. Therefore, it becomes quite necessary to carry on thorough discussion and free debate on all controversial matters. Only by this can we really tell the right from the wrong and distinguish the essence from the dregs, thus achieving the purpose of making the past serve the present and weeding through the old to bring out the new. This is also true with the city construction of Beijing, as well as the cultural construction of the whole nation, only the problem is even more complicated.

In concluding my lecture, I would like to repeat the point that I brought up at the beginning of my talk, i.e. a new China is forging ahead towards modernisation along the road of the new Long March. For this purpose, we have to learn from the West everything that is advanced. Likewise, we shall also absorb all that is valuable from our historical and cultural heritage, which is more important and more complicated a problem in the construction of our new socialist culture. We are quite sure to greet the advent of a new era in our country, which may well be termed a "renaissance", by solving the above-mentioned problem step by step in the process.

It is a great pleasure for me to have obtained this opportunity to come here on the kind invitation of your university, and give a very inadequate introduction of one of the problems confronting my country and my people to my most amiable Canadian friends and colleagues, with the aim to help in my small way to promote mutual understanding and cultural exchange between our two countries, which has been my greatest wish.

Once more, let me give my heart-felt thanks to the revered President of the University of British Columbia, the honourable Chairman and members of Cecil H. and Ida Green Visiting Professorships and all who have come to my lecture today.

令人鼓舞的是，近两年来在我国又重新出现了百花齐放、百家争鸣的繁荣景象。解放思想、广开言路，已被认为是加速实现社会主义现代化的重要条件。

事实证明，在历史文化遗产批判继承的问题上，精华与糟粕并不总是黑白分明和一目了然的。因此，在一切有争论的问题上，充分展开讨论，进行自由争辩，乃是十分必要的。只有这样才能真正明辨是非，才能善加区别精华与糟粕，从而真正达到古为今用、推陈出新的目的。在北京城的城市建设上是如此，在全国的文化建设上来说，也是一样，只是问题会更加复杂罢了。

在结束我的讲演之前，我愿意再一次提出在一开始时我所讲到的那个论点：一个新中国，正在一个新长征的道路上，向着社会主义现代化的目标，努力前进。为此我们就需要向你们、向西方学习一切先进的科学技术，同时我们还需要从自己的历史文化遗产中去吸取一切有价值的部分，而这一点，在我们建设社会主义新文化的过程中，乃是更为重要——也是更为复杂的一个问题。我们满怀信心，在不断解决这个问题的实践中，去迎接我国一个也可以称之为社会主义的"文艺复兴"新时代的来临！

❷ THE TRANSFORMATION OF THE OLD CITY OF BEIJING, CHINA

A Concrete Manifestation of New China's Cultural Reconstruction*

In the modern world, China is both a developing nation and a newly emerging socialist state. Coming from an ancient cultural tradition, she now faces a new era of unprecedented social change. While overhauling her backward economy and actively pursuing reconstruction and modernization, she is also rapidly developing a new socialist culture. In the process of modernization and reconstruction, it is necessary for China to adopt the foreign science and technology according to her own needs. But the development of a new socialist culture, however, entails a more important and complex problem: how to identify and preserve the valuable part of China's own traditional culture.

It is impossible, of course, for China's new socialist culture to drop from the sky, or be imported intact from any particular foreign country. It can only grow from China's own native soil. This is not to say that all foreign cultural influence should be rejected, but it can only contribute positively to China's new, modern culture by being first fused with China's unique traditional culture. Taking into account this background of great social change, this essay attempts to describe and explain a concrete example of the issues which must be faced in creating the new socialist culture. In presenting the problem of transforming an old, historical city into a modern, new one, I can only offer the perspective of an historical geographer, not that of a specialist in city planning, but hope this discussion has some value in that context.

The Relevance of Ancient Chinese Planning Theory

With the growth of world urbanization in recent times, city planning as a specialized science has become more complex and more important each day. But it is not a new science, as it was already flourishing in some of the great civilizations of antiquity. Ancient China was no exception, and Paul Wheatley has drawn particular attention to the symbolic nature of the "ideal" planned layout of ancient China's cities, citing

贰 展望首都新风貌：北京旧城城市设计的改造*

一

在当代世界中，中国是一个发展中的国家，同时又是一个新兴的社会主义国家。在经历了具有悠久文化传统的历史发展之后，现在它正面临着一个前所未有的社会变革的新时代，在努力摆脱经济上的落后状态而积极进行现代化建设的同时，一个社会主义的新文化也正在发展中。在进行现代化建设的过程中，结合自己的具体情况，注意吸收外国一切先进的科学技术是必要的。但是在发展社会主义新文化的过程中，如何从自己的历史文化遗产中吸取一切有价值的部分，乃是一个更加重要也更加复杂的问题。绝不能设想一个社会主义的新文化会从天上掉下来或是从某一个外国移植进来，它只能从自己固有的土壤里发育成长。当然这并不排除外来文化的影响，但是这种外来的影响只有在被充分融化于具有自己特色的传统文化之中，它才有可能产生某种真正的社会价值，才能为创造具有时代特征的新文化作出贡献。正是在这一伟大的社会变革的背景下，本文试图以北京旧城城市设计的改造为例，就我们当前所面临的建设社会主义新文化的问题，作一个具体说明。作为一个历史地理工作者，我也只能着重从地理的因素上而不是从城市设计的专门技术上来提出一些个人的观点和看法，或许还可能有值得城市规划学者参考的地方。

二

随着当代世界性城市化的进展，城市规划作为一项专门的科学，已经变得日益复杂、也日益重要。但是这门科学在一些文明古国里，却已早有萌芽，这在古代中国也不例外。惠特利教授的巨著《四方之极》一书，就充分说明了这一点。他在这部著作中，特别强调了古代中国城市建设在理想化平面设计中的象征意义，引证了

corroborative evidence in the *Book of Artificers* (*Kao Gong Ji*). One of the outstanding features of the ideal layout is the north-south axis of the whole city, and "this axial design is superbly executed in Pei-Ching [Beijing]."[1]

The *Book of Artificers* was completed around the fifth century B.C. and deals primarily with manufacturing technology. It also records the plan for the construction of the imperial capital, which is somewhat ambiguous and has been subject to varying interpretations and reconstructions. The main points of the plan include the following. First, the capital should be laid out as a square, surrounded by a city wall; each side should extend nine *li* (Chinese mile, equal to about 1/2 kilometer) and contain three city gates. Second, within the city there should be nine longitudinal and nine latitudinal thoroughfares, or three longitudinal and three latitudinal thoroughfares, each consisting of three chariot lanes. Third, in the center of the capital is the Imperial Palace of the emperor. On the left side of the Imperial Palace is the "Tai Miao," where the emperor pays homage to his ancestors. On the right side is the "She-ji Tan," where he worships the gods of soil and grain. The front part of the Imperial Palace is the emperor's administrative center, and to the rear of the Imperial Palace is the capital's main market and commercial center.

These declarations in the *Book of Artificers* refer to the capital and largest city of the empire; "left," "right," "front," and "back" refer to the four cardinal directions (respectively east, west, south, and north). The Imperial Palace of the emperor faced true south and was located in the geometric center of the whole city. Tai Miao (the Imperial Ancestral Temple) lay to its east, She-ji Tan (the Altar of Soil and Grain) lay to its west, and the city market to its north. The city was aligned along a north-south axis, facing the south and with its back to the north. This orientation bore a close relationship to the residential traditions of the lower reaches of the Yellow River (Huang Ho), where Chinese civilization originated. The plains of the lower Yellow River, small ones such as the Jing-Wei and Yi-Lo Basins as well as the great North China Plain, have a flat and open topography. They are located in the temperate zone, characterized by strong prevailing monsoons and four distinct seasons, with hot, rainy summers and cold, blustery winters. In order to maximize ventilation in summer, while in winter providing maximum exposure to the sun and shelter from the cold north wind,

《考工记》一书关于都城的平面设计作为一例，进行了饶有趣味的探讨。他还对北京旧城城市设计中象征性的格局，作了高度的评价。[1]

在这里，对于《考工记》中的有关记载，再作些进一步的阐述，或许是必要的。

《考工记》大约写成于公元前 5 世纪左右，主要是讲工艺制作，其中也记载了帝王都城建筑的平面设计，不过文字的描述过于简略，后人也有不同的说明和图解。如果就其主要内容加以阐述，可以包括下列几项：

（1）都城作正方形，四边筑有城墙，每边长 4.5 公里，各开三个城门。

（2）城内有九条直街，九条横街。也可解释为三条直街、三条横街，每街各有三条并列的车马大道。

（3）全城的中央是帝王的宫城。宫城的左边是太庙，也就是帝王祭祀其祖先的地方；右边是社稷坛，也就是帝王祭祀土地和五谷之神的地方。宫城的前面是朝廷，也就是帝王临朝听政的地方；后面是市场，也就是全城的商业中心。

《考工记》的上述记载，指的是帝王的统治中心，也就是国都，是规模最大的城市。记载中的"左祖"、"右社"、"面朝"、"后市"，都是按照正南正北和正东正西的方向排列的。帝王的宫城面向正南，正处于全城中轴线的中心位置。太庙在其东，社稷坛在其西，全城市场在其北。这种城市布局有一条显然存在的南北中轴线，确定了背北面南的主导方向。这一主导方向，和中国古代文明起源的黄河中下游地区有密切的联系。这里的平原地带，大者如华北平原，小者如泾渭盆地、伊洛盆地，地势平坦开阔，又是季风盛行的北温带。春夏秋冬四季分明，夏季高温多雨，冬季北风凛冽。为了夏季通风和降温以及冬季御寒和采光，

residential structures in this area were built to open toward the south, with their backs to the north. Over time, these evolved into the *si-he-yuan* (house built around a courtyard). The *si-he-yuan* has structures facing the center on all four sides, with the principal one, called the *zheng-fang*, on the north.

The *si-he-yuan* is, in fact, the "cell" of traditional Chinese city structure. If the streets and alleys defined by rows of *si-he-yuan* are arranged in a certain pattern and surrounded by a wall, a city is formed. The emperor's palace in the national capital was simply a grand *si-he-yuan*, or a collection of them, surrounded by a palace wall and referred to as the Gong Cheng or Imperial Palace. The Imperial Palace was supposed to have a dominant position, at the center of the city's primary north-south axis, and this central location symbolized the center of the cosmos. Also, according to ancient custom the "Tai Miao" could only be built in the nation's capital.

China is an agrarian nation, and the "She-ji Tan" was an important symbol of the emperor's authority. As for the market, it was a necessity of city life. All these basic elements of the city were clearly set forth in the *Book of Artificers*. Of all the written works concerning the construction of the capital city which have been passed down from antiquity, this is the earliest and most important, and had the greatest influence on the actual design of the ancient capitals.

Of the several imperial capitals in Chinese history, the last built was Beijing, or more specifically, that part of modern Beijing referred to as the "Old City," and it is the actual design of this city that comes the closest to expressing the ancient principle of "palace in front, market in back, ancestral temple on left, altar of soil and grain on right." After the foundation of New China, the capital was re-established in Beijing, with its center in the Old City, and work commenced to build a "people's capital" for the new socialist era. Thus, the redevelopment of Beijing's Old City plan became an urgent task. In order to fully understand the nature of this task, it is necessary to examine the plan of Beijing's Old City in some detail.

Early Planning and the Rise of Dadu City

Although Beijing is an ancient city with a history spanning three thousand years, it has been in its present location only since the establishment of Dadu City by the Yuan Dynasty (1271-1368) in the thirteenth century. The previous location was in what is now the southwest suburbs of the city. The last and largest

住宅建筑中的主要房舍，都是背北面南的，由此而发展成为普遍流行的所谓"四合院"。虽然四合院四面房子都面向当中的庭院，但最主要的住房是北房，也叫正房。实际上这种四合院就是城市建筑在结构上的"细胞"。把这些细胞成条地排列起来就是街巷，把大小街巷有计划地组织起来就是方方正正有城墙包围的城市。作为一国的都城，帝王的宫室就是特大的住宅，或是几组住宅的综合体。周围绕以宫墙，这就是宫城。宫城布置在全城最重要的位置上，这就是全城南北中轴线的中心所在地。同时也是宇宙中心的象征。其次，按照古代的传统来说，只有在一国的都城之内，才有皇家太庙的建筑。至于像中国这样一个以农立国的国家，"社"的建筑、或称"社稷"，又是用来作为帝王统治天下的象征。至于市场，更是城市生活中所必有的。因此，这些基本要素都已经明确地包括在《考工记》所记载的关于帝王都城的理想设计之中了。这是保存到现在的中国古代著作中关于都城规划设计的最早也是最重要的记载，对后来的都城建设是有影响的。但是最为近似也可说是最完整地体现了这一理想设计"面朝"、"后市"、"左祖"、"右社"以及全城街道布局的基本特点的都城，只有一个，那就是历代帝王都城中最后建成的北京城，也就是现在所说的北京旧城。新中国成立后，又决定建都北京，并以北京旧城为中心，开始营建社会主义新时代的人民首都。因此，北京旧城的改造，也就成为当务之急。为了充分说明这一点，就有必要把北京旧城的规划设计，详细介绍如下。

三

北京是一个有三千多年历史的古城，不过她现在的城址是从 13 世纪中期元朝（1271—1368）大都城的兴建开始的。北京的古城址原在大都城的西南郊。在这个古城址上所建立起来的最后也是最大的

city built in this old location was Zhongdu, the capital of the Jin Dynasty (1115-1234). The establishment of Zhongdu marked the beginning of Beijing's emergence as a national political center.

To the northeast of Zhongdu City there was a scenic area with a natural lake, which was utilized by the Jin emperor. The lake was expanded on its southern part and two islands were created and an imperial retreat, called Tai-ning Palace (Palace of Great Tranquility) was built (Fig. 2-1). In the year 1215, the army of the Mongolian leader Genghis Khan swept down from the north, occupying Zhongdu City and razing the Imperial Palace. But Tai-ning Palace outside the city was spared.

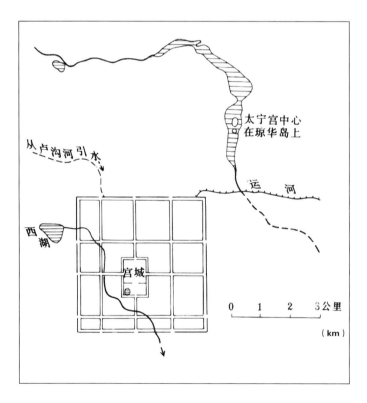

2-1 Beijing's early urban nuclei: Zhongdu City and Tai-ning Palace　金朝中都城与太宁宫位置略图

Imperial Palace 宫城	West Late 西湖	Aqueduct from Lu-gou River 从卢沟河引水
Canal 运河		Main buildings of the Tai-ning Palace on the Qiong-hua Island 太宁宫中心在琼华岛上

Forty-five years later, Genghis Khan's grandson, Kublai Khan, in order to consolidate his rule over China, decided to establish his capital in Zhongdu. But the Imperial Palace there was in ruins and would have been extremely difficult to rebuild. Worse yet, Zhongdu had but a meager water supply from a small lake (West Lake, now called Lotus Lake) just west of the city. The complex problems of providing water for the city, and especially channels for water transport, became more critical day by day.

Man-made canals were needed, primarily to ensure that the capital could be supplied with the large quantities of grain it required. During the Jin Dynasty, an aqueduct had been constructed to divert the water of the Yongding River (then called Lu-gou River) eastward, following the natural topography, to the north moat of Zhongdu City. From there a canal continued eastward to Tong-zhou (east of present-day Beijing). The plan was to bring together river shipments of grain and other

一个大城，就是金朝（1115—1234）的中都城。中都城是古代北京城上升为全国性政治中心的开始。

中都城的东北郊外，原有一带天然湖泊，金朝的统治者曾利用这一带湖泊上的自然风光，在其南半部的中心一带，开拓湖面，修筑岛屿，营建了一处风景佳丽的离宫，命名为太宁宫（图2-1）。1215年崛起于北方的蒙古族首领成吉思汗的骑兵南下，攻占了中都城，当时中都城中豪华的宫殿惨遭焚毁，可是城外的太宁宫幸得保全。1260年成吉思汗的孙子忽必烈，决定以中都作为他的统治中心，策划统一中国，但是中都宫殿已成废墟，难于重建。更重要的是中都城的地表水源，只是来自城西的一个小湖——西湖（今莲花池），供水有限。随着城市功能的日益复杂，对于地表水源的需要也日益增加，特别是对于水上运输的要求，更为迫切。因为每年都需要有大量的粮食运送到城市，开凿人工运河尤为必要。金朝的统治者曾开凿了一条人工渠道，把城西永定河（当时叫做卢沟河）的河水，顺地形的自然坡度东流，通过中都北护城河，继续向东直达通州，计划把从华北平原上征收的粮食和物资，沿天然河流北运、集中到

material at Tong-zhou for transshipment to Zhongdu. But when the Yongding River flooded, however, it could not be effectively controlled, and the scheme proved to be unworkable.

Kublai Khan therefore decided to abandon old Zhongdu City and commissioned the Han scholar Liu Bing-zhong, who was acquainted with the ancient classics as well as experienced in city construction, to draw up plans for a new city centered on the lake by Tai-ning Palace. Liu Bing-zhong and his student Guo Shou-jing, an expert astronomer and hydraulic engineer, began directing the construction of the new city and its canal system in 1267, but the work was not completed until 1285. What they created was the historically renowned Dadu City. It was during the construction of Dadu that Marco Polo visited China and became an official of the Yuan Dynasty. Later, after his return to Italy, he recalled the grandeur of Dadu and the splendor of the palace in his account of "Khanbaliq" in *Marco Polo's Journal.*

This account of the founding and initial construction of Dadu City is well enough documented, but the decisions concerning planning and design of the city are more obscure since no official papers or other accounts have been passed down. The only direct evidence for the city's internal organization consists of a restored map of Dadu City and some incomplete historical records. My own reconstruction of the city's plan development is as follows.

First, it was decided that the north-south axis of the city would be located close by the east bank of the northern part of the lake, which at that time was called Ji-shui Tan (Fig. 2-2). The north end of this axis was set at the northeast bank of Ji-shui Tan. The emperor's palace, surrounded on four sides by a palace wall, was located on the east bank of the southern part of the lake and centered on the city's north-south axis.

On the west bank were two palace complexes, the southerly one being the palace of the crown prince and the northerly one the palace of the

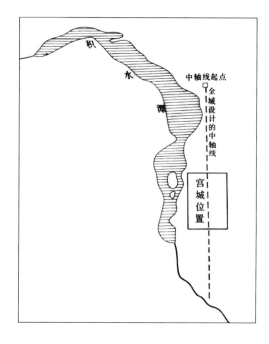

2-2 Set of the axis and location of the
emperor's palace
大都城中轴线的选择与宫城位
置的确定

Ji-shui Tan 积水潭

Main axis of the city 全城设计的中轴线

Starting point of the main axis 中轴线起点

Location of the Imperial Palace 宫城位置

通州，然后转运中都城下。但是遇到永定河洪水暴涨，难以控制，终未收到预期的运输效果。由于上述原因，忽必烈决定放弃中都旧城，改以太宁宫的湖泊为中心，命令熟悉古代典章制度并且有筑城经验的汉族学者刘秉忠，进行规划设计，另建新城。刘秉忠和他的一个学生，即长于天文历算和水利工程的郭守敬共同合作，从1267年开始，直到1285年，才把新城连同它的运河系统全部兴建完成。这就是历史上赫赫有名的大都城。正是在大都城修建期间，马可·波罗来到这里，并且出仕元朝。后来他回到意大利，在追忆中对大都城规模的宏伟、宫殿的精美，极口称赞，这就是见于《马可·波罗游记》中的汗八里城。

大都城的修建过程略如上述。至于大都城的规划设计，没有任何档案资料保存下来，因此只好根据已经复原的大都城平面图，参考有关的一些历史记载加以分析。根据个人所见，依照可能的设计程序，试作说明如下：

（1）首先是紧傍北部湖泊——当时叫做积水潭的东岸，选定了全城南北中轴线的位置（图2-2）。这条中轴线的北端，确定在积水潭的东北岸上，皇帝的宫殿则确定在南部湖泊的东岸，是为宫城。宫城平面设计的中心，也就正好落在已定的南北中轴线上。

（2）其次，在南部湖泊的西岸，又分别兴建了南北两组宫殿。

emperor's mother, or "empress dowager." These two complexes were also surrounded each on four sides by a palace wall, and faced the emperor's palace from afar across the lake. In the middle of the lake, equidistant from the three palaces, was a small island, which remained from the old Tai-ning Palace complex, called Ying-zhou. Bridges extending from Ying-zhou Island to the east and west shores of the lake connected the three palaces together. North of Ying-zhou Island was a larger island, called Qiong-hua Island, upon which was the main concentration of buildings of Tai-ning Palace. Surrounding the three palace complexes was a city wall, which defined what was known as the "Royal City." Henceforth the south lake was surrounded by the Royal City, and according to tradition, was given the name "Tai-ye Chi" (Supreme Liquid Lake). Around the shore of Tai-ye Chi an imperial park was planned.

Since the northern part of the lake now lay outside the Royal City, and being separated from the southern part, a canal was constructed to divert its outflow around the east wall of the Royal City and on toward the south suburbs. At the same time, a new source of water was found for the Royal City's Tai-ye Chi; an aqueduct was dug connecting the lake to a spring at the foot of Yu-quan (Pearl Spring) Hill northwest of the city. The outflow from the lake passed along the front of the Royal City, then out to join the canal which drained Ji-shui Tan. (Fig. 2-3)

南为皇太子的宫殿，北为皇太后的宫殿。这两组宫殿的四面，也都筑有宫墙，和湖泊东岸的皇帝宫城，遥遥相望。旧日的太宁宫，正好居于这三者中间，湖中的一个小岛，原名瀛洲。从瀛洲通向东西两岸，各建一桥，把三组宫殿联系在一起。瀛洲北面另有一个大岛，叫做琼华岛，则是旧日太宁宫主要建筑所集中的地方。三组宫殿的四周又绕以城墙，是为皇城。从此南部湖泊遂被圈入皇城之中。按照传统的惯例，命名为太液池。沿太液池周围开辟为皇家园林。至于北部湖泊因为已经隔在皇城之外，遂另开人工渠道，引水南下，绕经皇城东墙之外，流出南郊。与此同时，又为圈入皇城之内的太液池，另辟新水源，把城西北玉泉山下的泉水，经过人工渠道，直接引入太液池。其下游流经宫城的前方，向东流出皇城，注入积水潭下游的水渠。（图 2-3）

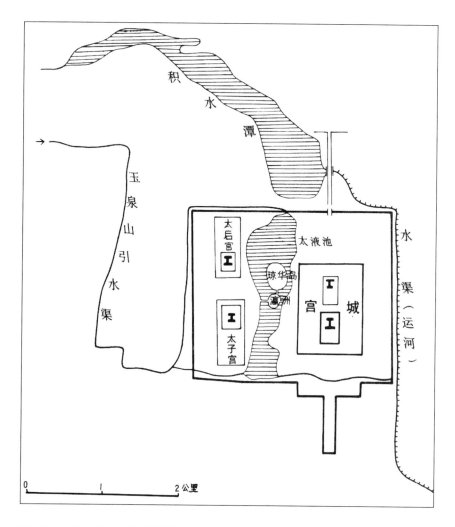

2-3 Kernel of Dadu City 大都皇城平面略图

Imperial Palace 宫城	Palace of the emperess dowager 太后宫
Palace of the crown prince 太子宫	Tai-ye Chi 太液池
Ying-zhou Island 瀛洲	Aqueduct from the Yu-quan Hills 玉泉山引水渠
Ji-shui Tan 积水潭	Canal 水渠（运河）

A large secular city was constructed around the Royal City. The plan for the large city placed its geometric center at the north end of the axis of the Royal City. At that site a platform was built, and on it were inscribed the four characters "Zhong Xin Zhi Tai," meaning "Central Platform." This shows clearly the careful measurement that went into the city's layout. From the Central Platform on the east to its western end, Ji-shui Tan is about 3.3 kilometers in east-west extent. The location of the west wall of the enlarged city was set a little farther than this from the city center. Ideally, this should have been the standard distance determining the location of the east wall of the enlarged city. The land at that easterly location, however, was swampy and unsuitable for heavy construction, so the east wall could not be placed that far out. The south wall of the enlarged city was located about 3.75 kilometers from the Central Platform, that being the distance which allowed the Royal City to be included within the enlarged city. It was then decided that the north wall should be placed at the same distance. Consequently, the shape of the enlarged city after the construction of the four walls was that of a slightly elongated rectangle.

The east, west, and south walls of the enlarged city each had three gates, but the north wall only two. Inside the southernmost gate of the east wall was built the Tai Miao, and inside the southernmost gate of the west wall was built the She-ji Tan. Spanning the area between the eleven city gates, which were spaced at approximately equal distances from one another, were wide avenues. Including the "wall streets," which ran along the insides of the city walls, there were nine aligned north-south and nine east-west. Many smaller lanes were laid out running east-west between the primary north-south avenues. Thus, the basic layout of all of Dadu City was accomplished (Fig. 2-4).

（3）皇城之外又兴建大城。大城设计的几何中心，就定在皇城中轴线的北端，在这里筑台立碑，石碑上刻有四个大字"中心之台"。

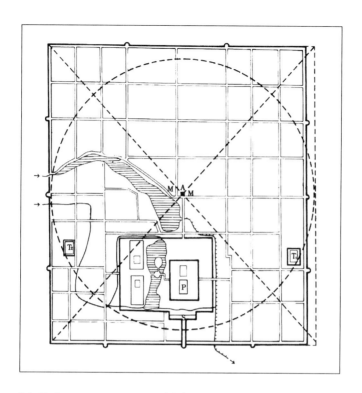

2-4 The layout of Dadu City (Beijing) 大都城平面设计示意图

A: Central Platform 中心之台   P: Imperial Palace 宫城   M: Market 市场
S: The Palace Square 宫廷广场   T₁: Imperial Ancestral Temple 太庙   T₂: Altar of Soil and Grain 社稷坛

这就充分说明，全城的平面设计是经过了精密测量的。从"中心之台"向西直到积水潭的西端，约3.3公里，这就是整个积水潭的宽度。以此宽度作为标准稍向外延，确定了大城西墙的位置。本来应该以同一标准尺度确定大城东墙的位置，只是在这一位置上原有一块洼地，不宜筑墙，因此大城东墙的位置，只好稍向内移。从"中心之台"向南，选定相去约3.75公里的距离，确定大城南墙的位置，这样就可以把皇城适当地包括在大城之内。然后再以同等的距离，确定大城北墙的位置。结果，四面大城的城墙建成之后，略呈长方形。东、西、南三面城墙，各开三门，北城墙只开两门。在东城墙最南一门之内，兴建了太庙。在西城墙最南一门之内，兴建了社稷坛。在全城11个城门内以及各个城门中间，大约以相等的距离，开辟了基本上相互正交的宽阔街道，连同紧靠四面城墙之内的所谓"顺城街"在内，全城中正南正北和正东正西的大街，各有9条。然后在南北平行的大街之间，又规划了相互平行的东西向"胡同"。这样，整个大都城的平面格局基本完成。（图2-4）

At this point, it is important to note the special significance of the location of the central gate of the south city wall, at the south end of the city's north-south axis. Along the sides of the "Imperial Road" which connected this city gate to the south gate of the Royal City, a T-shaped square was built. This was equivalent to the so-called "Wai Chao" (Outer Court) of antiquity. Precisely located along the central axis of the whole city were the chief buildings of the emperor's palace, as well as the emperor's throne. The purpose of this was to demonstrate that the emperor was "number one under heaven," a concept with great symbolic meaning.

The last major project in the construction of Dadu was the tapping of the springs of the mountains to the northwest to provide the city's water supply (Fig. 2-5). All these springs, except for those of Yu-quan Hill which were used exclusively to feed the Royal City's Tai-ye Chi, were brought together into a single channel which flowed into Dadu City's Ji-shui Tan. From there, these waters were channeled southward around the east wall of the Royal City, joining the old Jin Dynasty canal in the southern suburbs which led to Tong-zhou. At Tong-zhou this joined with the historically renowned Grand Canal, which linked the area to China's southern regions. The northern terminus of the Grand Canal system therefore was Ji-shui Tan, which became a bustling port, crowded with boats laden with grain and goods from the lower valley of the Changjiang (Yangtze River). An area on its northeast shore, including the vicinity of the Central Platform and a street along the north side of the lake, became the most prosperous commercial center of the city (Fig. 2-6).

这里应该着重说明的是大城南面正中一门，正当南北中轴线的起点，位置特别重要。从大城南门以内，直到皇城南门之间，沿着中心御道的两侧，开辟了一个丁字形的广场，相当于古代所谓"外朝"。从皇城南门进入宫城，恰好是在全城的中轴线上，兴建起皇宫中最主要的宫殿，而宫殿内正中的宝座也就正好落在这条中轴线上。

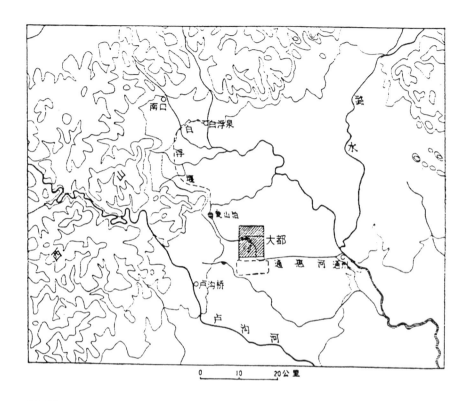

2-5 Watercourses in the vicinity of Dadu City 大都城近郊水道略图

Dadu City 大都　　　　　　　Tong-hui River 通惠河　　　　　　　Lu-gou Bridge 卢沟桥
Lu-gou River 卢沟河　　　　　West Mountains 西山

这一设计的主题，即在说明皇帝"普天之下，唯我独尊"的思想，是具有十分浓厚的象征色彩的。

（4）兴建大都城的最后一项工程，就是从西北山下利用泉水为新建的大都城开辟新水源（图2-5）。当时曾把西北沿山一带的泉水，除去玉泉山的泉水专为皇城内的太液池供水之外，都汇聚入一条渠道，流注大都城内的积水潭，然后绕经皇城东墙外南下，流出城外，与金朝所开旧渠相接，直达通州，这就是历史上有名的南北大运河最北的一段。这大运河航行的终点就在积水潭。运河开成之后积水潭上停泊了满载食粮和南货的江南船只。它的东北岸上"中心之台"周围一带，包括沿湖北岸的一条斜街，就成了全城最繁华的商业中心（图2-6）。

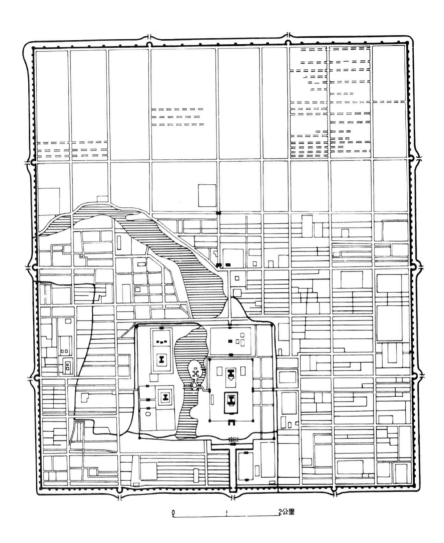

2-6 Reconstruction of the layout of Dadu City (Beijing) during the Yuan Dynasty

元朝大都城平面复原图

Dashed double lines indicate street locations identified by archeological evidence;
in empty areas, archeological evidence is lacking.
双虚线表示经考古证据显示的街道的位置，空白处表示考古证据缺乏。

The Yuan Dynasty's construction of Dadu City required eighteen years from beginning to end. If the design of Dadu is compared to the elements of ideal city layout set forth in the *Book of Artificers*, such as "palace in front, market in back, temple of ancestors on left, altar of soil and grain on right," and the street plan, it can be seen that these principles were completely realized in the construction of the city. Thus, the design of Dadu City without question had its origins deep in Chinese culture. But it was not just a machine-like copy of the ancient ideal form; its sides were not built in the form of a perfect square, but rather the ideal was modified to meet the requirements of reality to produce a creative work. By building the city around a wide body of water and extending its north-south dimension, it was possible to create a great city which combined grandeur with beautiful scenery. Moreover, the main elements of the ideal plan were still strongly represented, and this was no mean achievement.

元大都城的兴建，历时近二十年终于落成。如果把它的平面规划和《考工记》的理想设计作一比较，不难看出《考工记》中"左祖"、"右社"、"面朝"、"后市"以及街道布局的几项基本要素，都在大都城内完全体现出来。由此可见在大都城的规划设计中，是有着深厚的文化渊源的。但是它并非机械地照抄古代的理想设计，不拘泥于大城四面均等的正方形轮廓，而是结合地方上的地理特点和现实要求，进行了创造性的发展，利用一片辽阔的水面为中心，扩大了全城在南北方向上的深度，从而规划出一座规模宏伟而且具有优美自然风光的大城，并强有力地显示了它在设计上的主题思想，这不能不说是一种卓越的成就。

Planning Changes in the Ming and Qing Periods

Less than a century after Dadu City was built, an uprising in the lower reaches of the Changjiang (Yangtze River) resulted in the establishment of the Ming Dynasty (1368-1644), which eventually extended its rule over the whole of China. The Ming Dynasty originally had its capital at Nanjing. After it occupied Dadu, it changed that city's name to Beiping or "North Pacification." During the reign of the third emperor, who intended to rule from Beiping, to begin with the name was changed to Beijing, or "Northern Capital," and then the capital function itself was moved from Nanjing to Beijing. Concurrently, a major reconstruction of the city was begun (Fig. 2-7). First, the north city wall was moved about 2.5 kilometers to the south, leaving the northwest part of Ji-shui Tan outside the city. Then both the south city wall and the emperor's palace were rebuilt a little to the south. This reconstruction produced the new emperor's palace, or the Forbidden City, which has been passed down to the present, and is today's Palace Museum. Within the Ming Dynasty's Forbidden City, the most important buildings were a row of six great palaces, built along the city's main axis, which symbolized the supreme power of the emperor. The geometric center of the whole

四

大都建成后不到百年，兴起于长江下游的明王朝（1368—1644）夺取了全国的统治权。明朝最初建都南京，攻占大都后先改称大都为北平，其后迁都北平，遂改名北京。北京一名就是从这时开始的。与此同时，又大兴土木，改建了大都城（图2-7）。最初是把北城墙南移2.5公里，因而把积水潭西北一区的水面隔在了城外。其后又把南城墙以及整个宫城的位置稍向南移，因此又重建新宫城，这就是一直保留到现在的紫禁城（即今故宫博物院）。紫禁城内最重要的建筑，也就是象征皇帝至高无上的统治权的前后六座大殿，仍一律建筑在全城的中轴线上，只是全城设计的几何中心，已经不在原来"中心之台"所在的地方，

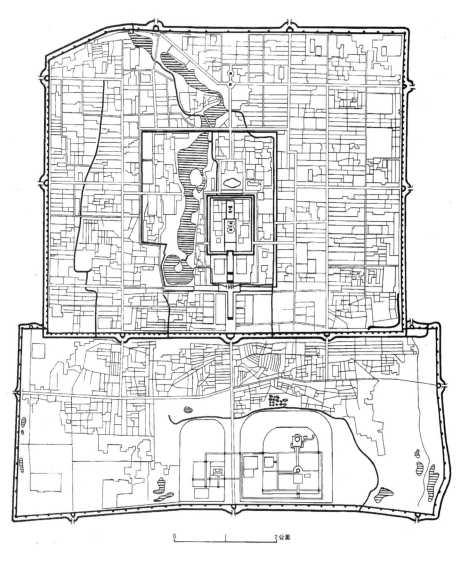

2-7 Plan of the capital of the Ming Dynasty 明代北京城平面示意图

city was no longer at the Central Platform, but had shifted south to a point just north of the new Forbidden City. In order to clearly mark the new city center, soil excavated from a new artificial lake at the southern end of the Tai-ye Chi and from a newly constructed moat of the Forbidden City was used to build a hill about forty-seven meters high. This was named Wan-sui Shan (Long Life Mountain) and symbolized the eternal ruling power of the emperor.[2] In addition, the Tai Miao and She-ji Tan were moved from their old locations inside the east and west walls to new locations just outside the south gate of the Forbidden City. They were still placed on the left and right sides of the meridional axis, respectively, in keeping with the tradition of "Tai Miao to the left and She-ji Tan to the right." At the same time, the south, north, and east walls of the Royal City were extended a bit, so the Tai Miao, She-ji Tan, and the new lake south of Tai-ye Chi were all contained within them.[3]

More importantly, two major new groups of buildings were constructed in the southern suburbs, one east and one west of the meridional axis. To the east was the Tian Tan (the Temple of Heaven), where the emperor paid homage to the gods of heaven, and to the west was the Shan Chuan Tan (the Altar of Mountain and River), where he paid his respects to the gods of mountain and river.[4] Up until 1553, this southern part of Beijing was outside the city wall; then an "outer wall" was built to formally incorporate the above-mentioned temple and altar into the city. The middle gate of this new outer wall was situated on the center axis, between these two groups of buildings. The main north-south road within the gate was built along the axis.

At the northern end of the axis, where the old Central Platform was located, two new buildings were constructed: the Bell Tower to the north and the Drum Tower to the south. The newly extended north-south axis had a full length of almost eight kilometers. The Forbidden City occupied the most important location on the axis; to its north, standing like a picture screen, was Wan-sui Shan; to its south, on the left and right, were the Tai Miao and the She-ji Tan. Between these two temples was the Central Imperial Avenue, which started at the Wu Men (Meridional Gate) at the center of the south side of the Forbidden City and extended to the Tian-an Men (Gate of Heavenly Peace)[5] at the center of the south side of the Royal City. After passing through the Tian-an Men, the avenue widened into a T-shaped palace square. The square was bounded on three sides by red brick walls. Inside the east and west walls, long corridors

而是相应地南移到新建的紫禁城的正北面。为了充分显示这一新定的全城中心，就以新开凿的太液池南端的湖泊和新挖掘的紫禁城护城河的泥土，在这里堆筑了一个中峰高约 47 米的土山，命名为"万岁山"，借以象征皇帝的统治权万世长存。[2] 此外，还把原在东城墙以内的太庙和西城墙以内的社稷坛，分别迁建到紫禁城南门之外的左右两侧，仍然保持着"左祖"、"右社"的传统规制。同时又把皇城的南、北、东三面城墙稍向外移，于是太庙、社稷坛以及新开凿的太液池南端的湖泊，都被包入皇城之中。[3] 更重要的是在全城正南方的郊外，分别兴建了东西两组重要的建筑群，在东边的是天坛，在西边的是山川坛，是皇帝分别祭天和祭山川之神的地方。[4] 这两组建筑群的正中间，也正是全城中轴线向南郊垂直延伸的地方。到了 1553 年又在北京大城的南面，修筑外城，遂把上述两坛正好包入城中。外城正南门就建在这两组建筑中间的全城中轴线上。门内的南北大道就是沿着这条中轴线开辟的。至于中轴线的北端，则是旧日的"中心之台"所在的位置，为此又在这里新建了南北两座大建筑，在南边的是鼓楼，在北边的是钟楼。这条新延长的南北中轴线，全长接近 8 公里。紫禁城占据了这条中轴线上最重要的位置，北面有耸立如画屏的"万岁山"，南面有左右并列的太庙和社稷坛。两者之间的中心御道，从紫禁城正南面的午门开始，向南通过皇城正南面的天安门[5]，便是进一步发展了的丁字形宫廷广场。广场三面有红墙包围，沿红墙修建了连檐

called the "Corridor of a Thousand Steps" were built. Outside the south central gate of the square was the south central gate of the inner city wall. This gate was known as the Zheng-yang Men, or Front Gate, and the part of Beijing which lay beyond it was called the outer city. Along the main axis of the city, which had been extended, the fundamental principles of the design of Dadu City were further developed, and a higher aesthetic level was achieved.

The Qing Dynasty (1644-1911), the last imperial dynasty in China's history, also established its capital in Beijing. Besides erecting more palace buildings in the Forbidden City and in the imperial park around Tai-ye Chi, it did not do much to change the layout of the city. Thus Beijing City—or as we now call it, Beijing's Old City—was preserved until the eve of the birth of New China. Starting with the principles set forth in the *Book of Artificers* with adjustments made to accommodate local geographical characteristics, and then having gone through numerous reconstructions, Beijing has finally come down to us as the ultimate expression of the ideal traditional Chinese city. (Fig. 2-8)

It is just this Beijing City that has been the object of high praise from Western urban planners. For example, the renowned Danish architect Steen Eiler Rasmussen, in the preface to his book *Towns and Buildings*, wrote:

> There are excellent German and Japanese guide books giving detailed information about every single palace and temple in Peking. But they do not contain a single mention of the fact that the entire city is one of the wonders of the world, in its symmetry and clarity a unique monument, the culmination of a great civilization.[6]

Another example is provided by the distinguished American city planner Edmund Bacon, who was Executive Director of the Philadelphia Planning Commission for twenty years and made an important contribution to historic preservation and restoration in that city. In his book *Design of Cities* he wrote this regarding Beijing's Old City:

Possibly the greatest single work of man on the face of the earth is Peking. This Chinese city, designed as the domicile of the Emperor, was intended to mark the center of the universe. The city is deeply enmeshed in ritualistic formulae and religious concepts which do not concern us now. Nevertheless, it is so brilliant in design that it provides a rich storehouse of ideas for the city of today.[7]

通脊的"千步廊"。出广场的正南一门，就是内城正南面的正阳门。出正阳门，便是外城。这个进一步改造过的北京城，城市轮廓呈凸形，它通过进一步延长的全城中轴线，把大都城平面设计的主题思想，又作了进一步的发挥，从而取得了更高的艺术效果。

清朝（1644—1911）——也就是中国历史上最后的一个封建王朝，继而在北京建都，除去增建宫室和继续辟治以太液池为中心的皇家园林之外，对于整个北京城并没有更大的改变。这个北京城——现在我们称它为"北京旧城"，一直被完整地保留到新中国诞生的前夕。它正是以《考工记》的理想设计为出发点，结合本地的地理特点进行规划，一再改造，终于达到了中国古典城市在建筑上的最高典型（图2-8）。正是这个北京城，获得了西方城市规划学家的高度评价。例如丹麦著名建筑与城市规划学家罗斯穆森，在其所著《城镇与建筑》一书的序文中，就曾这样写道：

[……] 整个北京城的（平面设计）匀称而明朗，是世界的奇观之一，是一个卓越的纪念物，一个伟大文明的顶峰。[6]

又如在美国，曾主持故都费城城市规划达二十年之久并作出了重要贡献的培根，在他的《城市设计》一书关于北京旧城的一节中也曾写道：

在地球表面上人类最伟大的单项工程，可能就是北京城了。这个中国城市是作为封建帝王的住所而设计的，企图表示出这里乃是宇宙的中心。整个城市深深浸沉在仪礼规范和宗教意识之中，现在这些都和我们无关了。虽然如此，它的（平面）设计是如此之杰出，这就为今天的城市（建设）提供了丰富的思想宝库。[7]

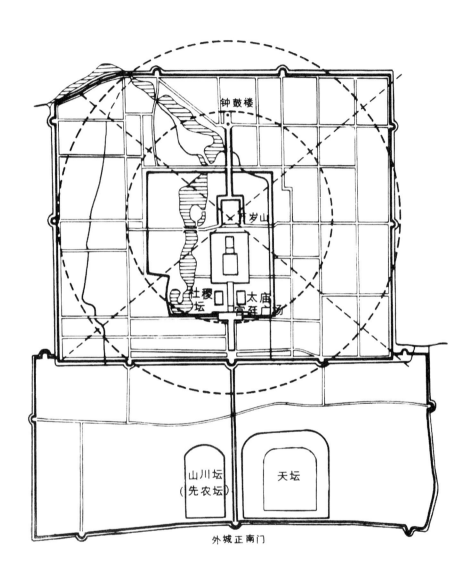

2-8 Dadu City's transformation into Beijing City under the Ming Dynasty 明清北京城平面设计示意图

Wan-sui Shan 万岁山 Tai Miao 太庙   She-ji Tan 社稷坛

Palace square 宫廷广场 Bell Tower and Drum Tower 钟鼓楼

Tian Tan 天坛   Shan Chuan Tan (Xian-nong Tan) 山川坛（先农坛）

Bacon's comment is noteworthy. As a center of imperial rule, he said, it was a great design achievement and should be studied by city planners today. At the same time, he points out that it contains much that does not serve the needs of the present. This clearly reveals the dilemma we face today.

Plan Changes in the New China Era

Following the progress of history and the passage of time, old cities—especially those of intricate design—unavoidably face the necessity of continuous redevelopment. This is especially true in the case of Beijing's Old City, since the single underlying motif of all its splendid architecture and ingenious design—namely, symbolizing the supremacy of a medieval sovereign—stands in such sharp contrast to the spirit of the present time. The establishment of New China represents the beginning of a new, socialist era. As Beijing is the nation's capital in this new era, the reconstruction of the city should reflect the fact that the people are now the true masters of their country.

培根的这一评论是很值得重视的。它既肯定了北京旧城在过去作为帝王统治中心进行建造的卓越成就，以及它在今天城市设计上所能提供的参考价值，同时也指出了它包含的某些主要内容，现在已经不合时宜。实际上，他所指出的这种不合时宜的地方，也正是我们目前在计划改造北京旧城时所面临的一个主要问题。

随着历史的发展和时代的前进，古老的城市——特别是经过详细规划设计的城市，必然要面临着不断改造的问题。这个问题在北京旧城的改造上之所以显得特别突出，最根本的原因，就是北京旧城在规划设计上以非凡的艺术手法集中表现的封建皇帝"唯我独尊"的主题思想和当前的时代精神，是完全矛盾的，也是根本不能调和的。新中国的建立，标志着社会主义新时代的开始。北京作为这个新时代人民的首都，人民就有理由要求它在全城的规划上能充分表现出人民的权威、人民的力量、人民已经成为这个国家的真正主人翁的主题思想。

How can this reconstruction effectively be carried out? First, it must be seen that this is not simply a matter of engineering and technology, but also a problem concerning our custodianship of a venerable historical and cultural inheritance, as well as the challenge of creating a new socialist civilization.

All of Beijing's Old City is part of China's historical and cultural inheritance. It is a symbol of the magnificent development of China's culture in imperial times. As Rasmussen pointed out, it is a significant monument to the highest achievements of a great civilization. The new Beijing City, as the people's capital and a symbol of the new socialist culture, can only rise from this historical foundation. But as we assume our charge over this historical and cultural legacy, we must adhere to the principle of maintaining a critical perspective. We can neither totally deny the legacy nor totally accept it. It is important to distinguish between the "wheat" and the "chaff"; we must accept and make full use of the wheat, while criticizing and giving up the chaff. In this way we can follow the principles of "making the past serve the present" and "weed through the old to bring forth the new," in order to use our historical foundation to create something new. We must note, however, that the standards for distinguishing the "wheat" from the "chaff" have changed through time. Today, we place a high value on all things which benefit the masses or fully express the people's creative abilities. That which truly embodies this populist spirit should be accepted and developed. That which does not should be criticized and given up. Today, this principle must be applied to the reconstruction of Beijing's Old City.

Some reconstruction work affecting the layout of Beijing's Old City has already been done since the establishment of New China. The most notable example of this is the reconstruction of Tian-an Men Square. As noted earlier the Tian-an Men was originally fronted by a T-shaped square. This was designed to serve as an imperial square—a place where the emperor performed important ceremonies (Fig. 2-9). On its east, west, and south sides were red walls which totally shut off public access. It was thus a great obstacle to east-west communications within the city. Viewed from the south end of this imperial square, the Tian-an Men loomed to the north as a lofty, ornate palace built upon a red platform. In old times, this sight served to create an impression of grandeur and solemnity.

怎样才能真正有效地进行这一改造，这首先不是一个单纯的工程技术问题。从本质上来说，这乃是一个如何对待悠久的历史文化遗产的问题，也是直接关系到如何发展社会主义新文化的问题。整个北京旧城正是中国历史文化遗产的一部分，象征着封建时代传统文化的高度发展，正如罗斯穆森所指出的：它乃是一个卓越的纪念物，一个伟大文明的顶峰。而新的北京城，象征着社会主义新文化的先进典型的人民首都，也就只能从历史形成的基础上脱胎成长。但是对于自己的历史文化遗产，我们必须坚持批判继承的原则，既不能全盘加以否定，也不能毫无区别地兼容并蓄。重要的是能区别其精华和糟粕。凡属精华的部分，必须继承和发扬；凡属糟粕的部分，则必须批判和扬弃。这样就可以达到"古为今用，推陈出新"的目的，就可以在历史形成的基础上获得创新。

但是，区别精华与糟粕的标准，也是因时代的不同而各有差异。在今天，我们认为凡是有益于人民群众的、充分表现出人民群众创造性的，也就是真正具有人民性的东西，就应该继承和发扬。反之，就必须予以批判和扬弃。在今天，这个对于古代文化批判继承的原则，也同样适用于北京旧城的改造。

新中国建立以来，在北京旧城的改造中，仅就原有的城市平面设计这一方面来说，已经取得了一定的经验。突出的一例，就是天安门广场的改造。

如前所述，天安门前原有一个 T 字形的广场，在当初是专门作为一个宫廷广场来设计的，是皇帝举行重要活动的地方（图 2-9）。它的东西南三面有红墙包围，严禁平民百姓进入其中，因此乃成为全城东西交通的一大障碍。从这个宫廷广场的南端，向正北遥望天安门，正是建筑在红色台基上的一座巍峨而华丽的殿堂，在旧日用以显示帝王宫阙的宏伟和庄严。

In 1911, after the overthrow of the last dynasty, Tian-an Men Square was opened and people were allowed to pass through, but the red walls were kept as before. On October 1, 1949, the declaration of the establishment of New China took place there. An important reason for this was that Tian-an Men Square was the site of the outbreak of the May 4th Movement of 1919, which set the stage for the New Democratic Revolution. Thus it is one of the places in Beijing's Old City with an honorable revolutionary tradition.

The Tian-an Men, which stands above the square, expresses the full talent and intelligence of China's working people in the art of construction. It could be considered a masterpiece among the ancient structures of Beijing. As for the red walls on the east, west, and south sides of the square, they still obstructed the movement of people and were actually a public nuisance. Therefore, on the tenth anniversary of the founding of the nation, the red walls surrounding the square were totally demolished, and a new square appeared which was several times larger than the old one. On the west and east sides of the square, two modern buildings were constructed. On the west arose the Great Hall of the People, and on the east was built the structure containing the Museum of Chinese History and the Museum of Chinese Revolution. In the center of the square stands the Monument to the People's Heroes. On the eve of the 30th anniversary of the revolution, the Memorial Hall of Chairman Mao was built on the south side of square, just inside the Zheng-yang Men. The transformation of Tian-an Men Square to the center of political activity was essentially complete. Although its location remains the same, its nature and function have totally changed, and it has an entirely new appearance (see Fig. 2-9).[8]

At the beginning of the reconstruction of Tian-an Men Square, its left and right wings extending along Chang-an Street (the street's name was derived from the former left and right Chang-an Men on either side of the old square) were widened and extended to become a broad, tree-lined thoroughfare. This thoroughfare extended to the east and west suburbs and created a major new axis for the whole city (Fig. 2-10). On one hand this reinforced the primacy of Tian-an Men Square's location in the layout of the whole city, and on the other hand it relegated the location of the old Forbidden City to "backyard" status. That ancient symbol of imperial primacy thus lost its exalted position relative to the rest of the city.

1911 年中国历史上最后一个王朝被推翻之后，天安门前的广场开放通行，可是三面红墙保存如旧。1949 年 10 月 1 日新中国的开国大典，就是选定在这里举行的，一个重要的原因就是这个广场正是 1919 年揭开了新民主主义革命序幕的五四运动爆发的地方，因此也是北京古城里最具有光荣革命传统的地方。屹立在广场正面的天安门，充分显示了古代劳动人民在建筑艺术上的智慧和才能，算得是古代建筑的精华。至于包围在它东、西、南三面的红墙，却依然是影响人民参加广场上群众活动的一大障碍。因此在建国十周年的时候，广场上的红墙被全部拆除，一个扩大了数倍的新广场展现在人们面前。新广场的西侧和东侧，分别建立起两座现代大建筑，西边的是人民大会堂，东边的是中国历史博物馆和革命博物馆，中间矗立着巍峨高大的人民英雄纪念碑。到了建国三十周年的前夕，又在广场的南部、正阳门的内侧修建了毛主席纪念堂。作为人民首都政治活动中心的天安门广场，从此基本建成。它的位置虽然依旧，可是它的性质和作用已经完全改变，它的面貌也已经是焕然一新（见图 2-9 ）。[8]

在天安门广场开始扩建的时候，作为它左右两翼的东西长安街——取名于旧日宫廷广场的东长安门和西长安门——也大为加宽和延长，成为一条宽阔平坦的林荫大道，一直伸向东西郊外，从而形成了一条横贯全城的新轴线，它一方面加强了天安门广场在全城平面布局上的中心位置，另一方面也就等于把旧日的紫禁城推到了"后院"的位置（图 2-10 ）。相形之下，旧日那条象征帝王统治中心的南北中轴线，也就失去了它在全城中独一无二的支配地位。

94

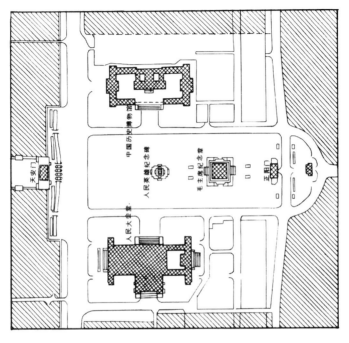

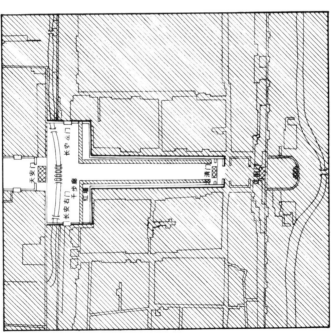

2-9 From imperial square to people's square at the Tian-an Men, Beijing 清朝天安门前"丁"形广场与今日天安门前人民广场的对照

Tian-an Men 天安门	Left Chang-an Men 长安左门	Right Chang-an Men 长安右门	Red walls 红墙
Da Qing Men 大清门	Zheng-yang Men 正阳门	Corridor of a Thousand Steps 千步廊
Great Hall of the People 人民大会堂		Museum of Chinese History 中国历史博物馆
Monument to the People's Heroes 人民英雄纪念碑		Memorial Hall of Chairman Mao 毛主席纪念堂

Although work remains to be done in the reconstruction of Tian-an Men Square, its position as the center of political activity in the city has been established. The old buildings on the square, such as the Tian-an Men and the Zheng-yang Men, and the modern buildings, such as the Great Hall of the People and the Museum of Chinese History and the Museum of Chinese Revolution, all go together very well, showing at the same time continuity with the past and the new spirit of the present. The principle of "weed through the old to bring forth the new" has been fully realized. With regard to the improvement of the layout of Beijing's Old City, it cannot be said that this was not a success.

There are still many opportunities for today's city planners to apply their creative talents, in accordance with this principle, to the reconstruction of Beijing's Old City. For instance, one such case is the question of what to do with the old Ji-shui Tan. Should we consider it an obstacle to the city's development and fill it in to create land for buildings? Or should we consider it a place of historical significance in the development of the city and protect and improve it?

现在天安门广场的改建虽然还有发展余地，但是它作为全城政治活动中心的地位，已经完全确定。广场上古老的建筑如天安门、正阳门和现代的建筑如人民大会堂和历史与革命博物馆，十分和谐地联系在一起，既反映了悠久的历史文化背景，又显示了新时代的精神和面貌，充分体现了"古为今用、推陈出新"的原则。在改造北京旧城的平面设计上，这不能不说是成功的一例。

根据这同一原则，在旧城的改造中，也还大有余地正等待着当代的城市设计者去发挥他们艺术创造的才能。在这里也可姑举一例，作为说明。这就是北京城内旧日的积水潭，今后应该如何去处理它，是把它视同城市发展的障碍而任意填塞改为建筑用地呢？还是应该看到它在城市发展中的重要作用而加以保留和改造？

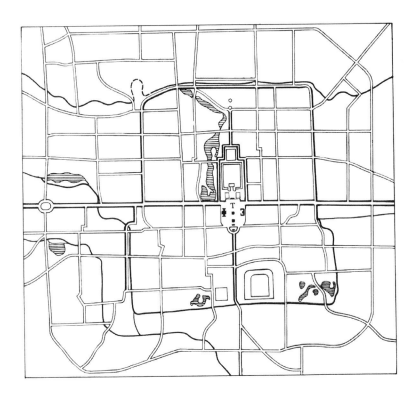

2-10 Chang-an Street, Beijing, extending east and west from the Tian-an Men

从天安门广场向东西延伸的林荫大道

The Ji-shui Tan of antiquity, as discussed earlier, had a great influence on the location and layout of Beijing's Old City. The city's main axis was set next to the eastern shore of Ji-shui Tan, and the width of the lake determined the location of the east and west city walls. It could be said that had Ji-shui Tan not existed, Beijing would not exist in anything like its present form. In Dadu City of the Yuan Dynasty, Ji-shui Tan was of great importance as the northern terminus of the Grand Canal. After the early period of the Ming Dynasty, when the north city wall was moved southward 2.5 kilometers, the northwest part of Ji-shui Tan was excluded from the city, and the area of the lake inside the city was greatly reduced. Subsequent reconstruction of Beijing's Old City, while further developing the primary themes of the original city plan, resulted in the filling of the Grand Canal's bed within the city and the elimination of its upper reaches. All that remained was the spring from Yu-quan Hill, which flowed into Ji-shui Tan and thence on to Tai-ye Chi. After this rearrangement of Beijing's water system, Tai-ye Chi, which was inside the Royal City, was again enlarged by the addition of a new lake at its southern end. The trees and structures around it increased in number, and it developed into the most scenic park district in the city. The lake became known as the "Three Seas"—the "South Sea" (Nan-hai), the "Middle Sea" (Zhong-hai), and the "North Sea" (Bei-hai). The "North Sea" has now been opened to the public; known as the Bei-hai Park, it is renowned for its most beautiful scenery. This was the location of the Jin Dynasty's imperial retreat, Tai-ning Palace.

Ji-shui Tan, which lay outside the Royal City, has a much different fate than the "Three Seas," with their imperial parks and gardens. Throughout

如前所述，旧日的积水潭和北京旧城的建址关系至为密切，因为从一开始，全城设计的中轴线，就是紧傍积水潭的东岸确定下来的。同时最初大城东西两面城墙的位置，也是以积水潭的宽度为标准而决定的，因此可以说如果没有积水潭，也就不会有现在的北京旧城。在元朝大都城内，积水潭作为南北大运河的终点，是受到一定的重视的。明初把大都北城墙南移2.5公里之后，竟把积水潭的西北部隔在城外，因此城内湖泊的面积大为缩小。其后进一步改建北京城，虽然把原有的全城平面设计的主题思想作了进一步的发展，但是城内大运河的故道已被阻绝，上游渠道也遭淤废。只剩下玉泉山下的泉水，这时被全部引入积水潭，然后流注太液池。经过这次水道系统的重新调整之后，由于太液池南端已开凿了一个新湖，因此圈在皇城之内的太液池的水面又有所开拓，沿湖一带的园林建筑也与日俱增，终于发展成为北京城内规模最大、景色最为秀丽的园林区。这时园中的湖泊已有"三海"之称，即南海、中海和北海。现在北海已经开放，这就是以风景名胜著称的北海公园。它的前身也就是金朝的离宫——太宁宫。

和三海的皇家园林命运悬殊的是隔在皇城之外的积水潭。

the Ming and Qing dynasties and up to the establishment of New China, it never received much attention from the highest rulers. Thus it has not benefited from any definite plan or development, and has quite naturally become a neglected backwater. The lake shrank into three parts, and only the northwesternmost part was still called Ji-shui Tan. A larger part of the lake, to the southeast, was called Shi-cha Hai. The area remained, however, one of the most scenic parts of the city. Especially lovely was the view looking west from the east shore of Shi-cha Hai; the reflected peaks of West Mountains seemed like part of the city landscape. Therefore this region in old times, especially during the Qing Dynasty, attracted some of the imperial nobility. They built great houses near the lake shore and channeled lake water into their private gardens. In addition, a number of large, wealthy temples were established around the lake. But, apart from the nobles' houses and temples, the greatest part of the lake region became a public recreation place for the common people. The southern part, especially, evolved naturally into a real "people's park." Concurrently there arose in that place a common people's market, where prices were low and merchandise was good. Because of a profusion of lotus growing along the lake shore there, this market came to be called the "Lotus Market." Up to the eve of the birth of New China, this region remained a haven for the common people, where they could relax and enjoy life in a rustic setting. This informality contrasted sharply with the detailed planning and arrangement of Tai-ye Chi and its imperial gardens.

Now, inside Beijing's Old City, this overlooked lake is still there, and along its shores there are still patches of greenery and glimpses of its former beauty.

Further planning and reconstruction of the Ji-shui Tan district has already been scheduled as part of the effort to improve and reconstruct Beijing's Old City, in coordination with the overall plan for greater Beijing (Fig. 2-11). As this process goes forward, we must consider the historical importance and value of this region. We must consider the strong association of the common people with this place and the present necessity of creating more spacious, pleasant and culturally meaningful recreation areas for our citizens. We must consider the potential for improving the natural environment and making the city a more beautiful place. We must also build our plan upon the historical base we have inherited, all the while maintaining a critical attitude and doing our best to realize the principle of "weeding through the old to bring forth the new." Ji-shui Tan is waiting for us to make this effort.

积水潭自明清以来，一直到新中国成立之前，再没有受到最高当权者的重视。因此也从来没有进行过统一的规划和开发，只是听其淤塞湮废。湖面也被收缩为三部分。最西北的部分仍然叫做积水潭，东南的大部分改名为什刹海。但是沿湖一带仍是旧城之内富有自然风光的一带地方，特别是从什刹海东岸掠过浩瀚的水面，遥见西山峰峦，如在眼前。因此这一带湖上风光，在旧日——特别是在清代，曾经吸引了一些皇室贵族，在沿湖一带修建府第，并引湖水辟治私家园林。另外也有一些富有的寺庙，环绕湖泊周围就地兴建起来。但是在这些贵族府第和大小寺庙之外，广阔的湖滨地区却成了城市广大居民群集游憩和进行娱乐活动的场所，特别是在它的南部，自然形成为一处真正的民间乐园。同时这里也是一处物美价廉的平民市场。后来由于湖泊西岸广种荷花，因此这处市场也就被叫做荷花市场了。直到新中国成立的前夕，这里仍然不失为平民百姓的游乐场所，这和旧日太液池上精心设计、逐事增华的皇家禁园，形成了鲜明的对照。现在，在北京旧城的腹地，还保留着什刹海这一区残存的湖泊以及滨湖一带若断若续的绿地。考虑到它在历史上的重要作用和价值，考虑到过去它所具有的强烈的人民性、群众性，同时还考虑到它在改善自然环境、美化首都市容上所具有的极大的可能性，以及为广大人民群众创造更广阔、更美好、更富有意义的历史文化风景区的必要性，如何进一步规划和开发这一地区，现在已经提到改造北京旧城的议事日程上来，并已列入北京城市建设的总体规划之中（图2-11）。这也应该是在历史形成的基础上，坚持批判继承的原则，力求能做到古为今用、推陈出新的一个例子，只是还有待我们努力去实现它。

2-11 Land use plan for metropolitan Beijing, 1983 北京市区规划示意图（1983）

1. Industry and warehouse 工业仓库　2. Office and residential areas 工作居住　3. Parks and recreation areas 绿地体育　4. Streets and roads 道路用地　5. Railroads 铁路

Conclusion

This essay examines only two examples, from the geographical perspectives of city location and design, in an attempt to assess what attitude we should have and what basic rules we should observe in the process of reconstructing Beijing's Old City.

In July of 1983, the Chinese Communist Party Central Committee and the State Council approved in principle the Master Plan for the City Construction of Metropolitan Beijing. This plan clearly evaluates Beijing's Old City, and while pointing out those strengths and notable traditional characteristics which should be preserved in the process of reconstruction, it also emphasizes the creation of a new style characteristic of the people's capital in the new era.[9] Thus, we have reason to believe that by the end of this century a new Beijing City will emerge, one which will maintain not only its ancient cultural tradition, but with a new face reflecting a prosperous, new socialist culture. At the same time we also hope that this new culture, which is still developing, can make an important contribution to the civilization of all mankind.

　　本文只是从城址的地理特点和城市的平面设计这两个方面，举出两个例子，借以说明在改造北京旧城的过程中，我们所应该坚持的基本态度和应该遵循的基本原则。

　　1983 年 7 月，中共中央和国务院已经原则上批准了《北京城市建设总体规划方案》，这个方案对北京旧城作了明确的评价，指出在旧城的改造中，要注意继承和发扬旧城原有的独特风格和优点，又要体现出作为社会主义新时代人民首都的新面貌、新格局。[9] 为此我们有理由相信，到本世纪末，一个足以显示具有悠久文化传统的新北京城，将会以崭新的面貌，出现在我们面前，它象征着一个社会主义的新文化已经在这个古老的国家里，发育成长，欣欣向荣！同时，我们也希望这个正在发展中的新文化，也能为全人类的文化发展，作出应有的新贡献。

❸ VIEWS ON THREE MILESTONES IN THE CONSTRUCTION OF BEIJING CITY*

1

'If you do not understand the past of Beijing City, you are unable to know the present of it and of course it is impossible for you to estimate the future of it too. The development of a city is a continuous process in which the past, present and future are situated on the same chain of time.'[1] Beijing is a world-famous city of history and culture, whose planning and construction has deep historical and cultural origins. Especially on the newly selected location through the Yuan and Ming dynasties, the favorable conditions of river and lake water system were fully utilized. The convex contour of closely combined inner and outer cities in spatial structure was finally completed in accordance with the planning principles which come down in one continuous line of the construction of capital city in China since the ancient time and above all with the consecutive renewals and reforms. At the center of it, there goes through a middle axis from north to south, i.e. starting from the Gulou and the Zhonglou (the Drum-tower and the Bell-tower) in the north running down to the Yongdingmen (a city gate) in the due south, the length of which is approximately 8 kilometers. This spatial structure of organic combination of inner and outer cities had been perfectly preserved up to 1949, the year of the establishment of New China.

New China established its capital again in Beijing and according to the needs of time has carried out the city planning and construction in succession, taking the old city as the core. Judging from the spatial structure of the whole city, the most important thing, and foremost thing too, was the enlargement of the Tian'anmen Square, i.e. to convert the enclosed square of imperial court of old days into a broad and magnificent city square. At the same time, two wings of the Tian'anmen Square, the eastward and westward Chang'an Boulevards, were also broadened and extended, thus making a scene just like a horizontal axis from east to west crossing the vertical axis of old days from north to south at the Tian'anmen Square.

Along with the demolishing of city wall of old days, the construction of the Second, Third and Fourth Ring Roads was carried out one by one. All these ring roads have naturally led to the extension of north-to-south middle axis inside the old city. This had been fully shown in the city planning map of the early stage. The south extension line of middle axis inside the old city had as its basis the road bed stretching from the Yongdingmen Gate down to the Dahongmen

叁 试论北京城市规划建设中的三个里程碑[*]

一

"不了解北京城的过去，就无法认清北京城的现在，当然也就不可能预测北京城的未来。城市的发展是一个连续的过程，过去、现在和未来处在同一时间之链上。"[1]北京是举世闻名的历史文化名城，它的规划建设有着深厚的历史文化渊源。特别是经过元明两代在新选择的城址上，充分利用河湖水系的有利条件，根据自古以来我国关于都城建设一脉相承的规划特点，又加以不断的更新和改造，终于在空间结构上完成了内外两城紧相毗连的"凸"字形轮廓，中间贯以自北而南的中轴线，北起鼓楼与钟楼，南至全城正南方的永定门，长近8公里。这一内外两城有机结合的空间结构，一直完整地保留到1949年新中国的成立。

新中国重新建都北京，根据时代的要求，相继进行了以旧城为核心的城市规划和建设。从全城的空间结构上来看，最重要的，也是首先进行的就是天安门广场的扩建，把旧日封闭式的宫廷广场，转变为恢宏开阔的城市广场。同时又将广场两翼的东西长安街加以拓宽和延长，有如一条东西横轴线与旧日自北而南的纵轴线交会在天安门广场上。

其后随着旧日城墙的拆除，又开始进行了二环路、三环路和四环路的设计。这些环路从构图上自然导致旧城内南北中轴线向外的延伸，这在早期的城市规划图上已经充分显示出来。旧城中轴的南延长线，已有从永定门通向南苑大红门的路基作为依据。至于旧城中轴的北延长线，

Gate at Nanyuan. As for the north extension line of the middle axis, there is no basis available because the area from the Gulou and the Zhonglou to the north Second Ring Road was totally blocked by the dwellings. This was directly related to the practice of breaking the historical tradition of the Jin Zhongdu, the middle capital of the Jin Dynasty, and not establishing the due north gate at the time of founding the Yuan Dadu, grand capital of the Yuan Dynasty. There is also no basis available for the further extension to the due north after crossing the residential areas, and there was the blocking of important buildings in between as well.

Therefore, except the portion inside the old city wall, this north extension line of the middle axis hadn't started being opened up until the eve of the convening of the Eleventh Asian Games in 1990, so that it could be linked with the north Fourth Ring Road under construction for the same purpose at that time. The northern portion of it is Beichen Road now. The location of the then-established main venue of the Asian Games, that is, the National Olympic Sports Center, is on the east side of the intersection of Beichen Road and north Fourth Ring Road. To the north sits the Beijing International Convention Center constructed at the same time, and the two face each other across the Fourth Ring Road. This place is just situated to the due north of the old city, wide in area, nearer to the capital airport and rather convenient for the international communication. So far as the selection of geographical location thereof is concerned, therefore, it is very suitable too for this grand international activity, with the call for 'Unity, Friendship, Progress', to have this place as the center to take place.

In fact, it is just the successful convening of the Asian Games in Beijing and the decision of constructing the National Olympic Sports Center thereupon that makes me become conscious that in the planning and construction of Beijing City, the concept which can be called 'Three Milestones' is taking form (Fig. 3-1). The study reads as follows:

The First Milestone is the core construction of the Beijing City in history, the Forbidden City. It has been 570 odd years old since it was built, representing the core of the Beijing City construction under the rule of feudal dynasties and being a masterpiece in China's traditional art of architecture as well. Up to now it still erects at the center of the spatial structure of the whole city, but it is not only the art wealth of the Chinese people but has been classified as the 'World Cultural Heritage' with global reputation also.

The Second Milestone is the Tian'anmen Square which symbolizes outstandingly that a new age has arrived after the founding of New China.

则无所依据。因为从钟鼓楼到北二环，完全为民居所阻隔，这与元大都城初建立时就打破历史传统不设正北门有直接关系。越过这一带民居再向正北方延伸，也同样是无所依据的，其间也还有重要建筑的阻隔。所以这条全城中轴的北延长线，除去旧城墙内的一段外，直到为了迎接 1990 年第 11 届亚运会的召开，这才开始打通，以与为了同一目的也正在开辟中的北四环路相接，其北段就是现在的北辰路。当时兴建的亚运会主会场，也就是国家奥林匹克体育中心，就选建在北辰路与北四环相交处的东侧，在其北面隔四环路相望的就是同时兴建的国际会议中心。这里恰处北京旧城的正北方，地域开阔，又去首都机场较近，国际上的来往也比较便捷。因此从地理位置的选择上来说，这次盛大的以"团结、友谊、进步"为号召的国际活动以这里为中心召开，也是很相宜的。实际上也正是由于这次亚运会在北京的胜利召开，以及由此而决定的国家奥林匹克体育中心的建设，才开始使我意识到在北京城的规划建设中，可以称之为"三个里程碑"的设想正在形成中（图 3-1）。试论如下：

第一个里程碑是历史上北京城的中心建筑紫禁城。它的建成至今已有五百七十余年，代表的是封建王朝统治时期北京城市建设的核心，也是中国传统建筑艺术的一大杰作。到今天它依然屹立在全城空间结构的中心，但已不仅仅是中国人民的艺术财富，而且已被列为"世界文化遗产"，享誉全球。

第二个里程碑就是新中国建立之后，在北京城的空间结构上，突出地标志着一个新时代已经来临的天安门广场。

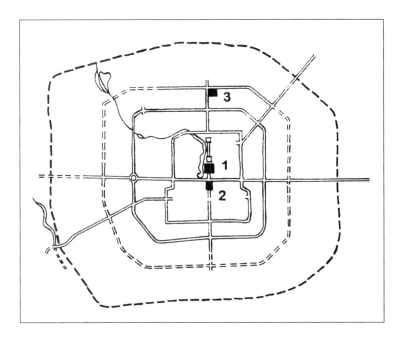

3-1 Views on Three Milestones in the construction of Beijing City
北京城市规划建设中的三个里程碑的初步设想

1. Forbidden City (Palace Museum) 紫禁城 (今故宫博物院)
2. Tian'anmen Square 天安门广场
3. National Olympic Sports Center 国家奥林匹克体育中心

It has gifted the middle axis of the whole city of long tradition with wholly new significance, reflecting the characteristics of 'making the past serve the present; weeding through the old to bring forth the new' of the age in city construction and the special meaning of inheriting the past and ushering in the future in cultural tradition.

The Third Milestone, as mentioned above, is that in the beginning it was only due to the convening of the Asian Games and the construction of the National Olympic Sports Center that it started showing the arrival of the age of Beijing marching towards an international metropolis. The first time I openly put forward this idea was May 14, 1991 when I was making a report at the academic discussion in Architectural College, Qinghua University. At that time I only indicated it orally and did not write in the text of speech.[2]

Now three years have passed. Facing the 21st century and inheriting the fine tradition of various master plans since the 1950s, the latest Master Plan of Beijing City has further put forward the new target of establishing the modern international metropolis under the new situation of reform and opening to the outside world and of establishing socialist economic system. It is also pointed out in the target 'to protect the famous historical and cultural cities under the consideration of the whole, especially to do this from the view of macroscopic environment of urban layout'.

What was first and foremost to put forward thereon was the 'protection of middle axis of the old city' and the direction that on the north and south extension lines of the middle axis of the old city, the following symbolic planning and design were to be made out respectively: 'the south extension line should embody the image of the South Gate of the city; along the north extension line should be retained the broad green belts, on the

它赋予具有悠久传统的全城中轴线以崭新的意义，显示出在城市建设上"古为今用，推陈出新"的时代特征，在文化传统上有着承先启后的特殊含义。

第三个里程碑如上所述，最初是由于亚运会的召开和国家奥林匹克体育中心的兴建，才开始显示出北京走向国际性大城市的时代已经到来。我第一次公开提出这一设想，是 1991 年 5 月 14 日在清华大学建筑学院的一次学术报告会上，当时也只是做了口头上的陈述，并没有写出书面的讲稿。[2]

而今时过三年，面向 21 世纪的《北京城市总体规划》，继承了 50 年代以来历次城市总体规划的优良传统，又在改革开放和建立社会主义经济体制的新形势下，进一步提出了建设全方位对外开放的现代化国际城市的新目标。其中也包括了"历史文化名城的保护与发展"的重要项目，并且指出"要从整体上考虑历史文化名城的保护，尤其要从城市格局的宏观环境上保护历史文化名城"。

其中首先提出的就是"保护传统城市的中轴线"，并且决定在旧城中轴线的南北延长线上，分别进行下列征性的规划设计，即"中轴南延长线要体现城市'南大门'形象；中轴北延长线要保留宽阔的绿带，在

two sides and north point of which the public building complex should be the culmination and the termination of the city axis, reflecting outstandingly the new style and features of the capital in the 21st century'.

What should be specially noticed here is that the west and east sides of the north extension line of middle axis are the very sites of the National Olympic Sports Center and the Chinese Nation Garden under construction. As for the north point of it, it is going to be built into the public building complex, and its completion in accordance with the plan in the area will really be considered the Third Milestone in the history of the city's planning and construction (Fig. 3-2).

2

It is necessary to explain further too that the extension towards the due north of this middle axis of the whole city in the planning is actually a new development against historical tradition.

其两侧和北端的公共建筑群作为城市轴线的高潮与终结,突出体现 21 世纪首都的新风貌"(着重号系作者所加)。

这里应该特别注意的是这中轴北延长线的东西两侧,正是国家奥林匹克体育中心和正在兴建的中华民族园所在之地。至于其"北端",也就是要作为城市轴线的"高潮"和"终结"的所在处,还要建成"突出体现 21 世纪首都的新风貌"的公共建筑群。因此,这一区公共建筑群按计划的完成,就真正可以看作是北京城市规划建设中的第三个里程碑了。

总结以上所述,《北京日报》1994 年 4 月 1 日"图解新闻版"为介绍《北京城市总体规划》所刊载的一幅示意图,正好可供参考,转载如下(图 3-2)。

在这里还可以进一步设想,上文提出的三个里程碑在建筑设计上还是应该各有其时代特征的。例如紫禁城作为第一个里程碑,它那巍峨壮丽的宫阙,就充分显示了皇权时代帝王至上的思想。天安门广场作为第二个里程碑,它在扩大宫廷广场为城市广场的基础上,又融合古今建筑为一体,从而呈现出继往开来的新气象。现在作为第三个里程碑,又处在整个城市空间结构的顶点上,其总面积还将超过旧日的紫禁城,对于这一区公共建筑的总体

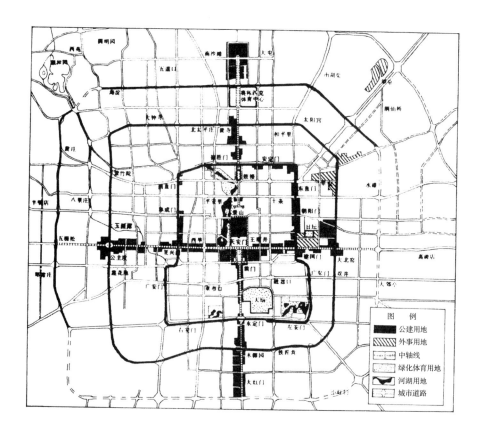

图 例
■	公建用地
▨	外事用地
	中轴线
	绿化体育用地
■	河湖用地
	城市道路

3-2 The north extension of the middle axis of Beijing City 北京城市中轴线的向北延伸

Public Construction areas 公建用地   Foreign affairs areas 外事用地
Parks and Recreation areas 绿化体育用地   Middle axis 中轴线
Rivers and Lakes 河湖用地   Streets and roads 城市道路

(From *Beijing Daily*, April 1, 1994 摘自《北京日报》, 1994 年 4 月 1 日)

规划必须早做考虑，更重要的是如何设计和营建方能"突出体现 21 世纪首都的新风貌"，这就为当代建筑学家提出了一个十分重要的新课题。愿拭目以待，早观厥成。

二

还应该进一步说明的一点，就是在北京城总体规划上这条全城中轴线向正北方的延伸，乃是一反历史传统的新发展，是具有划时代意义的。

The original middle axis inside the Beijing old city was defined at the time when the Yuan Dadu, the capital city of the Yuan Dynasty, was first constructed, but its historical origins in fact existed very long. What is more important is that it in a concentrated way embodied the traditional thought in the days of the imperial power: Facing the South to Be Emperor, i.e. the emperor should face the due south to rule the world. This was reflected conspicuously in the beginning of the planning and design of the Yuan Dadu.

The planning and design of the Yuan Dadu can be traced up to the description of 'The Way the Craftsmen Build the City-state' in *Kaogongji* of *Zhou Li* (the book recording the work of craftsmen at the Warring States Period, 475-221 B.C.), but the design of the city walls was in fact totally different from the description of the book. Now it is explained separately as follows:

So far as the layout of the core buildings in 'The Way the Craftsmen Build the City-state' is concerned, it reads like this: the Imperial Ancestral Temple on the left side, the Altar of Land and Grain on the right side, Court facing ahead and Market on the back side (*zuozu youshe, mianchao houshi*).

3-3 The sketch map of Dadu of the Yuan Dynasty
"左祖右社，面朝后市" 思想在元大都布局中的体现

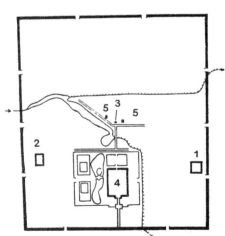

1. Imperial Ancestral Temple 太庙
2. Altar of Land and Grain 社稷坛
3. Central Terrace 中心之台
4. Imperial Palace 大内
5. The distribution area of market 市场分布区

(Redrawn according to Hou Renzhi, *Historical Atlas of Beijing*, Beijing Publishing House, 1988, pp. 27–28. 侯仁之绘制,《北京历史地图集》, 北京出版社, 1988, 第 27—28 页)

By comparison, it is analyzed with the help of sketch map of the Yuan Dadu that by the so-said *zuozu* it means in fact the Imperial Ancestral Temple at the foot of the east wall inside the city. By *youshe* it means in fact the Altar of Land and Grain at the foot of the west wall inside the city. By *mianchao* it denotes the place analogous to the 'Grand Inner Portion' on the extension line from the 'Central Terrace' towards the due south inside the city, i.e. the predecessor of the Forbidden City. By *houshi* it denotes the bazar area near the 'Central Terrace' on the due north of the 'Imperial Palace' (the Grand Inner Portion) (Fig. 3-3).

In accordance with the above mentioned comparison, it explains just as it is in 'The Way the Craftsmen Build the City-state', that the 'left' is the east, the 'right' is the west and the 'back' is the north. Only the site where the royal court was located is specially called 'court facing ahead' not 'in front'. Why? After pondering over it scrupulously,

北京旧城以内原有的中轴线，是元大都初建时所确定的，但是它的历史渊源却由来已久。更重要的是它还集中体现着一种皇权时代的传统思想，即："面南而王"，也就是说皇帝要面向正南来统治天下。这一点在大都城的规划设计中，从一开始就突出地反映出来。

大都城的规划设计，其核心建筑的布局，可以追溯到《周礼·考工记》中"匠人营国"的描述，这是明显易见的；可是大都城四面城墙的设计，却与"匠人营国"的描述大相径庭。分别说明如下。

"匠人营国"关于其核心建筑的布局是这样写的："左祖右社，面朝后市。"对比之下，借助于元大都的略图，进行分析，所谓"左祖"，就是大都城内东城墙下的"太庙"；"右社"就是大都城内西城墙下的"社稷坛"；"面朝"所指，相当于大都城内自"中心之台"向正南方延长线上的"大内"，也就是紫禁城的前身；"后市"所指，就是"大内"正北"中心之台"附近一带的市场（图 3-3）。

根据以上的对比，恰好说明"匠人营国"中的"左"就是东，"右"就是西，"后"就是北，只是朝廷所在独称"面朝"，而不称"前"，这是为什么？

I think if the 'court facing ahead' is understood as 'court in front', it seems not so exact. Because the word 'facing' (*mian*) contains the meaning 'looking forward to', that is to say: if you sit in the middle looking forward to the due south, that will be the court; if you turn back looking towards the north, that will be the site of market. Here it implies the meaning of giving priority to the south.

In fact, in the Chinese history, the main palaces of the capitals of successive dynasties all faced the due south in the planning. After the Yuan Dadu in the Yuan Dynasty, the further developed Beijing Capital City of the Ming and Qing dynasties further embodied this point in concentration, i.e. the well-preserved Forbidden City and two sides thereof, the Imperial Ancestral Temple (now the Working People's Palace of Culture) and the Altar of Land and Grain (now the Zhongshan or Sun Yat-sen Park).

Having been aware of above mentioned points, let us now analyze further the general planning of the Yuan Dadu—why it is totally different from the planning system of 'The Way the Craftsmen Build the City-state' on the city outline and the installation of city gates.

In accordance with the design of the big city in 'The Way the Craftsmen Build the City-state', it is square, each side being nine *li*, with three gates on each side (*fang jiuli, pang sanmen*). However, the Yuan Dadu is not a square, but a rectangle slightly longer from north to south. Besides three gates each for the east, west and south sides, there are only two gates, the east and west ones, on the north side with the middle portion totally closed. This kind of difference is utterly not accidental.

The reason why the plane structure of the Yuan Dadu is rectangle is directly related to the full use of the natural lakes and rivers which flow from northwest to the due south inside the city. I have another special article to elaborate this and will not talk too much here.[3] As for the fact that there is no gate right in the center of the north city wall is concerned, it is against the traditional regulations of 'The Way the Craftsmen Build the City-state', hence a very unique issue worth attention.

Actually, it is due to the very fact that the north gate was deliberately omitted that the middle axis running from north to south, which was the basis for the design of the whole city, taking the 'Central Terrace' of the whole city as the starting point, only stretched to the south. Just under such circumstances, when the Yuan Dadu was rebuilt at the early years of the Ming Dynasty, it was further extended southward along the original middle axis on the basis of reducing the northern city first, and the Wansui Hill (now the Jing Hill) was piled up in place of

细加思索，如果把"面朝"二字只是理解为"前有朝廷"，似乎还不甚确切。因为这里的"面"字，含有"前瞻"的意思，也就是说：要居中向正南方望去是朝廷，转身反顾身后的北方，就是市场所在。这里就暗示着以"南"为上的含义。事实上，中国历代都城在规划设计上，其主要宫殿都一律面向正南。继元大都之后，又进一步发展了的明清北京城，更是集中表现了这一点，这就是现在保存完好的紫禁城，以及进一步迁移到紫禁城前方左右两侧的太庙（今劳动人民文化宫）和社稷坛（今中山公园）。

在明确了上述各点之后，再来进一步分析元大都城的总体规划，在城市轮廓和城门设置上，又是如何与"匠人营国"的规制大相径庭的。

按"匠人营国"关于大城的设计是"方九里，旁三门"。而大都城的营建，并非四面等同的正方形，而是南北略长的长方形，而且除去东西南三面各有三门外，北面却只有东西两门，正中间却是完全封闭的。这种差异，绝非偶然。

大都城的平面结构呈长方形，这与充分利用城内从西北转向正南的一带天然湖泊，有直接关系，作者另有专文说明，此不赘言。[3] 至于在北面城墙的正中央不设北门，却有悖于"匠人营国"的传统规制，是十分突出的一个问题，应该引起重视。实际上也正是有意识不设北门，因此自北而南作为全城设计依据的中轴线，也只是以全城的"中心之台"为起点向南延伸。正是在这一情况下，明朝初年改建大都城，在首先减缩北城的基础上，又进一步沿着原有的中轴线，继续向南开拓，重新堆筑了万岁山（今景山）以代替

the original 'Central Terrace' as the symbol of center for designing the new city. At the same time, on the due south of Wansui Hill, the Imperial Palace, now the Forbidden City, was constructed along the middle axis.

Besides this, the Imperial Ancestral Temple in the east part and the Altar of Land and Grain in the west part of the Yuan Dadu were respectively moved to the east and west sides of the due south part of the Forbidden City, which was still fit for the ancient system of *zuozu youshe, mianchao houshi*. Then the newly built six big halls on the middle axis inside the Forbidden City further embodied the traditional system of Facing the South to Be Emperor (Fig. 3-4).[4]

After the completion of the Yuan Dadu, the middle axis of the whole city kept extending towards the south suburb again in accordance with the tradition of Praying to the Heaven in the South Suburb (*jitian yu nanjiao*). After crossing a small river which flew from west to east, the axis had two imperial building complexes separately built on the east side and west side, the Temple of Heaven on the east and the Altar of Mountain and River (now the Xian Nong Tan) on the west. After that, the city walls on three sides, east, west and south, were built, enclosing these two important complexes inside the city walls, as a result of which, Beijing started having inner and outer parts.

原来的"中心之台"作为新城设计中心的标志。同时又在万岁山的正南方，继续沿着中轴线新建大内，也就是现在的紫禁城。此外，又将大都东城下的太庙和西城下的社稷坛，分别改建到紫禁城正南方的东西两侧，依然符合"左祖右社"的古制。于是紫禁城中中轴线上兴建起来的前后六座大殿，也就更进一步体现了"面南而王"的传统体制（图3-4）。[4]

就在上述大城之内核心地区的规划建设完之后，又根据"祭天于南郊"的传统，将全城的中轴线继续向南郊延伸，在越过一条自西而东的小河之后，又分别在东西两侧，兴建了两组皇家建筑群。在东侧的为天坛，在西侧的为山川坛（后改称先农坛）。其后又兴建东、西、南三面城墙，将这两组重要建筑群圈入城内，于是北京始有内外城之分。

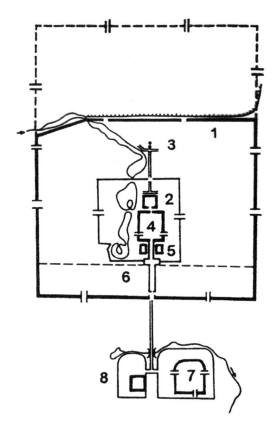

3-4 Surface planes of Beijing City in the middle age of the Ming and Qing dynasties

明中叶北京城空间结构的核心部分最后定型，清代继承不变

1. The rebuilt and newly built north city wall at the beginning of the Ming Dynasty 明初改建、新建北墙

2. Wansui Hill (now Jing Hill) 万岁山（景山）

3. Bell Tower (north) and Drum Tower (south) 钟楼（北）、鼓楼（南）

4. Forbidden City 紫禁城

5. Imperial Ancestral Temple 太庙

6. Altar of Land and Grain 社稷坛

7. Temple of Heaven 天坛

8. Altar of Mountain and River (now Xian Nong Tan) 山川坛（先农坛）

(Source: Same as Fig. 3-3, pp. 31–32. 来源同图3-3，第31—32页。)

From that onwards, Beijing City, the combination of inner and outer parts, became the last built capital city in the times of the ruling of imperial power. It further embodied the thought 'Facing the South to Be Emperor' in the traditional ideology, and was preserved intact until the birth of New China in 1949 (see Fig. 3-4).

Now only after having the full knowledge of the theme which is embodied in concentration in the original planning and construction of Beijing City, can we really learn that today the creation of the northern extension line of the middle axis of the whole city and the further construction of public architectural complex at the north point thereof, 'reflecting outstandingly the new style and features of the capital in the 21st century', are of epoch-making significance.

3

Finally, what is to be explained more is that it has been emphasized more than once above that in the palace construction of various dynasties in China, the traditional thought of 'Facing the South to Be Emperor' was embodied from the beginning to the end, and the southward extension of the middle axis of the Beijing City in old days again and again was also influenced by this traditional thought. Then from where did come this kind of traditional thought?

So far as the answer of this question is concerned, the discovery by archaeologists has provided the most important reference materials.

In the early 1970s, the ruins of a palace of no later than the early Shang Dynasty were excavated at Erlitou, Yanshi County, Henan Province. At the middle part of the site, there is an obvious rammed terrace base, about 0.8 meter high above the present ground, 108 meters in length from west to east, 100 meters in width from north to south. At the center of the southern part of the terrace base, there are ruins of doors with eight bays in width. In the middle of the northern part of the terrace base rose the pisé foundation 3.1 meters high, 36 meters from east to west,

25 meters from north to south. In accordance with the arrangement of the pillar holes round it, it can be concluded that this building is eight bays in width and three bays in length. Slightly north of the pisé foundation is the relic of the hall, 30.4 meters from west to east and 11.4 meters from north to south. The whole building structure, with the hall as the principal part, faces southwards as shown in the Fig. 3-5.[5] In accordance with the restored figure made out of the above mentioned discovery, the characteristic is much more explicit that the whole construction of the palace faces the due south (Fig. 3-6).[6]

从此这内外合一的北京城，就成为皇权统治时代最后建成的一座都城，它又进一步体现了传统的意识形态中"面南而王"的思想，并且完整地保存下来，一直到1949年新中国的诞生（见图3-4）。

现在只有充分认识到北京这座历史文化名城在其原有的规划建设上所集中体现的主题思想，才能真正体会到今天开辟全城中轴北延长线以及进一步在其北端兴建"突出体现21世纪首都的新风貌"的公共建筑群，确实是有着划时代的意义的。

三

最后，还应该说明的是：上文一再强调中国历代宫殿建筑，都始终体现了"面南而王"的传统思想，而且旧日北京城的中轴线一再向南延伸，也同样是这一传统思想的影响。那么这种"面南而王"的传统思想又是如何产生的呢？

关于这个问题的答案，考古学的发现提供了最重要的参考。

70年代初，在河南省偃师县二里头，发掘出至少是早商时期的一处宫殿遗址，其中部，有一明显的夯土台基，高出地面约0.8米，东西长108米，南北宽100米。台基南侧的中央，有门址遗迹，面阔8间。殿堂地居台基中央之北部，有夯土台，土层厚3.1米。殿堂东西长36米，南北宽25米，根据周围柱洞的排列，可以断定该建筑面阔8间，进深3间。基地中央稍北为殿堂遗址，东西长30.4米，南北宽11.4米。以殿堂为主的整体结构面向南方，如图3-5所示。[5]根据上述发现制为复原图，则整体宫殿建筑面向正南的特点，就更加显明（图3-6）。[6]

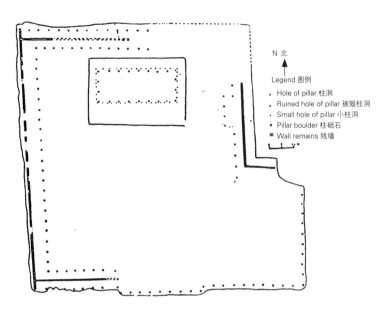

Legend 图例
· Hole of pillar 柱洞
· Ruined hole of pillar 被毁柱洞
· Small hole of pillar 小柱洞
· Pillar boulder 柱础石
▬ Wall remains 残墙

3-5 Plan of No. 1 palace base at Erlitou, Yanshi County 偃师二里头早商一号宫殿基地平面图

(From: *Archaeology*, No. 4, 1974《考古》，第 4 期，1974)

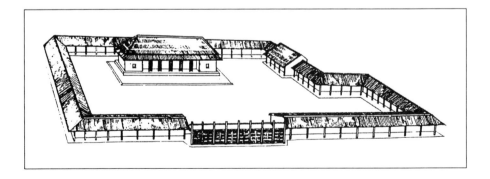

3-6 Drawing of the restored palace 偃师二里头早商一号宫殿复原图

(Redrawn according to *Ancient Architecture of China*, 1983, p. 24 根据《中国古建筑》重制，1983，第 24 页)

Therefore, it can be imagined that the palace hall in the Central Plain Region (comprising the middle and lower reaches of the Yellow River) in China from the ancient time on faced the due south. Thereafter, this rule was inherited in successive dynasties without exception. Hence, the so-called thought of Facing the South to Be Emperor gradually took shape in the ideology. This speciality of the dynasties established in the China Central Plain is reflected in the capital planning and design.

The forming of this characteristic was closely related to the geographical environment of the Yellow River Valley. The Yellow River Valley is located just at the region where the semi-tropical monsoon climate of the northern hemisphere is most typical. In winter, the high atmospheric pressure in the northwest of Asian continent is formed and the cold and strong north wind attacks the middle and lower parts of Yellow River with the severe cold lingering on for months. In summer, the center of high atmospheric pressure moves towards the southeast Pacific Ocean and the south monsoon bringing rain makes the temperature rise in such a way that summer heat even becomes unbearable. As a result of that, it is most suitable for the facade of the house to face the due

由此可以设想，中国中原地区自古以来的宫殿建筑就是面向正南方，此后历代相承，莫不如此。因此在意识形态里逐渐派生出所谓"面南而王"的思想。这一特点在中国的中原王朝中，正是历代都城在规划设计上的一大特色。这一特色的形成，和黄河流域的地理环境是有密切关系的。黄河流域正处于北半球亚热带季风气候最为显著的地区，冬季在亚洲大陆西北内部形成高气压，寒冷强劲的偏北风，袭击着黄河流域中下游，气候严寒，长达数月。夏季高气压中心转向东南太平洋上，来自南方致雨的季风，又使温度上升，甚至暑气逼人。于是房屋建筑面向

south with the closure of the northern side to avoid wind and coldness of winter. The opening of doors and windows towards the southern side is not only convenient to get winter sunshine obliquely coming into rooms, but also for the air circulating in summer time. It can be imagined that in order to adapt to this climatic characteristic, the earliest palace buildings in Yellow River Valley since the ancient time, have adopted the style of facing the south with the back to the north, as it is seen in the archaeological discovery at Erlitou, Yanshi County. Having been existing for a long time, this practice became a custom. When it was recorded in 'The Way the Craftsmen Build the City-state', it was quite enough to make clear upon noticing 'the Imperial Ancestral Temple on the left side, the Altar of Land and Grain on the right side, Court facing ahead and Market on the back side' their relative positions. Here the words 'facing ahead' are of great importance. It denotes fronting the southern direction, as a result of which the tradition of so-called 'Facing the South to Be Emperor' in the ideology finally came into being.

In accordance with the geomancy theory in later times there is also explanation concerning the question of facing the south in construction design. For example, Zhang Ziwei of the Song Dynasty wrote in his book entitled *Yu Sui Zhen Jing* that temples, courts, palaces, and prefecture and county offices all face the south without any exception, the reason of which is to manage in the face of brightness.[7] There is no record concerning whether in the beginning of the Yuan Dynasty the absence of the gate of due north was owing to the impact of geomancy theory or not. So let us lay it aside for the time being. However, it is very obvious that the geographical conditions of the Yellow River Valley led to the construction of palace facing the south in the beginning.

Translated by Li Guanghui

正南最为相宜，北侧封闭以御冬季风寒，南侧开设门窗，既便于冬季阳光斜射室内，又有利于夏季空气流通。可以设想，为了适应这一气候特点，从古代起，黄河流域最早的宫殿建筑，如偃师县二里头的考古发现所见，就采取了背北面南的形式。这一特点长期延续下来，相沿成习。到了《周礼·考工记》"匠人营国"的记载中，只要记述"左祖右社，面朝后市"，就足以说明彼此之间的方向，而"面朝"的"面"字在这里就特别重要，它指明了是面向南方，由此终于衍生出意识形态中所谓"面南而王"的传统。按后世的风水学说，就建筑设计面向南方，也有解说。例如宋人张子微在所著《玉髓真经》一书中就曾写道："庙朝宫殿府县治廨，无不向南，盖取向明而治之义。"[7]元初规划大都城，不设正北门，是否也有风水学说的影响，未见有明文记载，姑不具论。只是追本溯源，黄河流域的地理条件，导致了最初宫殿建筑取向正南，则是十分明显的。

❹ FROM BEIJING TO WASHINGTON

A Contemplation on the Concept of Municipal Planning*

I. Recommendation of the Topic

Beijing and Washington are two capital cities of two countries with totally different social systems. The design and planning of the two cities have their unique features respectively. Chronologically, there is a long interval between their initial constructions, yet their design and planning both reflect the depth of their own cultural and historical background. The original plan of old Beijing is a masterpiece of city planning in feudal China, while the plan of Washington inherits the elegance of the sixteenth-century Renaissance tradition and the graceful urban design of Western Europe, and is a marvellous specimen of the achievement in the era of rising capitalism.

China, after the lapse of feudal dynasties, suffered from the oppression of semi-colonialism and semi-feudalism. She is now in the era of socialist construction. America, on the other hand, is a highly developed capitalist nation, still following the capitalist road and even casting her influence abroad. The two capital cities, which are the focal point of expression for their respective national cultures and histories, would be confronted with different problems in city planning and design.

For city planning and design, Beijing and Washington share some similarities in form, but they are fundamentally different. The most prominent feature in common is the decision at the infant stage of city construction to fix a central axis line for the layout of the whole city. Nevertheless, their fundamental difference consists in the respective themes to be represented owing to the totally different social systems in the very beginning of their planning.

II. The City of Beijing (Peking)

● **Changes of Beijing's City Sites and Its Present Location**

The origin of the primitive settlement of Beijing could be dated back to over 3,000 years ago. It was located at the southwest part of present Beijing city which had not begun to be built until about 720 years ago (1267 A.D.). The lake district of the ancient Gaoliang River was chosen to

肆 从北京到华盛顿——城市设计主题思想试探*

北京和华盛顿是社会制度完全不同的两个国家的首都，但在城市的规划设计上，却各有千秋。从历史的发展来看，北京和华盛顿尽管在开始营建的年代上相去很远，但是在规划设计上，却各有自己深厚的文化历史渊源。北京城原有的规划设计，可以说是封建社会时期我国都城建设的一个杰出典型。华盛顿城中心部分的规划设计，从建国之初开始，就继承了自16世纪"文艺复兴"盛行以来欧洲城市建设的优良传统，堪称资本主义上升时期西方国家都城规划的一个光辉范例。

我国在封建王朝衰落之后，又经历了灾难深重的半殖民地半封建社会，现在已经进入了建设有中国特色的社会主义的新时代。

美国作为一个高度发达的资本主义国家，还在沿着它原有的道路徘徊前进，甚至伸张其势力于域外。

因此，这两个首都作为两个国家历史文化集中表现的地方，在其规划设计上所面临的问题，也就各不相同了。

在过去的规划设计上，北京和华盛顿既有形式上的类似之处，又有本质上的区别和差异。在形式上的类似之处，最突出的一点，就是两者从建城之始就各自选定了一条中轴线作为全城设计的出发点。在本质上的区别和差异，则在于两个城市在其最初规划设计上，由于社会性质的根本不同，所力图表达的主题思想，也就大不一样了。

一、北京城

（一）今城的建址与城址的演变

北京城原始聚落的起源，距今已有三千多年。早期的城址原在今城的西南部。今城的建设则是七百二十年前（即公元1267年）才开始的。当时选择了古代高粱河上的一带天然湖泊作为中心进行规划设计，建设

be the center for the design and plan of the new city, that is, the Dadu City (the Great Capital) of the Yuan Dynasty (1271-1368). The city underwent some reconstruction in the early days of the Ming Dynasty (1368-1644) and a new name Beijing was given to it. In 1553 A.D., an outer wall was added in the southern part of Beijing city. Thus, we have an inner city and an outer city of Beijing, both encircled by city walls. The two combined took the shape of a Chinese character "凸", occupying an area of 62 sq. km. Hence the surface plan of Beijing city was fixed, and it had been preserved as it was until 1949 A.D., when the New China was born. It is now called the Old City of Beijing.

At the beginning of building old Beijing, the southern half of the lake was enclosed within the city and was designed as the central part of the royal garden in the Imperial City. In accordance with the feudal tradition, it was named "Tai Ye Chi" (the Holy Water Pond). In the early part of the Ming Dynasty a new lake was dug at the southern tip of the Holy Water Pond. This is the present Nan Hai (the South Sea). The upper part of the original lake left out of the Imperial City was called Ji-shui Tan (the Reservoir). It was also in the early years of the Ming Dynasty that the northern city wall of the capital was moved south-ward, thus excluding the northwestern part of Ji-shui Tan from the city. The excluded part was called Tai-ping Hu (the Peaceful Lake), which was filled up during the Cultural Revolution. And the other part inside the northern wall of the great city but outside of the Imperial City is the Shicha Hai of today, made up of Qian Hai (the Front Lake), Hou Hai (the Back Lake) and Xi Hai (the West Lake). The southwestern tip of Qian Hai had also been filled up and reclaimed for building sites recently.

In sum, the original lake district furnished essential geographical conditions for the establishment of the Old City of Beijing. Its original appearance had long been altered, but it still occupies an important place. There is a plan to connect the six south and north lakes (that is, Nan Hai,

Zhong Hai and Bei Hai in the south and Qian Hai, Hou Hai and Xi Hai in the north), which is part of the general plan for developing the new Beijing. In order to illustrate the theme of the plan of the Old City, it's better to show the changes of watercourses and city sites of old Beijing in the following figure. (Fig. 4-1)

- **Theme of City Plan**

As shown in Figure 4-1, we see clearly that several changes in the shape of the Old City of Beijing, from rectangular to the ingenious shape

新城，这就是元朝的大都城。明朝初年又历经改建，始称北京。到了明朝中叶，也就是公元 1553 年，又在北京城南加筑外罗城，于是又有北京内城和外城之分，各有城垣环绕，合成凸字形，面积约计 62 平方公里。全城的平面布局，至此定型，并且一直完整地保留到 1949 年新中国的诞生，这就是今天所说的北京旧城。

在北京旧城建设的过程中，城内湖泊的南半部，从一开始就圈入皇城之内，作为皇家园林的中心部分进行营建，并按照封建传统，命名为太液池。明初又在太液池南端新凿一湖，遂有南海、中海和北海之称，流传至今。至于被隔在皇城以外的原始湖泊的上游，原名积水潭。明朝初年，缩减北城，竟将积水潭的上游部分隔在城外，这就是在"十年动乱"期间才被填掉的太平湖。保留在城内的部分就是今天的什刹海，习惯上又分别叫做前海、后海和西海。前海的西南隅一部分也已被填为建筑用地。

总之，为北京旧城的建址提供了重要地理条件的原始湖泊，今天虽然已经不是本来的面貌，却仍然占有十分重要的地位，并且已经有贯通南北六海（即南部的南海、中海、北海和北部的前海、后海、西海）的设想，纳入北京城的总体规划之中。为了便于揭示北京旧城城市设计的主题思想，应将北京旧城河湖水系的变迁与城址的演变，作图说明（图 4-1）。

（二）城市设计的主题思想

从插图中可以明显地看到北京旧城的轮廓虽然从长方形到

126

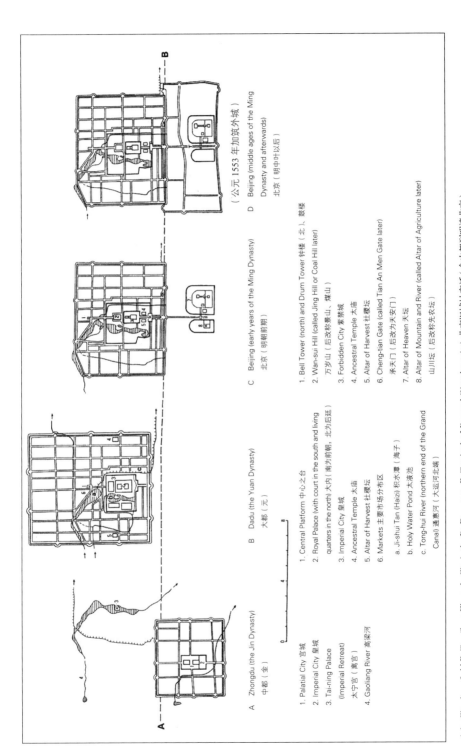

4-1 City sites of old Beijing (from Zhongdu City in the Jin Dynasty to Beijing in the Ming and Qing dynasties) 北京旧城址变迁（金中都到明清北京）

(Broken line from A to B is a reference line to demonstrate the relative positions of city sites vertically AB 间虚线表示城址南北移动的相对位置)

A　Zhongdu (the Jin Dynasty)
　　中都（金）

1. Palatial City 宫城
2. Imperial City 皇城
3. Tai-ning Palace
　　(Imperial Retreat)
　　大宁宫（离宫）
4. Gaoliang River 高粱河

B　Dadu (the Yuan Dynasty)
　　大都（元）

1. Central Platform 中心之台
2. Royal Palace (with court in the south and living
　　quarters in the north) 大内（南为前朝，北为后廷）
3. Imperial City 皇城
4. Ancestral Temple 太庙
5. Altar of Harvest 社稷坛
6. Markets 主要市场分布区
　　a. Ji-shui Tan (Haizi) 积水潭（海子）
　　b. Holy Water Pond 太液池
　　c. Tong-hui River (northern end of the Grand
　　　　Canal) 通惠河（大运河北端）

C　Beijing (early years of the Ming Dynasty)
　　北京（明朝前期）

D　Beijing (middle ages of the Ming
　　Dynasty and afterwards)
　　北京（明中叶以后）
　　（公元 1553 年加筑外城）

1. Bell Tower (north) and Drum Tower 钟楼（北）、鼓楼
2. Wan-sui Hill (called Jing Hill or Coal Hill later)
　　万岁山（后改称景山、煤山）
3. Forbidden City 紫禁城
4. Ancestral Temple 太庙
5. Altar of Harvest 社稷坛
6. Cheng-tian Gate (called Tian An Men Gate later)
　　承天门（后改为天安门）
7. Altar of Heaven 天坛
8. Altar of Mountain and River (called Altar of Agriculture later)
　　山川坛（后改称先农坛）

of a Chinese character "凸", took place. However, the axis line running through the city from north to south, though extended, had no sideward shift. Actually the axis line was the basis of the surface plan of the capital. This is true of the design of the Inner City as it is of the Outer City. It must be pointed out that even before the building of the outer walls, two groups of architecture had been built in 1420 A.D., that is, the Temple of Heaven and the Altar of Mountain and River (later renamed the Altar of Agriculture). They were located symmetrically on the east and west sides of the prolonged axis line. And with building of the outer walls in 1553 A.D., a newly prolonged central axis line with a total length of 8 km., implicitly linking the Inner City and the Outer City, took shape, which impressed one with the sense of unity so much that it appeared that the two parts of the city had been planned and completed at the same time. And the "凸"-shaped capital, when compared with Dadu of the Yuan Dynasty and Beijing in the early years of the Ming Dynasty, renders a greater sense of stableness and security. It is this feature of the layout of the city that has won enormous appreciations and praise from Western architects and city planners for its aesthetic value. The Danish architect S. E. Rasmussen remarked

凸字形经过了几次变化，但是自北而南隐然存在的纵贯全城的中轴线，只有延长，并无改变。实际上这条中轴线，也正是全城平面设计的依据。在内城是如此，在外城也不例外。因为外城城垣未建之前，就先已于 1420 年兴建了天坛和山川坛（后改称先农坛）这两组建筑。其东西并列的位置，显然是由内城中轴线的延长部分所决定的，后来加筑外城（1553 年），终于出现了纵贯内外两城长达 8 公里的新轴线，并且给人一种整体感，好像内外两城是同时设计，一气呵成的。这也显示出凸字形的城垣轮廓，比起任何一种矩形轮廓（如元大都和明初北京城的轮廓），更能给人以一种稳定感。正是这种全城平面布局上的特点，从美学观点上引起了西方建筑学家和城市规划学者的无限赞叹。丹麦的 S. E. Rasmussen 称道说：

Beijing as "one of the wonders of the world, in its symmetry and clarity a unique monument, the culmination of a great civilization."[1] The American city planner E. N. Bacon praised highly of it, saying "Possibly the greatest single work of man on the face of the earth is Peking.... [I]t is so brilliant in design that it provides a rich storehouse of ideas for the city of today." He also highlighted central axis line and the lakes adjacent in yellow and blue, which appeared prominent and vivid against the greyish surface plan.[2]

One should, however, note more the thought underneath the design of the surface plan. From the architectural perspective, two points should be clarified:

1. Relationship between building of city walls and city plan

According to Chinese tradition, all ancient cities were built with walls. Hence the Chinese character "城" (*cheng*) has a dual meaning. It may mean "a city" or "the wall of a city." It can also be used as a verb. For example, in "Cart Driving," one poem from Minor Odes, *Book of Poetry*, one of ancient classics, there is a line, "wall the place in the north." Here the word "wall," used as a verb, means "to build city walls." Building of city walls is most essential in the design and plan of a capital city. For example, *Kaogongji* (*A Study of Engineering*), a volume of the ancient classics *Zhou Li* or *The Rites of Zhou* completed during the Age of Spring and Autumn (770-476 B.C.), had a paragraph "The Way the Craftsmen Build the City," which summarized the experiences in city building since the founding of the Zhou Dynasty, and on its basis established a standard for capital city building as follows:

> A capital city should be square in shape, each side being nine *li* long. There should be three gates on each side. Within the city, there are nine thoroughfares running longitudinally and another nine latitudinally, each wide enough for nine chariots driving abreast. On the left side within the city an ancestral temple should be erected. And on the right side there should be an altar of harvest. The court should be built to face

the front while the market square should be placed at the rear of the court.

It is self-evident that the imperial court is in the center of the city. For this idea, reference can be made to He Ye-ju's *Research on the System of Capital City Building*, from which some quotation could be cited as follows:

Why was the imperial court located in the middle of the capital? I think this is closely related to the doctrine of "to choose the middle"

"北京城乃是世界的奇观之一，它的布局匀称而明朗，是一个卓越的纪念物，一个伟大文明的顶峰。"[1] 美国的 E. N. Bacon 又推崇它"可能是地球表面上人类最伟大的单项工程……它的平面设计是如此之杰出，这就为今天的城市建设提供了丰富的可供参考的实例"。同时他还曾用黄蓝两色把这条中轴线连同和它并列的一带湖泊，突出地显示在全城淡灰色的平面图上，给人以十分突出的印象。[2] 然而更加值得注意的却是隐然支配着这整个平面设计的主题思想，从其建筑上来说有最重要的两点，须分别加以说明如下：

1. 城垣建筑与城市设计的关系

根据我国的历史传统，最初的城市，都有城垣，因此"城"这个字有双重含义，既指城市，又指城垣，有时还可用作动词，如《诗·小雅·出车》："城彼朔方"，即指在朔方筑城，而城垣的修筑，又与整个城市的规划设计密切联系在一起。例如，成书于春秋时期（公元前 770—前 476）的《周礼·考工记》在"匠人营国"一节中，总结了周初以来营建国都的经验，又加以规范化，并做了如下的描述：

匠人营国，方九里，旁三门，国中九经九纬，经涂九轨。左祖右社，面朝后市。

这段记载的大意是说：国都的营建，应是一座方城，每边长九里，各有三门。城内纵横大道各九条。左有太庙，右有社稷坛。面向外朝，后为市场。这里不言而喻的是帝王的朝廷位居全城的中央。关于这一点，贺业钜在《考工记营国制度研究》一书中有所说明，摘录如下：

为什么要把宫廷区布置在全城中心，这和周人所崇奉的

esteemed by the people of Zhou and it cast great influence on the determination of the location of a capital. To build the capital in the middle of a kingdom is not only convenient for the subjects from different directions to pay tributes to the king, but also easier for the king to reign over the country from the center.[3]

It should be noted that of all the capital cities built in the feudal dynasties in China, the Dadu City of the Yuan Dynasty is the one built according to the standards closest to those set by "The Way the Craftsmen Build the City." Certainly this was directly related to the main designer of the city Liu Bingzhong (Liu Kan). Liu was a practically-minded person and well versed in classics. He had lectured in the Zijin College at the eastern foot of the Taihang Mountains, where the famous astrologist and expert on water conservancy Guo Shoujing studied under him. Before the establishment of the Yuan Dynasty, Liu had been ordered by Kublai Khan to design on the northern shore of the Shandian River on the upper reaches of the present Luan River, Kaiping City (called Shangdu City later), whose remains can still be found today. This achievement won Liu the recognition of Kublai Khan, so the latter bestowed him the name "Bingzhong" (Adherence to Loyalty). In 1260 A.D., Kublai Khan entered and got stationed in Zhongdu, the last big city that developed on the site of the primitive settlement. Seven years later he decided to build a new city around the Taining Palace (an imperial summer retreat in the lake district) to the northeast of Zhongdu City, and he again appointed Liu in charge of the task. Guo Shoujing was also recommended to participate and made great contribution especially to water conservancy and construction of the Grand Canal.

It is necessary to point out that the shape of the Great Capital was rectangular with the north-south walls longer than the east-west walls, rather than square as prescribed in "The Way the Craftsmen Build the City." This was out of necessity to fully utilize the watercourses. Another discrepancy was that residential palaces in the "Grand Inner Portion" (equivalent to the later Forbidden City) did not lie at the geometric center of the capital but slightly south of it, though it was still situated on the axis line in the plan, which also fitted into the doctrine of "to choose the middle."

From the construction of Dadu of the Yuan Dynasty to the supplement of outer walls in the middle ages of the Ming Dynasty, the surface plan of this city had underwent several alterations, and thus become vastly different from the ideal described in the classics, but the basic concept

"择中论"的规划思想是分不开的。"择中论"是我国奴隶社会选择国都位置的规划理论，这种理论认为择天下之中建王"国"（即国都），既便于四方贡献，更有利于控制四方。[3]

这一说明指出了国都设计的理论根据，值得注意。按中国历代都城的建设，只有元大都城的规划设计和上述"匠人营国"的描述最为近似。这自然与大都城的主要设计人刘秉忠有直接关系。刘秉忠原名侃，是位熟通经史而又务实的学者，曾设坛讲学于太行山中，元代著名天文历算学家、水利学家郭守敬即出其门下。蒙古首领忽必烈入主中原，建立元朝之前，曾命刘侃在今滦河上游闪电河北岸设计兴建开平城（后改称上都，今遗址尚在），深得忽必烈赏识，因赐名秉忠。1260年忽必烈进驻当时金朝中都城，也就是在北京原始聚落上发展起来的最后一座大城，1267年决定在中都城外东北郊一座湖上离宫（太宁宫）的周围，另建大都新城，仍然任命刘秉忠为主要负责人。郭守敬也被推荐参与其事，特别是在河湖水系的利用与大运河的修建上，做出了卓越的贡献。

这里需要指出的是大都城垣，南北纵长，而非正方，与"匠人营国"的规划稍有区别，这显然是由于在全城的平面布局上要充分利用河湖水系的结果。其次是"大内"（相当于后日的紫禁城）的寝宫，并不在全城的正中央，也与"匠人营国"所暗示的不尽一致，而是稍向南移，但是仍然处于全城设计的中轴线上，也是合乎"择中论"的规划思想的。

元大都建成之后直到明中叶北京外城的兴建，其平面布局历经改造，与"匠人营国"所描写的原始形制，已经相去甚远，但是它所体现

the city was trying to express was still the same. Moreover, it had been more prominent, especially owing to prolonging the axis line twice. Therefore, the following part will be devoted to the discussion of the design of the axis line and the concept beneath.

2. Implications of axis line design and its historical and cultural background

The artistic effect that the axis line rendered in the layout of the Old City of Beijing has been highly appreciated by city planners home and abroad, while its implications and historical and cultural background are to be further explored.

In another paper "On the Remolding of the Old Beijing City"[4] by the author, it is recorded that Kublai Khan decided to build the new capital before the founding of the Yuan Dynasty and the geometric center of the plan of the capital was fixed on the northeastern shore of the lake Jishui Tan. At this spot was erected a stone tablet with four characters "中心之台" (The Central Platform) carved in it. Taking the platform as the starting point, a straight line was drawn closely along the eastern shore of the Jishui Tan as the central axis of the whole city. The imperial palaces were built on the eastern shore of the Holy Water Pond, exactly in the middle of the axis, so that the front court Daming Palace (Palace of Brilliance) and the residential palace Yanchun Ge (Prolonged Spring Palace) occupied the most significant sites of the city. Hence, the idea embodied by the central axis became very clear, that is, the absolute power of the emperor. The Ancestral Temple and the Altar of Harvest, the two complexes of symbolic significance, were placed on the left and right sides of the palaces respectively within the city walls as prescribed by "The Way the Craftsmen Build the City." Later, as the capital was rebuilt by the Ming emperors, the original geometrical center of the Inner City was moved south to the Central Peak of the Jing Hill, which was the original site of the Prolonged Spring Palace during the Yuan Dynasty. And these two groups of buildings were also moved southward to the two sides in front of the Forbidden City. The result of this is that the concept embodied by the design of the axis becomes more prominent. With the building of the Temple of Heaven and the Altar of Mountain and River in the southern suburb, the axis was further prolonged to the south. Its influence on the planning and design of the Old City of Beijing became even more significant, also making the theme represented thereby more prominent.

Another question to be further clarified is: How is it decided that the axis of the capital as it appeared on the surface plan runs perpendicularly

的基本内容，却依然未变。不仅如此，它所传达的主题思想却更加突出、更加明显。这一主题思想就集中表现在两度延长的全城中轴线上。因此这条全城中轴线的设计和它所集中表现的思想内容，正是本文所应该进一步探讨的核心问题。

2. 全城中轴线设计的含义及其历史文化渊源

北京旧城的中轴线在全城平面布局上的艺术效果，虽然屡为中外规划学家所称道，但是它的含义及其发生和演变的历史文化渊源，还有待进一步阐明。

拙作《论北京旧城的改造》[4]一文已经说明在元朝国号未建以前兴建大都城时，首先在积水潭的东北岸上确定了全城布局的几何中心，就地刻石立碑，命名为"中心之台"，然后以中心台为起点，紧傍积水潭东岸，定下了全城设计的中轴线，从而把宫城"大内"，恰好布置在太液池东岸，也就是中轴线的中间部位上，其结果是大内的前朝大明殿与后宫延春阁，也就占据了全城最重要的位置，这就十分突出地显示了这条中轴线在全城设计上的主题思想，如果用文字来说明，那就是封建帝王的"唯我独尊"。至于宗庙社稷这两组具有象征意义的建筑群，遵照"匠人营国"的原则，相应地布置在大内左右，也就是东西两面城垣的内侧。其后经过明朝的改建，内城的几何中心虽然由原来的中心台南移到景山中峰（也就是元朝延春阁的旧址），宗庙社稷两组建筑也分别移到紫禁城前的左右两侧，结果是全城中轴线在设计上的主题思想，不仅没有减弱，反而加强。特别是随着南郊天坛和山川坛的兴建，中轴线又继续向南延长，终于使得它在全城平面布局上的支配地位更加突出，它所代表的主题思想也就更加显明。

但是在这里必须进一步说明的一个问题，就是在北京旧城平面设计上不断得到发展的中轴线，它的自北而南的垂直走向是怎样确

from north to south and extends this way? The question seems simple, but it concerns the issue of orientation in the design and planning of a capital, that is, it must face towards the due south. From it derives the doctrine of "facing the south to be king." There is no direct reference in documents to when this idea applied to city planning originated. However, in "The Way the Craftsmen Build the City" in *Kaogongji, Zhouli*, there is an implication that the city should be built towards the south. As for the layout of the capital, there are such prescriptions, "left for the Ancestral Temple and right for the Altar of Harvest"—"left" refers to east and "right" west, and "court in the front (south) and market at the rear (north)." The north-south orientation of city had long been accepted by Chinese as a tradition and passed down. Archaeological discoveries have provided concrete evidence. All the ruins of the foundations of the palaces from the early Shang Dynasty attest to that the original structures above were facing south.[5] Two foundations found in the Shang ruins indicate that the palaces not only faced southward but also stood on the same north-south line with one in front of the other, which should be the primitive form of the principle —"court in the front and living quarters at the rear."[6] The foundations of city walls were also excavated in the capital relics of Shang; they appeared almost square, only the palaces were in the northeast of the city.[7] Most probably the idea of building the palaces in the middle of the city, i.e. on the central axis, hadn't took shape or established as a rule until the Zhou Dynasty. This is the initial thought from which the traditional principle recorded in the classic of *Zhouli* developed. These became the rules for workmen to follow in the building of a capital in later times. The theory of "to choose the middle" was a reflection of that thought as it appeared in the passage of "Judge the Situation" (*Shenshi*) in *The Book of Spring and Autumn by Lü Buwei* (*Lüshi chunqiu*) in the later part of the Warring States Period (475-221 B.C.) that "All rulers of ancient times did choose the middle place under the Heaven to establish their kingdoms."

The facts mentioned above show that in designing the plan for a capital, the concept was to arrange the building of the city to face southward. This is deeply rooted in historical and cultural background and tradition. This fact is that the central part of China is located in the monsoon land of the northern hemisphere, where strong northwesterly winds blow with fierce coldness in winter. In summer southeasterly winds prevail causing the weather to be hot and humid with heavy rainfall. Thus to keep out the bitterly cold wind and to get

定下来的？这个问题看似简单，实际上却涉及我国都城在规划设计上的一个基本定向的问题，那就是城市布局的主导方向，一定要面向正南。由此而派生出来的一个封建统治者的正统观念，就是所谓"面南而王"。这个"面南而王"的思想，在城市的规划设计上最初体现出来始于何时，没有直接的文献记载可供参考，但至少《周礼·考工记》的"匠人营国"一节，已经间接说明了当时的城市建设计划，其主导方向必是面向正南。因此在文中讲到国都的平面布局时，只用"左祖"与"右社"以代表宗庙在东，社稷坛在西；只用"面朝"与"后市"以代表朝廷在南，市场在北。可以设想，这一既定的主导方向，是早已相沿成习而后遗传下来的。关于这一点，考古发现提供了有力的佐证。迄今所见早商时代的宫殿基址，说明当时的宫殿建筑，都是正面朝南。[5] 又商代的宫殿基址中还显示出有两座殿址，不仅坐北朝南，而且前后并列，从规划上判断，应即后代"前朝后寝"的原型。[6] 其次，商代都城已发现有略呈方形的四面城垣，但宫殿建筑偏在城内东北部。[7] 有计划地把面向正南的宫殿修建在方形城垣的中央——也就是全城的中轴线上，应是到周代才成为定制的，这就是《周礼·考工记》中"匠人营国"所根据的传统原则。其后，到了战国末年，为秦国统一天下提供思想武器的《吕氏春秋·慎势》篇中所谓"古之王者，择天下之中而立国"的"择中论"，就是这一历史事实的反映。

上述事实说明，在都城的规划设计上，以面向正南为主导方向，是有很深厚的历史文化渊源的。追求其原因，很显明的是和地处北温带的季风地区有关，这里冬季西北寒风强烈，气候严酷；夏季转以东南风为主，炎热多雨。为了避寒和采光，居室的设计，

the most sunshine and warmth, it was advisable and reasonable to build the houses with windows and doors facing south and the high walls in the back facing north. This requirement of building principle and rule of "facing south" gradually prevailed in the design and planning of municipal construction. And from this principle and rule derived the doctrine of "facing the south to be king." Such a tradition can be traced to the time of slave society. It became a confirmed system during the feudal era. Beijing, a famous historical and cultural city, has preserved these characteristics in the planning and design of its buildings.

- **The Essential Task of Transforming Old Beijing and the Achievements**

With the birth of New China, the task of transforming Old Beijing into the capital of the People's Republic of China was put on the agenda. This is to say, while preserving the special characteristics of this famous historic city of cultural richness, we must supply new concepts which reflect the spirit of the new era. This is not an easy task. What we have done in the past thirty years showed that we have committed some irretrievable mistakes and damage. Nevertheless, we have had some achievements among which the transformation of Tian An Men Square is one.

Tian An Men Square was once the imperial court of feudal sovereignty. It was surrounded on three sides by red walls, along the inside of which there was a long corridor each made up of rooms whose eaves and ridges were connected successively. It was called "A Thousand Steps Corridor." The court within the red walls was in a "T" shape. It had been the place where royal ceremonies took place showing off the absolute authority of the feudal emperors. The place was out of bounds to the common people. The court was located on the central axis which is symbolic in the sense that it expressed the feudal ideology of "the Emperor is the Almighty Sovereign."

Entering the gate of Tian An Men, one must pass through layers of enclosed space in order to reach the nuclei of the royal buildings. They are the grandest buildings in the Forbidden City—Tai He Dian (the Palace of Prosperity and Peace), Zhong He Dian (the Central Peace Palace), Bao He Dian (the Palace of Preserving Peace), and the royal residential palaces in the rear part of the Forbidden City—Qian Qing Gong (the Palace of Heavenly Purity), Jiao Tai Dian (the Palace of Mutual Prosperity) and Kun Ning Gong (the Palace of Feminine Calmness). (Fig. 4-2)

In 1911, the revolution led by Dr. Sun Yat-sen ousted the Manchurian imperial reign, thus ending more than two thousand years of feudalism and it was not until then that the imperial court in front of Tian An Men

背北面南最为合理。因此由个体建筑扩大到城市布局，逐渐发展为面向正南作为整体设计上的主导方向，进而派生出"面南而王"的传统观念，其起源可以上溯至奴隶社会时期，到了封建社会时期，已成定型。从这一点来说，北京作为历史文化名城，它所保存下来的最大的特殊风貌，也正表现在这里。

（三）旧城改造的一项根本任务及其成就

随着新中国的诞生，又重新建都北京，它所面临的一项根本任务，应该是在力求保护这座历史文化名城的特殊风貌的同时，赋予它以新的主题思想，从而反映出新的时代精神。这是极为困难的一件事。在过去三十多年的实践中，虽然出现了一些难以挽救的损失，但是也取得了一定的成就，天安门广场的改造就是一例。

现在天安门广场的前身，原是封建王朝统治时期的一个宫廷广场，三面筑有红墙，沿红墙内侧筑有联檐通脊的千步廊，中间广场呈"T"字形，过去只有炫耀封建帝王无上权威的重大典礼在这里举行，庶民百姓严禁涉足。因此在全城中轴线上所集中表现的封建帝王"唯我独尊"的主题思想，首先在这里显示出来。进入天安门之后，还要穿过层层封闭的空间，才能来到紫禁城内的核心建筑，即雄踞全城之上的前朝三大殿——太和殿、中和殿、保和殿，以及后廷三大宫——乾清宫、交泰殿、坤宁宫。（图4-2）

1911年的辛亥革命推翻了历时两千多年的封建王朝的统治，天安门前的宫廷广场才得开放通行，其结果也正是在这里爆发了

was open to all. It was in 1919 in Tian An Men Square that the famous May 4th Movement first started and began the overture of the neo-Democratic Revolution. This is one of the most important incidents which took place in the Square in the heart of Beijing. It was the spark that started the prairie fire of a national revolution of the people. Under the leadership of the Chinese Communist Party and after thirty years of struggle, the People's Republic of China was born. The inauguration of the People's Republic of China took place in Beijing in the year 1949, on the first of October in Tian An Men Square. This incident gave a new significance to the Square. This grand and gorgeous old building obtained a new significance which symbolized the rebirth of an ancient civilization. When creating the emblem of the People's Republic of China, Tian An Men was designed in the middle of the emblem. In spite of this, the old red walls were still there hindering the common people from going into the Square for their various social, recreational or political activities. Therefore, it was of practical necessity to transform the Square. In order to celebrate the tenth anniversary of New China, Tian An Men Square underwent massive transformation. The old red walls were completely demolished and the Square itself was thereby expanded. Two grand structures were built. They were, on the east the Museum of Chinese History and the Museum of Chinese Revolution, and on the west the Great Hall of the People, which stands for the power of the Chinese people. In the middle of the Square, a monument in memory of the heroes of the people was erected. Thus on the same old location, Tian An Men Square showed its new face and new significance. Here the old concept of "the Almighty Sovereign" was totally eradicated, and in its place the new concept of "the Almighty People" was expressed. The basic layout of the Square was set, although there was much to be improved. All those who have visited Tian An Men Square could grasp the concept of a new era embodied in the Square that is situated on the original axis of the city. Hence, the transformation should be considered successful (Figs. 4-2, 4-3).

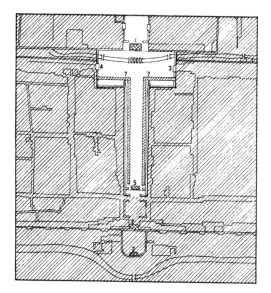

1. Tian An Men 天安门
2. Zheng Yang Gate and Archery Tower
   正阳门及其箭楼
3. Left Chang An Men 长安左门
4. Right Chang An Men 长安右门
5. Da Qing Men of the Qing Dynasty
   大清门
6. The Red Walls 红墙
7. A Thousand Steps Corridor 千步廊

4-2 Imperial square before Tian An Men in the Qing Dynasty 清代天安门前宫廷广场

1919 年伟大的五四运动，从而揭开了新民主主义革命的序幕。这是发生在北京城里的具有重大意义的历史事件。以此为起点，经历了整整三十年的革命斗争，在中国共产党的领导下，终于迎来了新中国的诞生。1949 年 10 月 1 日万民欢庆的开国大典，选择在天安门前举行，这一事实本身就开始赋予天安门以崭新的意义，从此这座由历史上劳动人民在被迫服役下所兴建起来的庄严壮丽的古建筑，以全新的含义出现在中华人民共和国的国徽上，象征着一个古老文明的新生。但是旧日严防庶民百姓涉足广场的红墙依然存在，这就严重阻碍了日益增多的人民群众进入广场开展各项有意义的活动。广场的改造，势在必行。为了迎接建国十周年的纪念日，开始对天安门广场进行了大规模的改造。旧日的红墙被彻底清除，广场的面积因之大为扩展。又在东西两侧分别兴建起中国历史与中国革命博物馆和代表人民权力中心的人民大会堂。广场中央巍然矗立起人民英雄纪念碑，从此天安门广场开始以崭新的面貌出现在人们面前，其他地点依旧而气象一新，它在旧日设计上所力求表达的"帝王至上"的主题思想，已经完全为一个崭新的主题思想所代替，这就是"人民至上"。尽管现在天安门广场尚有若干细节有待改进，但是它的基本格局已定。在旧城原有的中轴线上它所体现出来的新时代的主题思想，是身临广场的任何人都感受到的，因此应该承认它的改造是成功的（图 4-2、4-3）。

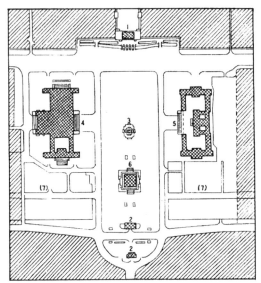

1. Tian An Men 天安门
2. Qian Men (Zheng Yang Men) and Archery Tower 前门（正阳门）及其箭楼
3. Monument of the People's Heroes 人民英雄纪念碑
4. Great Hall of the People 人民大会堂
5. Museum of Chinese History and Museum of Chinese Revolution 中国历史博物馆与中国革命博物馆
6. Chairman Mao's Memorial Hall 毛主席纪念堂
7. Dong and Xi Jiao Min Xiang 东、西交民巷

4-3 The enlarged Tian An Men Square after the founding of New China

新中国成立后扩建的天安门广场

In addition to this, the East and West Chang An Streets were broadened and prolonged and so became a major horizontal axis from west to east across the city. This horizontal axis, to a certain extent, neutralized the dominating effect of the original perpendicular axis from north to south. Meanwhile, it also broadened the field of perception. The Forbidden City, which had always been the focal point of the capital, has now become "the backyard" and support to Tian An Men Square. Its present function as the "Palace Museum" is more appropriately represented. The objective effects mentioned above can clearly be seen on the surface plan of Beijing. Its characteristics as the political centre of China are fully expressed by this transformation of Tian An Men Square (Fig. 4-4).

So much for the discussion of the plan and design of Old Beijing and its future development and transformation. Let us now turn to an exploration of the design and plan of the city of Washington. Comparisons will be made between Beijing and Washington in the discussion.

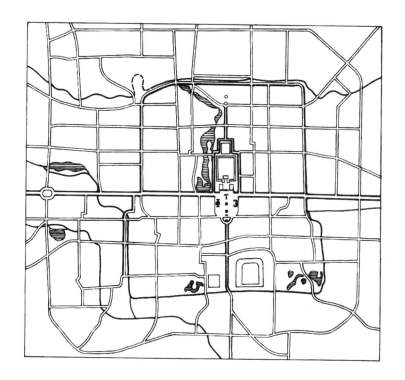

4-4 Boulevards extending eastward and westward from Tian An Men Square respectively—
East and West Chang An Streets 从天安门广场向东西延伸的林荫大道——东、西长安街

不仅如此，随着天安门广场的左右两翼在东西长安街原有的基础上又扩建和延长，从而形成了一条横贯新北京全城的东西轴线，既抵消了那条自北而南的旧轴线在全城布局上独一无二的支配地位，同时也就产生了一种宏观效果，即把旧日全城中心的紫禁城，推移到了类似天安门广场"后院"的位置上，这就更加符合它作为"故宫博物院"的作用。上述的客观效果，从城市的平面布局上来看都是明显可见的。北京城作为全国政治中心的城市特点，已经在改造后的天安门广场上充分显示出来（图4-4）。

关于北京旧城城市设计的主题思想以及它的改造和发展，就先写到这里。以下想就华盛顿城市设计的主题思想，从比较的观点上，再做些探讨。

III. The City of Washington

- ### Choice of the Site and the Original Design of the City

Early in 1791 (the 56th year of the reign of Emperor Qianlong), the site of Washington was decided and the planning began, and it was only eight years after the announcement of Declaration of Independence.[8] From the very beginning the issue of choosing a permanent seat of government had aroused much controversy and the decision was difficult to make, so it was long delayed. Finally, the Congress authorized President George Washington to decide on the site of the capital. The president surveyed and inspected in person the prospective location and finally decided on the present site of the capital. It is situated in the central part of the Atlantic seacoast, in a triangular area between the Potomac River and its eastern tributary called the Anacostia River or the Eastern Branch. The site is a plain with slightly inclining slopes. There is a hill in the middle of the plain. It looked prominent and was called, at that time, Jenkins Hill. Borderlines of private properties crisscrossed the whole area. Most of the land was covered by wild woods, with marshlands dotted on the plain. It was in fact an area not wholly cultivated. On the northern part of the triangular district, the land rose and several rivers and creeks flowed down the slope. The most well known was Goose Creek which flows along the foot of Jenkins Hill and then turns westward to join the Potomac. Two small settlements were respectively established on the tip of the triangle and at the northwestern corner. Only a few residents lived there, though grid-like streets were shown on the map drawn in the primary survey. Georgetown, located at the northwestern corner opposite to Rock Creek, was the largest settlement of the time (Fig. 4-5).

The primary survey of the chosen site had been undertaken by Andrew Ellicott, and Pierre Charles L'Enfant responsible for the design and plan of the capital. L'Enfant was a French-born American engineer and architect, possessing great brilliance and passion. He was thirty-seven years old at that time. L'Enfant's father had been the imperial artist at Versailles, and there he had lived when he was a boy. Later he obtained his education at the Royal Academy of Painting and Sculpture in Paris, where his father taught. In 1777 L'Enfant and other French volunteers crossed the Atlantic Ocean to go to America and offer help to the people of the British colonies in their struggle against the British rulers for their independence. His achievements in military engineering won him high esteem from the Commander-in-Chief George Washington so that he was promoted to the rank of Major in the army. In 1791 he was assigned the duty of designing the plan of the capital. With enormous energy

二、华盛顿城

(一) 城址的选择与城市的初步设计

华盛顿城城址的选择和着手规划是从 1791 年（清乾隆五十六年）初开始的。当时离美利坚合众国的建国（1783）也只有八年。[8] 建国之初，定都问题颇有争议，迟迟难以决定。最后国会授权合众国第一任总统华盛顿选址建城。经过他本人的实地考察，终于选定了现在的城址。地当大西洋海岸中部，位于波托马克河（以下简称波河）与其东岸支流（以下简称阿河）之间的三角地带，地形平坦，微有起伏，中央最突出的一个小山丘，当时叫做詹金斯山，周围地界纵横，都属私产。大部分林莽丛生，间有沼泽，尚未完全开垦。两河间三角地带的北部，地形逐渐隆起，有几条小河，顺地形坡度下注，其中主要的一条原名鹅溪，流经詹金斯山下，西转注入波河。三角地的尖端和西北隅，各有一个小居民点，虽有方格状的街道见于最初测量的地图上，但住户寥寥无几。只有西北角上隔着一条石溪，遥遥相望的乔治镇算是这一地区一个真正的居民点了（图 4-5）。

城址选定之后，经过安德鲁·埃利科特的初步测量，即由皮埃尔·夏尔·朗方负责进行规划设计。朗方是位热情奔放又富有才华的法籍工程师，年方 37 岁。父亲原是法国凡尔赛的宫廷艺术家，朗方儿时就在那里居住过。年长肄业于他父亲任教的巴黎皇家绘画雕刻学院。1777 年朗方和其他的法国志愿人员，远涉重洋来到北美洲，支持英国殖民地人民正在进行的独立战争，在军事工程中，深得当时陆军统帅华盛顿的赏识，并获得少校军衔。1791 年初他接受规划首都的任务，以充沛的精力、

and amazing efficiency he had completed the task by the end of August of the same year and submitted the plan to Washington immediately. It was at the very beginning that L'Enfant had spotted Jenkins Hill and realized that it was the perfect foundation for the main buildings of the Federal Government. He thought of the site as God-sent. These buildings together with the later additions and improvements comprised the strikingly magnificent and dignified architecture of the present Capitol. As to Jenkins Hill, it has long since been renamed "Capitol Hill."

With Capitol Hill as the centre, L'Enfant designed the central axis in the plan of the capital. The axis was 5.5 kilometers long, starting from the eastern shore of the Potomac in the west to the western shore of the Anacostia in the east. Along the western section of the axis, that is, from the west of Capitol Hill to the east shore of the Potomac of that time, a space was to be reserved as a large green lawn for the recess and recreation of the people. This part, undergoing plans and development, was the famous "Mall" today. The presidential office and residence, that is, the present White House, was designed to be located to the north of the western part of the Mall rather than on the axis—it moved slightly westward to its present site, which commands a wonderful view of the wide expanse of the lower Potomac when one looks to the south. Linking the White House and Capitol Hill is a broad thoroughfare running in an oblique line, which is the present Pennsylvania Avenue. The west-east axis stands prominently in the surface plan, and the Mall for whom the space was previously saved, also looks outstanding. Besides, there is often a public square at the meeting point of roads intersecting with each other at right angles or diagonally. The lower section of Goose Creek, running through the centre of the city immediately along the northern side of the Mall before it pours itself into the Potomac, was planned to be canalized to connect with the canal at the foot of the Capitol Hill. It was named the Tiber River, after the Roman Tiber.

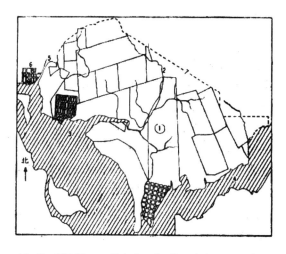

1. Jenkins Hill 詹金斯山
2. Goose Creek 鹅溪
3. Potomac River 波河
4. Anacostia River 阿河
5. Rock Creek 石溪
6. Georgetown 乔治镇
7. Borderline of the highland in the north 北部高地边缘

(This chart is a simplified copy of the original chart made in 1792 from a book kept in National Archives of the United States. 根据美国国家档案馆藏 1792 年旧图书复制品加以简化)

4-5 Site of Washington with the boundary lines of private properties
华盛顿城址初定时私人地产界线

惊人的速度，在同年 8 月底完成了他的规划设计，上报华盛顿总统。他在开始工作之初，就一眼看中了詹金斯山，认为这正是联邦政府中心建筑的天然基座，可以称得上是天造地设了。这座中心建筑经过后日的不断营建，就是现在最引人注目的国会大厦，詹金斯山的名称也早已为"国会山"所代替。

以国会山为中心，朗方拟定了全城设计的中轴线，西起波河东岸，东至阿河西岸，全长约 5.5 公里，沿这条中轴线的西段，也就是从国会山以西至当时波河东岸，保留为一条开阔的绿地，供人民群众游息其间，几经规划发展，这就是现在有名的绿茵广场。至于总统府也就是现在"白宫"的选址，并不在中轴线上，而是在绿茵广场西头的北侧（后来又稍向西移到现在的位置），由此南望，视野开阔，可以遥见波河下游的浩瀚水面。至于国会山与总统府之间，则由一条斜向的大道直接连接起来，这就是现在的宾夕法尼亚大道。自西而东横贯全城的中轴线在全城的平面布局上，显然占有支配地位，预定的绿茵广场，位置尤为突出。至于全城街道系统，纵横交错，或正交，或斜交，交接点上又多布置有大小广场。流经市中心区的鹅溪，其下游注入波河的一段，紧傍预定的绿茵广场的北侧，计划加以渠化，改为直通国会山下的运河，因仿罗马古城中的小河，改名为台伯河。

For the design and plan of the municipality, the two rivers were used as the boundary of the southern part and the borderline of the highland was to be the boundary of the northern part of the capital. And it was on this principle that the city of Washington was built, developed and expanded. We must acknowledge that without the plan and design by L'Enfant, there would not be the magnificent design of the central part of the world famous city of Washington. It is because of this that the central part of Washington proper is referred to by some people as "L'Enfant City" (Fig. 4-6).[9]

Here let me try to make a comparison between the plans of Old Beijing and Washington, which might help the audience understand the further discussion better.

Two essential points are worth our notice:

One, both cities have a central axis line. For Old Beijing, the axis was from north to south, closely following the eastern shore of the natural lakes. The orientation of the axis, though constrained by natural factors, was greatly influenced by cultural elements deeply rooted in the history, as we have discussed above. For Washington, the central axis was from west to east between the two rivers and it was decided solely by natural conditions. There were no historical or cultural factors involved.

Two, in the plan of the Old City of Beijing, the surrounding walls were an integral part of the whole city, while in Washington, rivers and highlands were utilized as the boundaries of the city for there was neither necessity nor tradition of wall building for a city. Actually no cities in the U.S. are equipped with walls.

The above mentioned differences, though superficial, reflect the differences of the cultural traditions between China and the West. It is even more important that such differences are embodied in the key concepts in the capital plan. As the topic pertinent to Beijing has been explored, we would confine the following part to the discussion of Washington's city plan.

1. Congress 国会
2. White House 白宫（总统府）
3. The green area of the Mall on the horizontal axis 全城中轴线上的绿茵带
4. Pennsylvania Avenue 宾夕法尼亚大道
5. Potomac River 波河
6. Anacostia River 阿河
7. Goose Greek (Tiber River) 鹅溪（台伯河）
8. The boundary region of the upland in the north 北部高地边缘

（The above diagram is a copy of the Ellicott's survey map from 1793. 根据 1793 埃利科特测量图绘）

4-6 Washington, as it was chosen to be the capital, with the central axis and main thoroughfares as designed by L'Enfant 华盛顿城址初定时的地形示意图及朗方设计的全城中轴线及主要街道轮廓

　　全城的规划，南半部以两河为界，北半部以高地边缘为界，现在的华盛顿城，就是在这一规划的基础上不断扩展而逐渐兴建起来的。如果当初没有朗方的设计，也就不会有今天以其中心地区宏伟壮观的空间布局而闻名于世的华盛顿城。因此，现在华盛顿城中心部分，还有人称之为"朗方城"（图 4-6 ）。[9]

　　在这里，不妨先将北京旧城与华盛顿城在规划设计的轮廓上做一对比，这或许有助于读者更好地了解以下的讨论。

　　首先值得注意的有两点：

　　第一，两者各有一条中轴线。北京旧城的中轴线自北而南，紧傍一带天然湖泊的东岸。其主导方向如前所述，虽有自然因素的制约，更有深厚的历史文化渊源。华盛顿城的中轴线，自西而东，正好介于两河之间，纯粹是自然条件所决定，不受任何历史文化传统的制约。

　　第二，北京旧城的规划设计，四面城垣是其有机的组成部分。华盛顿城的规划设计，则完全以河流与高地边缘为界限，没有必要修筑城垣，也没有修筑城垣的传统。实际上在美国就没有一个城市是建有城垣的。

　　上述区别，虽然只是表面现象，却也反映了我国和西方文化传统上的一些差异。当然更重要的是这一差异在设计的主题思想上也同样地反映出来。北京城在设计上的主题思想，已如上述，在这里仅就华盛顿城在城市设计上的主题思想，试做一些探讨。

- **On the Concepts of Municipal Design and Planning**

The concept of the design and plan of Beijing Old City originated in the Shang and Zhou dynasties when slavery still prevailed, and was written down in "The Way the Craftsmen Build the City" in *Kaogongji, Zhouli*. As the centralized reign of the feudal dynasties took shape, the concept of building a capital based on the doctrine of "Almighty Sovereignty" had varied in forms of expression. Then came the time when Dadu of the Yuan Dynasty was built, which not only inherited the standards and system of building a city prescribed in the classic of *Kaogongji, Zhouli*, but also utilized the natural distribution of the water sources, thus laying the foundation of Beijing, the capital city of the Ming and Qing dynasties. Hence, we can claim that the design and plan of the Old City of Beijing is an overarching masterpiece in building capital cities during the more than two thousand years of feudalism in China.

The historical background of the building of the city of Washington is totally different from that of Old Beijing. To study the basic concept embodied in the design and planning of Washington, we must first understand characteristics of its historical background.

1. The characteristics of the period and their reflection on the design and plan of the capital

The construction of the city of Washington was one of the victorious achievements gained by the North American people who fought against the colonization of its suzerain state the Great Britain. The nature of this struggle was fully expressed in the Declaration of Independence approved by the Second Continental Congress convened by delegates from the colonies in North America. The Declaration held "all men are created equal, that they are endowed by their Creator with certain unalienable Rights, that among these are Life, Liberty and the pursuit of Happiness." In the original draft there was a chapter concerning the abolition of slavery, but it was deleted for the opposition from the representatives of the State of South Carolina. Karl Marx highly esteemed the Declaration and he claimed that "[i]t is the first declaration of human rights"[10]. It was the time of the rise of capitalism in North America, and the people of all classes reacted enthusiastically to the Declaration, including the most oppressed blacks, who also joined in the struggle against the British oppressors and made significant contributions.

After the War of Independence, the ruling class of the new born country came to realize that their acquired social status and power must be further confirmed and consolidated. Hence they started the Constitution Movement, in an attempt to defend their acquired privilege by means of the establishment of the American Constitution. Two years

（二）城市设计主题思想试探

北京旧城城市设计的主题思想，胚胎于我国奴隶社会的商周时期，到了东周，就以《周礼·考工记》中"匠人营国"的文字描述表达出来。中央集权的封建王朝形成之后，在都城的建设上"帝王至上"的主题思想，曾有过不同形式的表现。及至元朝大都城的兴建，在继承《周礼·考工记》所描述的形制的同时，又结合了地方上河湖水系分布的特点，遂为明清北京城奠定了基础。应该说北京旧城的规划设计乃是我国长达两千多年封建王朝都城建设的最高典型。

华盛顿城市建设的时代背景，和北京旧城完全不同，在探讨其城市设计的主题思想时，应该首先从它建都时期的时代特征讲起。

1. 时代特征及其在城市设计上的初步反映

华盛顿城的建设，是北美洲人民团结起来反抗宗主国英国的殖民统治从而取得了胜利的结果之一，这一斗争由北美殖民地代表召开的大陆会议所通过的《独立宣言》充分表达出来。《独立宣言》宣称：人人生而平等，人民享有生存、自由和谋求幸福的天赋权力不可侵犯等等。在宣言的初稿中，原来还有反对奴隶制的一条，只因南卡罗来纳州的代表反对而被删去。马克思曾高度评价这一宣言，认为这是"第一个人权宣言"[10]。这时北美正处于资本主义上升时期，《独立宣言》在各阶层的人民群众中得到了强烈的反应，包括最受压迫的黑人在内，都卷入了革命斗争的行列，并做出了重要的贡献。

独立战争结束以后，美国统治阶级逐渐感觉到必须进一步巩固本阶级的阶级地位和权力，从而又发起了制宪运动，企图利用宪法作为手段以维

before the founding of the United States of America, in Philadelphia, the old capital or temporary capital before the building of the city of Washington, the Constitutional Convention took place[11] and created the United States Constitution, which formulated the three divisions of power—the Legislature, the Judiciary, and the Executive, as the principle of governmental organization. Later, when L'Enfant set out to plan the construction of the new capital Washington, this principle was also adopted as the guiding line, which was shown in the layout of the three main structures of the Capitol, the White House and the Supreme Court. It is difficult to identify the exact location of the Supreme Court in today's city plan. The present Supreme Court is built to the northeast of the Capitol, not far away from the latter. Nevertheless, such layout still indicates the idea of the division of power.

The most salient and influential feature of L'Enfant's plan is the determination of main axis line centered on the Capitol Hill, and along the axis he reserved the space for the Mall, which laid the basis for the development of the nuclear area of Washington in the future. This section of the axis resembled that part from the Scenic Hill (Jing Shan) to the Zheng Yang Men on the axis of the Old City of Beijing in its significance to the whole plan of the city. Nevertheless, the concepts represented by the two were totally different for the one in the Old City of Beijing emphasized the doctrine of "Almighty Sovereignty" while its counterpart in Washington tried to demonstrate the importance of human rights. Thus the approaches to municipal design and planning were also different. The former chose the strictly enclosed design, while the latter chose to be "completely open to all". Different concepts gave rise to different forms of expression.

2. Further development of the axis line and the objective effects of the main buildings

L'Enfant's blueprint for the design of Washington and his concept of building the city had not been appropriately noticed and appreciated for the entire century that followed. And the person who made such an outstanding contribution to the construction of Washington hadn't received appropriate acknowledgement in his lifetime either. He was very poor and destitute in the last years of his life. It was only with the financial aid and a piece of land offered by one of his friends that his body could be buried. Not until the beginning of this century were his talent and achievement acknowledged and his remains moved to the National

护其既得利益。在美利坚合众国正式建国前两年，在费城（全名费拉德尔菲亚，为华盛顿兴建之前的临时都城，因称故都）召开制宪会议[11]，制定联邦共和国宪法，以立法、司法、行政三权分立作为国家机构的组织原则。其后，朗方着手于进行新建首都华盛顿的规划，显然也是本着国家机构三权分立的原则设计的，这在国会大厦、总统府和最高法院三大主要建筑的布局上，明显地反映出来。只是最初设计的最高法院的位置，在今图上已难确指。现在的最高法院，正好建筑在国会大厦的东北方，相去甚近，仍然显示出三权分立的布局思想。

但是朗方设计最突出——也是影响最为深远的一点，就是他确定了以国会山为中心的主轴线，并把主轴线上计划作为绿茵广场的位置固定下来，从而为日后华盛顿城核心地区的发展奠定了基础。华盛顿城主轴线上的这一段和北京旧城中轴线上从景山到正阳门的一段，在全城布局上的重要性极为相似。但是彼此所反映的在设计上的主题思想，却截然不同。在北京旧城力求突出的是"帝王至上"，在华盛顿城则企图反映的是"人权为主"。因此，两者在空间处理上也就截然不同。前者是严格的封闭型，后者则是完全的开放型。思想内容不同，表达的形式也就因之而异了。

2. 中轴线设计的进一步发展及其主要建筑的客观效果

朗方为华盛顿城的规划所拟定的蓝图以及他所企图表达的主题思想，在相继而来的整整一个世纪中，并没有得到应有的重视，甚至这样一位为华盛顿城的建设做出了如此卓越贡献的人，在生前也没有得到应有的公正待遇。在他临终之前，生活穷困潦倒，死后靠友人的一片土地和资助才得下葬。直到本世纪初，他的贡献才得到承认，

Cemetery of Arlington and buried on top of the hill in 1909. On the headstone was carved the draft plan of the capital as a memorial to his achievement. Looking to the east from the tomb of L'Enfant, one can see the Mall situated on the original axis line as designed by him across the Potomac between the Lincoln Memorial and the United States Capitol. In fact, one can see all the important buildings laid out in the plan. Indeed, there is no better place for L'Enfant to have his permanent rest.

It seems advisable for us to recall some of the incidents that occurred during the one hundred years of the nineteenth century on the Mall to the west of Capitol Hill.

One, L'Enfant's plan to canalize the Tiber River to reach the foot of Capitol Hill had never been taken into serious consideration. As a result, the Tiber became a stinky sewer for litter and rubbish and was filled up and abandoned later. What remained to the date is a small sluice shed not far from the White House, marking the originally designated site of the canal.

Two, the Smithsonian Institution was built in 1847 without reference to L'Enfant's design of the boundary of the Mall, and the Institution went so far as to be situated inside the Mall. A proposal had once been made to tear down the building, but was turned down for the preservation of historical relics and architecture.

Three, the designated location of the White House was moved further westward to its present site.

Four, the present Washington Monument is not built on the originally planned spot due to the weak foundation there. It is now 40 meters south to the original site, and therefore not on the city's central axis line according to the original design. Nor does it fall on the perpendicular line leading southward from the White House, but is 120 meters east of that line. However, one would have such a visual impression that the Monument is still on the horizontal axis line.

Five, the most important change is that the marshy lowland to the south of the western extreme of the axis on the eastern shore of the

Potomac has been reclaimed. Thus the original axis line between the two rivers of the Potomac and the Anacostia was prolonged from 5.5 kilometers to 7.3 kilometers. Meanwhile, the broad riverbed of the Potomac was utilized and a narrow stretch of land reclaimed along the eastern shore from south to north, which is the present Potomac River Park beautifully dotted with lakes (Figs. 4-7, 4-8).

他的遗骸终于在 1909 年被隆重地迁葬于阿灵顿国家公墓的小山顶上，他所设计的城市蓝图的示意图也被镌刻在他的墓碑上，这是很有意义的一件事。从朗方墓东望，可以隔着波河遥望他所初步规划的中轴线亦即现在的绿茵广场，从林肯纪念堂一直延伸到国会大厦，整个布局上的主要建筑，历历在目，实在没有比这里更好的地方，可以使朗方永远安息了。

在这里，追述一下 19 世纪的一百年间，发生在国会山以西现在的绿茵广场上的以下几件事，是必要的。

第一，朗方利用台伯河加以渠化，改建为运河直达国会山下的计划，未受重视，结果河道变成了一条藏污纳垢的臭水沟，遂被填废，现在只有一座河边的小闸房在去白宫不远的地方被保留下来，作为当初运河旧址的一个标志。

第二，1847 年开始兴建国家博物馆，没有充分考虑朗方最初设计的绿茵广场的边界线，竟然侵入了广场界内。后来虽曾议论拆除，结果还是为了保护古建的原因而保留下来。

第三，原定白宫的位置又稍向西移，进行修建，这就是现在白宫所在的地方。

第四，建成了华盛顿纪念塔，只是原定的塔址，基础不够坚实，不得不稍有迁移。新址已不在原设计的全城中轴线上，而是南移了 40 米，同时也已不在白宫向南垂直延伸的轴线上，而是在其以东 120 米，但是从视觉上好像它仍然位于中轴线上。

第五，最重要的一个变化，是在全城中轴线西端的南面和波河的东岸，填筑了一片沼泽低地，从而使波河与阿河之间原定全城中轴线的长度，从约 5.5 公里延伸到 7.3 公里，同时又利用波河这一段宽阔的河床，沿东岸筑起了一个南北狭长的半岛，这就是现在有湖泊点缀其间的波河公园（图 4-7、4-8）。

The last change is most significant in its influence on the development of the capital's central axis line. It was on the reclaimed land on the western extreme of the central axis that the Lincoln Memorial was constructed in 1922. This signified graphically the starting point of the axis line from west to east of the capital. This horizontal axis of Washington from west to east is less than one kilometer shorter than the perpendicular axis of Old Beijing from north to south. In 1976 the Constitution Gardens on the northern side of the long narrow "Reflecting Pool" in front of the Memorial, were constructed in order to celebrate the 200th anniversary of Independence Day.

It should be highlighted that the construction of the Lincoln Memorial has not only further developed the original central axis designed by L'Enfant, but also furnished the underlying theme embodied by the central axis line with a new implication. The Lincoln Memorial is a structure of white marble, simple and dignified. Mounting the many marble steps in front of the Memorial, one comes to see an immense white marble sculpture of President Lincoln sitting and meditating in the middle of the hall. There is no other thing or decoration around except that in the far end of the hall the two famous speeches by Lincoln were carved on the north and the south sides respectively. One contains the

这最后一个变化，对后来全城中轴线上的发展至为重要。1922 年正是在中轴线西端所填筑的河边低地上，兴建了林肯纪念堂，明显地标志了全城自西向东的中轴线的起点。华盛顿这条自西而东的中轴线较之北京旧城自北而南的中轴线短了不到 1 公里。1976 年又在纪念堂前狭长的"映像池"北侧，开辟了"宪法公园"作为建国两百周年的纪念。

这里应该着重说明的是林肯纪念堂的兴建，不只是进一步发展了朗方最初确定的全城中轴线，而且还赋予这条中轴线在设计上所代表的主题思想以新的含义。林肯纪念堂这座白色大理石建筑，造型质朴庄严。从堂前多层白石台阶拾级而上，在殿堂内部广阔的大厅里所能看到的，只有白石雕刻的林肯座像，屹立在中央，环顾厅内，别无一物，仅在大厅尽处南北两壁宽阔的白

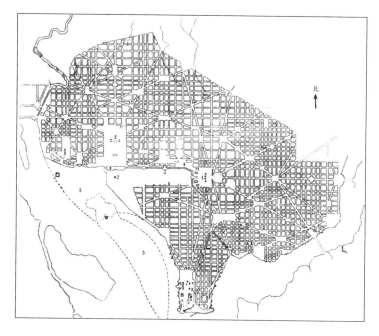

1. Site of the Capitol Building 国会大厦址

2. The original designated location of the Washington Monument 原定华盛顿纪念塔址

3. The original designated location of the White House 原定白宫址　　4. The Canal 运河　　5. Potomac River Park 波河公园

--- The dotted lines show the riverside after reclamation. 虚线表示填筑后的河岸

□ New starting point on the east shore of the Potomac. It is the location of the Lincoln Memorial built later.
中轴线在波河东岸的新起点，即日后修建林肯纪念堂的地方

○ The site for the Jefferson Memorial built later. The site of the White House on the above diagram was later moved to a site further west on the perpendicular line north of the Jefferson Memorial.
日后修建杰斐逊纪念堂的地方，此图上的白宫位置后来也稍向西移，与杰斐逊纪念堂在一条南北垂直线上

4-7　Reclamation of the marshland on the east shore and the shallow water area of the Potomac
波河东岸沼泽及浅水区填筑的陆地

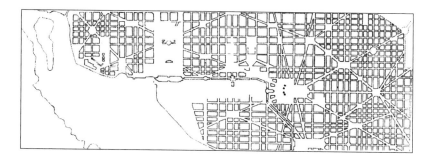

4-8　The original eastern shoreline of the Potomac where the starting spot of the axis line was located
波河东岸中轴线起点的原始河岸线

phrase he used to describe a government which has "a new birth of freedom," that is, "of the people, by the people, and for the people." When one comes to pay his/her respect to the Memorial, stands before the statue and looks back eastward beyond the tall Washington Monument and the great span of green lawn of the Mall to the big white dome of the Capitol, he/she would think of the great contribution President Lincoln made to the United States of America.

In spite of all these, we must also see that since the establishment of the Federal Government, the principles of human rights and the ideal that all men are born free and equal as expressed in the Declaration of Independence not only had not been truly realized, but the internal conflicts had become even more serious. Among them the major one was the rivalry between the North as represented by the employers of laborers, and the South as represented by the owners of slaves. When Lincoln was elected President of America in 1860, he declared his strong opposition to slavery, and issued the preliminary Emancipation Proclamation. By that time the Civil War had broken out, and the issue of the Proclamation made the situation even more tense. Although the North army won the final victory, Lincoln, after being elected President for the second time in November, 1864, was assassinated by a killer sent by Southern slave owners in April, 1865.

Although the struggle led by President Lincoln saved the United States from falling apart, the problem of racial discrimination still existed. In 1866, the year after Lincoln was assassinated, a group of Southern racists established a reactionary organization called the KKK (Ku-Klux-Klan), which brutally attacked and murdered black people. In August, 1963, the well-known anti-racism activist, Rev. Martin Luther King, Jr., delivered his famous speech "I Have a Dream" before over two hundred thousand people in front of the Lincoln Memorial to commemorate the signing of the Emancipation Proclamation. Unfortunately, he got assassinated by racists in April, 1968 when he went to Memphis, Tennessee to support a strike for equal pay for equal work, his "dream" yet realized by a long way.

Symbolically the construction of the Lincoln Memorial at the starting point of the central axis of the capital is a further development of the underlying theme prescribed by L'Enfant in his plan, that is, the idea of human rights. However, this ideal has never been fulfilled. Karl

石墙面上，镌刻了林肯的两个著名的演讲词，其中之一就有他用来描写重新获得自由的一个政府的六字形容词，即"民有、民治、民享"。因此来到这座殿堂的巡礼者，立足在林肯像前，回首东望，越过中央耸立的华盛顿纪念塔和辽阔的绿茵广场，自然就会把一个人的思路，一直引向白色穹顶的国会大厦，这也会促使人们联想到林肯为美利坚合众国的缔造所做出的重大贡献。

然而应该看到，自从美国的联邦政府成立以来，它在《独立宣言》中所标榜的天赋人权、人人自由平等的理想，不仅没有得到真正实现，内部的矛盾反而日益突出。其中最重要的是北方以雇佣劳动为主的资本主义制度和南方以奴役黑人为主的奴隶制，两者之间的冲突，越来越尖锐。林肯于 1860 年被选为总统以后，坚决反对奴役黑人，并颁布了《解放黑奴宣言》，当时已经爆发的南北战争，因此而更加激烈。结果北部军队虽然取得了这次战争的最后胜利，可是林肯却在第二次当选为总统（1864 年 11 月）之后，竟于 1865 年 4 月遭到了南方奴隶主刽子手的暗杀。

林肯领导的斗争虽然挽救了国家免于分裂，但是种族的歧视继续存在。1866 年，也就是林肯被暗杀的第二年，南方的种族主义者还成立了反动的组织"三 K 党"（Ku-Klux-Klan 的简称），对黑人进行残酷的袭击和杀戮。在本世纪内继续为反对种族歧视而奔走的黑人牧师小马丁·路德·金，也曾于 1963 年 8 月在林肯纪念堂前有二十万人参加的群众大会上，为纪念《解放黑奴宣言》的签署而发表了他的著名讲演《我有一个梦想》。可是他的"梦想"还远没有实现，而他本人却于 1968 年 4 月在田纳西州的孟斐斯城指导黑人工人争取同工同酬的示威中，也同样遭到种族主义者的暗杀！

从象征意义上说，林肯纪念堂兴建在华盛顿全城中轴线的起点上，应该看作是朗方最初所赋予它的天赋人权这一主题思想的一个

Marx once commented on the revolution led by Lincoln that it was "an earnest of a new epoch to come" and that "it fell to the lot of Abraham Lincoln to lead his country through the matchless struggle for the rescue of an enchained race and the reconstruction of a social world."[12] It is nevertheless an undeniable fact that the "new epoch to come" remains an age the American people have to strive for (Fig. 4-9).

3. A problem provoking further thinking

In a warm and sunny morning in the spring of 1980, I visited the Lincoln Memorial for the first time. It impressed me so deeply both emotionally and mentally that the memories never faded away. Later, I visited the United States three times and every time I paid my respects to the Lincoln Memorial to recapture the feeling that I had got on my first visit, no matter how pressing my schedule was. In the summer of 1984 when I visited there again, I came across a statue of three soldiers on the lawn unexpectedly in front of the Memorial in the west of the Constitution Gardens. When I approached the statue, I realized that it was a monument that honors U.S. service members who fought and died in the Vietnam War after the Second World War. The design of the memorial is an open lawn in a wide V shape which gradually sinks towards the interior angle beneath the ground. Along the two sides are two walls made of black gabbro, that is, the Vietnam Veterans Memorial Wall, on which are etched the names of the more than fifty thousand Americans dead in the Vietnam War with their rankings. As one walked down along the wall and looked at the names, a mournful sense would well up in the heart, so it was also called "America's Wailing Wall." One wing of the V-shaped memorial pointed to the Washington Monument in the southeast, and the other to the Lincoln Memorial in the southwest. This ingenious design was the work of a Chinese-American architect Maya Lin.[13] The implication of this design is also thought-provoking, for the American people had strongly protested sending troops to Vietnam and deemed the war as unjust. The site

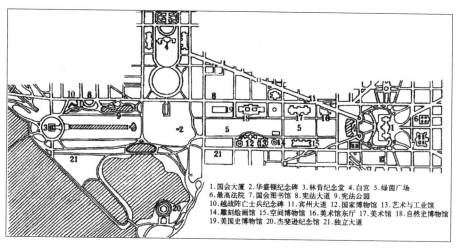

1. The Congress   2. Washington Monument   3. Lincoln Memorial   4. The White House   5. National Mall

6. Supreme Court   7. Library of Congress   8. Constitution Avenue   9. Constitution Gardens

10. The Vietnam Veterans Memorial   11. Pennsylvania Avenue   12. Smithsonian Institution

13. Arts and Industries Building   14. Hirshhorn Museum and Sculpture Garden

15. National Air and Space Museum   16. National Gallery of Art East Building

17. National Gallery of Art   18. National Museum of Natural History

19. National Museum of American History   20. Jefferson Memorial   21. Independence Avenue

4-9　The Mall of Washington on the axis line 华盛顿城中轴线上的绿茵广场

发展，可是这始终还是一个远未实现的理想。马克思也曾预言说："林肯来领导自己国家进行解放被奴役种族和改造社会制度的史无前例的战斗，是即将到来的时代的先声。"[12] 可是这个"即将到来的时代"，至今还有待美国人民自己去努力争取。这也是无可讳言的事实（图 4-9）。

3. 一个引人进一步思考的问题

　　1980 年春天一个风光明媚的清晨，作者初访华盛顿的林肯纪念堂，印象之深刻以及思想上的感受，至今难忘。其后又曾三次访美，每次途经华盛顿，总要挤出时间前往林肯纪念堂巡礼，重温初访的感受。可是 1984 年夏再到华盛顿又访林肯纪念堂时，就在纪念堂前宪法公园的西侧，出乎意料地看到有三个军人一组的雕像出现在草地上，走向前去，才知道这里乃是为第二次世界大战以后美国出兵越南阵亡士兵新建成的纪念碑。纪念碑现场的平面设计，是一个开敞式的"V"字形三角绿地。"V"字形两边以内的绿地，由地面开始向下倾斜，呈坦坡式，逐渐没入地面以下，直到尖端的最深处。沿着两边砌成黑色的石壁也就是纪念碑，碑上成排镌刻着侵越战争中五万多名阵亡士兵的姓名和军衔。沿着石碑走下去，阵亡者的名字历历在目，自然引起人们的悼亡之感，因而有"哭墙"之称。这"V"字形的两壁，一个向东南直指华盛顿纪念塔，一个向西南直指林肯纪念堂。从工程设计上来说，堪称独出心裁，是一位华裔女青年林樱的杰作。[13] 至于其含义，则更加耐人寻味，因为当年美国出兵越南，曾引起国内广大人民群众的反对，被认为是一场非

chosen for the Vietnam Veterans Memorial is on the Mall along the central axis. Looking down the extension of the two walls, one can see the Washington Monument and the Lincoln Memorial in the distance, which would remind one of the vast discrepancy in nature between the ideals embraced by the founding fathers of the United States of America and the unjust Vietnam War. When I, a foreign visitor, stood on the axis of the city of Washington and saw this memorial there, I could not help but think of the difficulties and hardships the common people of America must overcome in order to realize the ideals of their founding fathers.

IV. Other Mountain's Stone May Polish the Jade—Some Examples Which Can Be Referred to in the Construction of Washington

Right from the very beginning of urban construction, the sister cities of Beijing and Washington both tried their best to express their underlying concepts in the design of the central axis line. In spite of the differences in their historical background, they both aim to reflect the spirit of their ages. At the present time, the urban development of the two cities has far exceeded the original design and plan. Although the city walls of Old Beijing have been torn down and the city expanded rapidly to the areas which used to be outside the city, the Old City is still the nucleus of the overall plan for a new Beijing. The case is the same with Washington which has also exceeded the original limits of the two rivers and the northern highland, but the L'Enfant City still serves as the heart of the plan of the whole city. For Beijing, with the reformation of the social system in China, the problems that it was confronted with in its construction are much different from those for Washington. The most urgent task which should be addressed in its planning and construction is how to preserve the best of tradition and at the same time to add new conceptual elements, in order to reflect the initiation of a new era of socialism. In this respect, the issue of the central axis line is most delicate and important.

For example, the transformation of Tian An Men Square is successful in this sense. Furthermore, while considering inheriting the best tradition of China to utilize the old for the benefit of the present, we must also try our best to absorb the best of foreign experience for the benefit of China. We must concede that regarding the issue of urban construction, capitalist countries have a lot of experience worthy of learning, only it is necessary

正义的战争。这一阵亡士兵的纪念地，选址在全城中轴线的绿茵广场上，沿着其两壁向外的指向看去，华盛顿纪念塔和林肯纪念堂即遥遥在望。这又不能不使人联想到美利坚合众国的缔造者所怀抱的理想与信念，和出兵越南的非正义战争，这两者在性质上的差异，相去何啻天渊。作为一个异国的观光者，在华盛顿城市设计的中轴线上看到这一纪念地时，不能不想到：美国的人民群众为了最终实现其国家缔造者的伟大理想，正不知道还有多少崎岖不平的道路正等待着去跋涉呢。

三、他山之石，可以攻玉——华盛顿城市建设可供借鉴的几例

北京和华盛顿这两个姊妹城市，从建城之初就力求通过全城中轴线的设计来显示其主题思想，尽管两者的历史背景各不相同，但在力图反映其时代精神这一点上，却是一致的。现在北京和华盛顿的城市建设都已远远超出了最初设计的范围，北京旧城的城垣已被拆除，新市区在旧城郊外迅速扩建起来。但是北京旧城在新的城市建设总体规划中，仍然居于核心地位。华盛顿城的发展也早已超越了东西两河与北部高地边缘的界限向外迅速扩展，但是"朗方城"仍然是全城布局的中心。不过从北京城的建设来说，随着整个社会制度的改革，它所面临的主要问题就和华盛顿大不一样了。当前在北京城的城市规划和建设中，亟须注意的一件事就是如何在继承其优良传统的同时，又能赋予它以新的思想内容，从而反映出一个社会主义新时代的来临。这个问题在全城中轴线的处理上表现得最为敏感，也最为突出。例如天安门广场的改造，在这个意义上来说是成功的；其次，也要考虑到在继承自己优良传统以达到古为今用的目的的同时，还必须积极吸收外国的先进经验，以达到"洋为中用"的目的。应该

for us to know how to differentiate the truly advanced experience from the bad and to keep away from copying blindly. To learn indiscriminately would bring nothing but harms. Take the plan of Washington for example. Layout of all the buildings along the central axis line and their functions are properly regulated, on which lessons could be drawn. The Capitol stands on the central point of the axis and all other buildings in the city are not allowed to be built higher than it, which contributes to a special skyline of the city. The space stretching from the Capitol westward to the Mall in front of the Washington Monument is wide and level, commanding a broad view. To the south and north of the Mall, museums and galleries are arranged in order. On the southern side, there are the National Air and Space Museum, the Hirshhorn Museum and Sculpture Garden, the Smithsonian Institution (which contains an exhibition on the history of the capital planning) and others. On the northern side are the National Gallery of Art, the National Museum of Natural History, the National Museum of American History and further north is the National Archives. To the southeast of the Capitol is the world famous Library of Congress with its recently built annex building, standing side by side with the Supreme Court on a north-south line. The heart of the capital here is a concentration of the characteristics of Washington as the national centre of political and cultural activities. The design of the capital in its entirety is of dignity and diversity. All the museums and galleries on either side of the axis, though of the relatively same height, differ from one another in their architectural designs, varying from the classic redbrick-castle style of the Smithsonian Institution to the ultra-modern design of the National Air and Space Museum—they all express the characteristics of their age. And among them the most renowned is the East Wing extension to the National Gallery of Art built recently. This site used to be a piece of triangular land at the northeastern corner of the Mall not far from the Capitol Hill, making it not only the most important but also subtle to deal with in architectural design. Here the world famous Chinese-American architect Ieoh Ming Pei showed his talent and designed a unique building which adds charm to the Mall.

The above discussion reminds me of the construction of the Great Hall of the People and the Museum of Chinese History and the Museum of Chinese Revolution during the transformation of Tian An Men Square on the occasion of the tenth anniversary of New China, as mentioned earlier, which highlighted the identity of Beijing as the national cultural

承认在资本主义国家的城市建设上，确有不少先进的经验，值得我们学习。问题在于区别哪些是真正的先进经验，切忌盲目抄袭，否则有害无益。以华盛顿的城市建设为例，在它的全城中轴线上对所有建筑物的布局及其功能要求，就有可供借鉴的地方。它的国会大厦屹立于中轴线的正中央，城中所有的楼房建筑的高度都不得超过它，它就给整个城市的天际线带来一大特色。从国会大厦向西直到华盛顿纪念塔前的绿茵广场，地势平展，视野辽阔。广场的南北两侧，有博物馆、展览馆等，依次排列，在南侧的有航天空间博物馆、雕刻绘画馆、国家博物馆（内有首都城市规划设计史展览厅）等。在北侧的有美术陈列馆、自然史博物馆、美国历史博物馆等。北侧中间退后一方场地，还有一座国家档案馆。在国会大厦的东南侧与高等法院大楼南北并列的，则是举世闻名的国会图书馆及其最近扩建的新馆。在这个全城的心脏部位上，集中表现出华盛顿作为全国政治中心和文化中心的特点，整个布局严正而富有变化，两侧的各大博物馆、展览馆，虽然高度大体一致，而建筑形式各不相同，从国家博物馆红砖碉堡式的古典建筑，到航天空间博物馆的现代设计，各有其时代特征，其中最负盛名的是建成不久的美术陈列馆的东厅。这里原是绿茵广场东北角上的一块三角地带而又近在国会山下，地点至为重要，在建筑设计上也最难处理。正是在这里，著名华裔建筑学家贝聿铭显示了他卓越的才能，设计了这座独具一格的建筑物，为广场增辉。

写到这里，又不禁想到上文已经讲过，建国十周年时扩建天安门广场，同时兴建了人民大会堂和中国历史博物馆与中国革命博物馆，使得天安门广场在体现全国政治中心的同时，也兼有文化中心的象征。但是在设计的当时，北京作为全国的政治中心之外也是全

center besides its position of the national political center. However, at that time the dual role of this capital had not been fully recognized or elaborated. Considering the great significance of construction of the spiritual civilization and the requirements of building Beijing as the national cultural center, the overall design and planning of the city should be drawn on the basis of the historical characteristics of the layout of Beijing. The design of the central part along the axis line of Washington discussed above can serve as one of the examples for us.

Translated by Cheung Hon Cha
July 11th, 1988

国的文化中心这一特点，还没有得到充分的认识和说明，现在考虑到今后精神文明建设的重大意义和建设北京作为全国文化中心的要求，在全城的规划设计上，应该进一步结合城市平面布局的历史特点来加以考虑。上述华盛顿城中轴线上核心地区的建设，只是仅供参考的一例而已。

❺ OVERSEA COMMUNICATIONS BETWEEN CHINA AND EAST AFRICA BEFORE THE SO-CALLED DISCOVERY OF THE NEW SEA-ROUTE*

At the end of the fifteenth and the beginning of the sixteenth century, a series of long-distance sea voyages started out from Western Europe. The earliest and most widely publicized among them were (1) the trans-Atlantic voyage which in 1492 brought Christopher Columbus to districts now known as Cuba and Haiti; and (2) the voyage undertaken by Vasco da Gama, in the course of which he rounded the Cape of Good Hope, crossed the Indian Ocean and eventually reached the modern Kozhikode (formerly known as Calicut, mentioned in ancient Chinese records as *Kuli*) in South India in 1498. With this tremendous expansion of geographical vista, the Europeans landed in a continent where they had never set foot before and found a passageway hitherto unknown to the East. These events they commemorate under the imposing titles of discovery of the new continent and discovery of the new sea-route respectively. With these began the era of "great geographical discoveries", which looms large in the history of European geographical discovery and standard textbooks on European history.

The subsequent expansion of European colonialism has disseminated these ideas to practically every corner of the world. In reality, however, the achievements of Columbus and da Gama may be considered in a certain sense "discoveries" only if one postulates a limited view point— that of the Europeans. Any attempt to enlarge the viewpoint to take in other areas or to endow it with a world-wide significance would be seriously mistaken.

This essay purports to deal exclusively with what the Europeans call the discovery of the new sea-route.

To begin with, a brief retrospect of the historical facts is perhaps called for. The search for the new sea-route is commonly thought of as entering its last crucial phase with the effort of Bartholomew Diaz, who by continuing to cruise southward along the western coast of Africa in 1487 (many parts of which had repeatedly been touched by former navigators), finally reached the southernmost point of the African continent, later known as the Cape of Good Hope. It was not until ten years later that da Gama pushed the voyage yet further by sailing northward along the eastern coast of Africa, reaching in April, 1498 Malindi in Kenya (mentioned in Chinese records as *Malin* or *Malinti*).

伍 在所谓新航路的发现以前中国与东非之间的海上交通*

在 15 世纪末叶和 16 世纪初期，从西欧开始了一系列的远洋航行，为众所周知的最初两件大事，就是：一、1492 年哥伦布横渡大西洋，到达了现在古巴和海地等处；二、1498 年达·伽马在绕过好望角之后，越过印度洋，到达了现在印度南部的卡利卡特（中国古籍作古里）。欧洲人的地理视野从此大为扩大，他们登上了还从来没有登上过的大西洋彼岸的土地，找到了从来还不知道的到东方来的航路。前者他们称为新大陆的发现，后者他们称为新航路的发现。这就是欧洲地理发现史以及一般欧洲历史上所大书而特书的"地理大发现"的开始。

随着欧洲殖民势力的扩张，这种观点几乎被传布到世界各地。其实，无论是哥伦布的成就或是达·伽马的成就，只有从欧洲中心论的观点来看时，才能在某种意义上被认做是一种"发现"。如果把这一观点应用于其他地方，或扩大到世界的范围，那显然是错误的。

本文专就所谓新航路的发现这一问题加以讨论。

这里首先需要回顾一下所谓新航路的发现的简单经过。新航路的探寻被认为是从迪亚士才开始进入了最后的关键性的阶段，他在 1487 年沿着前人已经屡次到达的非洲西部的大部分海岸继续南航，终于来到了非洲大陆的南端（后称好望角）。十年之后，达·伽马又继续迪亚士的航程前进，沿非洲东海岸北上，于 1498 年 4 月到达现在肯尼亚的马林迪（中国古籍作麻林、麻林地）。

Then, starting out from Malindi, da Gama began the last and most important section of his voyage by crossing the Indian Ocean, ending up in Kozhikode in May of the same year.[1]

In this manner was "discovered" the much-vaunted new sea-route to the East. To the Asian and African peoples, however, the route was by no means new, so that any claim to have "discovered" it is out of the question. It can be confidently established that every section of the route had been traversed by Asian and African navigators and explicitly recorded in historical texts.

Let us first take up the route along the African coast. We know from the distinguished Greek historian Herodotus (484-425 B.C.) that the first cruise around the African continent dates back to about 600 B.C. In trying to show that the African continent (then called Libya), except being joined to Asia by a narrow isthmus, was completely surrounded by the ocean, he cited as evidence the following facts. In 600 B.C. or thereabouts, a fleet manned by Phoenicians, who were experienced sailors, left the Red Sea under the orders of the Egyptian Pharaoh Necos, and made its way southward into the open ocean. It took them two years to return safely to Egypt, having finished the voyage in accordance with Necos' plan which necessitated their entering the Mediterranean Sea via the Strait of Gibraltar.[2] That was an astonishing feat in the history of navigation.[3] We may suppose that in rounding the southernmost point of the African continent and sailing up northward, da Gama was not aware that he was following a route which had already been discovered by Phoenician sailors more than two thousand years ago, the only difference being that he was sailing in a direction opposite to that of his predecessors.

Indeed, besides that remarkable voyage made by the Phoenicians, history knows of other instances that men had sailed southward along the eastern coast of Africa, rounded the cape and entered the Atlantic Ocean. In the 1420s, or about seventy years before da Gamma's eastern voyage, an Arabian navigator had taken exactly that route.[4] The Arabs had then established extensive oversea trade along the eastern coast of Africa, which penetrated as far southward as Mozambique, and it was from none other than those Arabian traders that da Gama obtained the necessary information which enabled him to continue his voyage in a northward direction.[5]

从马林迪出发，达·伽马开始了在他全部航程中最后的也是最重要的一段，那就是横越印度洋的一段，并在 1498 年 5 月到达了他全程的终点——卡利卡特。[1]

欧洲一些人所盛加称道的到东方来的新航路就是这样被"发现"的。但是从亚洲和非洲人民看来，这既不能被认为是新航路，自然也就很难说是"发现"了。因为这一航路的每一段，都已经为亚非航海家所航行过，而且已经明确载入史册。

首先，我们来看非洲沿岸的航路。古代希腊大史学家希罗多德（公元前 484—前 425）告诉我们早在公元前 7 至前 6 世纪之间，就已经有环航非洲大陆的壮举了。当他在说明非洲大陆（当时称 Libya）除去和亚洲相连的一处外，其余各方面都为大海所环绕时，曾举出了如下的事实：公元前 600 年左右，埃及法老尼可派遣了一个由有名的航海者腓尼基人所驾驶的船队，从红海出航，向南驶入大洋。过了两年，他们终于按照尼可的命令，经由直布罗陀海峡进入地中海，安然返航到埃及，[2] 这是古代航海史上令人惊异的事件。[3] 当达·伽马绕过非洲大陆南端转而向北沿岸航行的时候，他大约还不知道这已经是腓尼基航海家在两千多年前所发现过的航路了，所不同的只是他在逆着他的先行者的航行方向而前进罢了。

其实，沿着非洲东岸南航，并且绕过大陆南端而驶入大西洋的，在历史上还不仅仅是腓尼基人那一次。例如 15 世纪的 20 年代，也就是达·伽马东来以前的七十多年，一个阿拉伯的航海家也已经那样航行过了。[4] 那时阿拉伯人已经沿非洲东岸自北而南，远到莫桑比克沿岸一带（至南回归线以南之伊尼扬巴内），建立了海上贸易，而达·伽马则正是从这些阿拉伯商人那里获得了有关向北继续航行的情报的。[5]

Another point to be stressed is that while the voyage from the eastern coast of Africa across the Indian Ocean to South India is justly regarded by the Europeans as the last and most important section of their so-called new route, since their final objective of reaching the East virtually hinged upon its successful completion, that very route had not only been opened up by the Asian and African peoples long before but had remained in constant use for a considerable period of time. Special mention should be made of Ibn Madjid, a great Arabian navigator, who came from a family of sailors and whose knowledge and experience about the sea was unrivaled in his day.[6] It was with his expert guidance that da Gama finally accomplished the last and most important section of his voyage.

Here it is necessary to recall the magnificent contribution made by the Asian and African peoples toward opening up the trade route across the Indian Ocean.

Trading relations connecting the South China Sea with the Indian Ocean had long existed prior to the end of the fifteenth century. The scale and financial prosperity of these ventures were such that hardly any other areas in the world could offer a contemporary parallel. On this topic, which forms an extremely important chapter in the history of ancient navigation and transportation, many dissertations and books have been written by Chinese and foreign scholars. The scope of this essay permits us merely to cite a few examples from Chinese documents by way of illustration.

The earliest mention in Chinese records of voyages over the South China Sea and the Indian Ocean goes back to the first and second centuries B.C.[7] Since then a long line of messengers, monks and merchants had used the same sea route, voyages back and forth between China and Ceylon[8] or India being especially frequent. A well-known example is that of the Chinese monk Fa Hsien, who in 409 sailed from *Tomoliti* (whose ancient site was located on the western bank of the Hooghly River, near the

Ganges Delta in modern India) to *Shihtzukuo* (now Ceylon); and in 412 boarded a large merchant vessel which brought him from *Shihtzukuo* back to China.[9] His contribution to the cultural exchange between China on the one hand and India and Ceylon on the other has become almost proverbial down to the present day.

The earlier seventh century saw the founding of the T'ang Dynasty (A.D. 618-906) in China and the rise of the Arab Empire (A.D. 632-1258) in Southwest Asia.[10] Contacts between the two were numerous,

其次是从非洲东岸横越印度洋到达印度南部的航路，这在欧洲一些人所谓新航路中应当是最后一段，也是最为重要的一段，因为只有完成这一段航路之后，他们到东方来的最后目的才算实现。然而正是这一段航路，不但久已为亚非人民所开辟，而且已经连续航行了一个很长的时期了。特别值得注意的是，达·伽马在完成这最后一段，也是最重要的一段航路时，正是借助于一位阿拉伯航海家的导航才顺利成功的，这就是出身于世传的海员家庭而又饱有航海经验和学识的伊本·马吉德。[6]

在这里，回顾一下亚非人民在开辟印度洋的航路上所作出来的卓越贡献，是必要的。

15 世纪末叶以前，从中国南海一直到印度洋上的来往贸易已经有了长时期的发展，其巨大规模和繁荣程度，在当时说来，也是世界任何地区所难以比拟的。这是古代世界航运史上非常重要的一部分，关于这一部分，中外学者已经写了不少的论文和专著。在这篇短文里，只拟根据中国的文献，举出几个例子，作为说明。

早在公元前 2 至前 1 世纪间，中国南海以及印度洋上的通航来往，已经见于中国记载。[7]此后，中国南海与印度洋——特别是从中国到锡兰[8]与印度之间，使者、僧侣和商人泛海来往，络绎不绝。例如著名的中国僧人法显在公元 409 年从多摩梨帝（故址在今印度恒河三角洲呼格利河西岸）航行到狮子国（今锡兰），又于公元 412 年从狮子国乘商人大船经海道返回中国。他在中国与印度以及锡兰之间的文化交流上所作出的贡献，至今传为美谈。[9]

到了 7 世纪前半叶，在中国有唐朝（618—906）的建立，在亚洲西南部有阿拉伯人大食帝国（632—1258）的兴起[10]，两者之间接触

and a new stage began in East-West trade over the South China Sea and the Indian Ocean. The volume of trade in the two-way traffic over the Indian Ocean continued to swell after the eighth century. In China, throughout the long period of the T'ang, Sung (Northern Sung 960-1127, Southern Sung 1127-1279 A.D.), and Yüan (1279-1368 A.D.) dynasties, there were chartered ports along the southeastern seacoast which made oversea trade their special business, and government officials were specially appointed to take charge of trading affairs. Among these ports, Canton had at first the largest amount of foreign trade.[11] Beginning from the middle of the thirteenth century, however, it was eclipsed by Chüan-chow (Zayton). In the latter, we possess lively sketches by a couple of contemporary witnesses, who arrived in China toward the end of the thirteenth century and in the middle of the fourteenth century respectively, namely the renowned Venetian traveller Marco Polo and Ibn Battuta of Tangier, Africa. This is what Marco Polo wrote:

> At this city you must know is the Haven of Zayton, frequented by all the ships of India, which bring thither spicery and all other kinds of costly wares... I assure you that for one shipload of pepper that goes to Alexandria and elsewhere, destined for Christendom, there come a hundred such, aye and more too, to this Haven of Zayton; for it is one of the two greatest havens in the world for commerce.[12]

Ibn Battuta was even more emphatic:

> I must tell you that the first Chinese city that I reached after crossing the sea was Zayton (now is called Chüan-chou-fu).... The harbour of Zayton is one of the greatest in the world; I am wrong: it is the greatest! I have seen there about one hundred of first-class junks together; as for small ones, they were past counting.[13]

Ships that voyaged over the South China Sea and the Indian Ocean during the T'ang and Sung dynasties included, besides Chinese ships, those of the following nationalities, all mentioned in Chinese records:

Persian ships, *Shihtzukuo* ships, ships from the Western Regions, or simply, "foreign" ships. These seagoing vessels had from a very early time made use of the monsoon in their voyages, which accounted for the fact that most vessels sailing from China started out between autumn and winter when the dry monsoon blew from the northeast whereas most ships coming to China chose the summer season when the wet monsoon blew from the southwest.

频繁，从而开始了中国南海与印度洋上东西通航的新阶段。8 世纪初叶以后，印度洋上东西往来的贸易，日趋繁盛。在中国，自唐历宋（960—1279，1127 年以前为北宋，以后为南宋）至元（1279—1368）在东南沿海一带，都有指定的港埠经营海外贸易，并设专官管理通商事宜。在这些港埠中，先以广州的外国贸易最为繁盛。[11] 到了 13 世纪中叶以后，泉州又凌驾广州之上。在 13 世纪后期和 14 世纪中叶先后来中国的大旅行家威尼斯人马可·波罗和非洲丹吉尔人伊本·拔都他，都曾亲到泉州，并作了简明生动的描述。马可·波罗记道：

> 你必须知道，印度所有商船前来泉州港十分频繁，运来的香料和其他贵重物品……我可以肯定地告诉你，如果有满载胡椒的一艘船只驶入亚历山大里亚或其他商港以供应耶稣教诸国，那么就会有一百艘或更多的满载胡椒的船只驶入泉州港，因为泉州乃是世界两个最大贸易港口中的一个。[12]

伊本·拔都他所写更为具体：

> 我必须告诉你，在我渡过海洋之后所到达的第一个中国城市刺桐（现在叫做泉州府）……泉州的港口乃是世界最大港口之一；我错了，它乃是所有港口中最大的。我看到港口里约有大海船百艘，至于小船那真是不可胜数了。[13]

唐、宋时期来往中国南海和印度洋上的船舶，除中国船外，其以国别或地域名称见于中国记载者有波斯舶、狮子国舶、西域舶或简单称为外国舶等，这些海舶从很早起利用了季风航行，因此从中国出航的海舶，多在秋冬东北季风风发之时，而前来中国的海舶，则多在夏季西南季风盛行之时。

In periods when China's foreign trade was exceedingly active, for instance, in the Sung Dynasty, the number of foreign traders in China was so large that special residential quarters were set apart for them in all chartered ports. Some of these traders elected to stay in China, or even assumed important posts in the Chinese government. A case in point is P'u Shou-keng, responsible official for trading affairs in Chüan-chow at the end of the Sung Dynasty, whom research showed to be the descendant of an immigrant Arab who settled in China.[14]

In the first three decades of the fifteenth century, the government of the Ming Dynasty (1368-1644) in China expended great efforts in developing oversea communications between China and the Indian Ocean. These efforts were crowned by the seven long-distance voyages led by Cheng Ho. As Cheng Ho's expeditions were by all odds the most impressive achievement in the history of navigation prior to the Europeans' sailing for the Orient, which did not begin till the end of the fifteenth century, a short description of those remarkable events may not be out of place here.

The seven voyages of Cheng Ho spanned a period of 29 years (1405-1433).[15] His fleet was composed of more than sixty galleys and a large number of smaller auxiliary vessels, making a total of well over two hundred. On his seventh voyage (1431), he was accompanied by various kinds of nautical technicians, soldiers, interpreters, scribes and medical and service personnel to the number of 27,550.[16] When we recall that sixty-one years later (1492) Columbus had only three ships and eighty-seven sailors with him in making his first trans-Atlantic voyage, and that sixty-six years later (1497) da Gama brought only four ships and one hundred and forty-eight (or, according to some authorities, one hundred and seventy) men to the Orient, we may arrive at a truer estimate of the size of Cheng Ho's expeditions.

The farthest points reached by Cheng Ho's fleet in the seven voyages, which headed in somewhat different directions, are: Hormuz (mentioned in Chinese records as *Hulumussu*) on what is now the Iranian Bay,

Jeddah (mentioned in Chinese records as *Chihta*) on the eastern coast of the Red Sea, and Mombasa (mentioned in Chinese records as *Manpasa*) on the eastern coast of Africa. The last of these voyages has bequeathed some very valuable legacies to us of the present day, including a tolerably complete sailing record and a copy of the original sailing chart.[17]

Cheng Ho's routes over the Indian Ocean require some attention. Variations were slight among those for east of Ceylon and South India, which may be passed over, but as we follow him further westward, we notice certain interesting features.

中外贸易最繁盛时如在宋代，前来中国的外商，人数众多，中国各通商港埠，都为外商划有一定的居住区。有的外商常住不归，甚至在中国担任了重要的官职。例如宋末元初在泉州负责管理通商事宜的长官蒲寿庚，就是在中国定居的阿拉伯人的后裔。[14]

到了 15 世纪最初的三十年间，中国的明朝（1368—1644）政府用了很大力量来发展中国与印度洋上的海上交通，其代表事件就是由郑和所领导的七次远航。由于这是 15 世纪末叶欧洲人东来以前最大规模的航海史上的壮举，因此有稍加介绍的必要。

郑和的七次远航，始于 1405 年，止于 1433 年，前后共历二十九年。[15]他所领导的船队有大海船 60 多艘，连中小船只计算在内，多至 200 余艘。第七次出航时（1431），随行各种航海技术人员、士兵以及翻译、书记、医生和服务人员，共计 27550 人。[16]如果我们想到六十一年后（1492）哥伦布第一次横渡大西洋时只有船 3 只、船员 87 人，或者想到六十六年后（1497）达·伽马前来东方时也只有船 4 只、船员 148 人（或作 170人），我们就可以体会到郑和的远航是在一种什么样的规模上进行的了。

在七次远航中，郑和的船队在不同方向上所到达的最远之地，是现在的波斯湾上的霍尔木兹（中国古籍作忽鲁谟斯），红海东岸的吉达（中国古籍作秩达），还有非洲东岸的蒙巴萨（中国古籍作慢八撒）。在这七次航行中，最后一次不仅保留了一个比较完整的航海记录到今天，而且还有一幅航海图经过翻刻之后也被保留下来，这是极可珍贵的。[17]

现在有必要把郑和在印度洋上的航路，再作些进一步的分析。这些航路自斯里兰卡和南印度以东的变化不大，可以从略，以西的却是值得特别注意的。

It should first be pointed out that the two sea routes leading from the western coast of South India to the Iranian Bay and to the Red Sea had both a long history behind them. However, in early times, oversea communications between those regions were presumably achieved by sailing along the coast. It was only when later navigators learned to make use of the monsoon, which was a familiar phenomenon in that area, that a direct route over the Arabian Sea was opened up.

Who was the first to notice and turn to account the monsoon that blew over the Arabian Sea and thus opened up the above-mentioned route? Some authorities ascribe the discovery of the monsoon to Hippalus, an Alexandrian in the employ of the Roman Empire c. A.D. 40- 50. Hence, as one historian puts it, "Hippalus deserves as much honour in Roman annals as does Columbus in modern history." Others contend that before Hippalus the Arabs had already made use of monsoon in sailing over the Arabian Sea. Still others would credit Nearchos, one of the generals who accompanied the Macedonian king Alexander in his Asian expedition in the fourth century B.C. with the so-called "discovery."[18] Be that as it may, the fact remains that navigators over the Arabian Sea had, from a very early time, learned to make use of the monsoon to strike out an oversea route, thus enabling themselves to abandon the tortuous coastal sailing. When Cheng Ho's fleet arrived in the Iranian Bay or entered the Red Sea, these routes were already scenes of busy trafficking.

There is another problem that deserves a far more thorough probing. Among the routes shown in Cheng Ho's chart (Fig. 6-1) is one that leads from the present Belligamme in the south of Ceylon or from Kozhikode on the western coast of South India to Brava or to Mogadishu on the eastern coast of Africa. When was this direct route first opened up? We know that oversea communications between the equatorial regions on the eastern coast of Africa and India or China also go a long way back. Indeed, descriptions of the sea coast in what is now Somalia and

Kenya may be found in Chinese records as early as the eighth and ninth centuries.[19] In 1071 (or the fourth year of Hsining in the Sung Dynasty), ambassadors from *Tsengtan*, a country on the eastern coast of Africa, after 160 days of sailing along the coast, landed in the city of Canton in China. A second embassy came in 1083. The Sung rulers obviously thought very highly of this diplomatic relationship and loaded the ambassadors with rich gifts.[20] Now *Tsengtan* is actually a scribal error

　　首先应该指出，从印度南部的西海岸，无论是通向波斯湾，还是通向红海口的航路，也都是具有悠久历史的两条航路，不过最早期的印度南部海岸与波斯湾及红海之间的海上来往，应该都是沿着海岸进行的。后来航海家由于认识和利用了这一地区盛行的季风，才终于开辟了上述穿越阿拉伯海的直达航路。

　　究竟是谁最先认识和利用了阿拉伯海上的季风，从而开辟了穿越海上的直达航路的呢？有人说最初发现阿拉伯海上的季风的是约在公元40—50年之间为罗马帝国服役的一个亚历山大里亚人，名字叫做希帕卢，因此认为"希帕卢在罗马编年史上应该享有像哥伦布在近代史上所享有的那么多的荣誉"。随后又有人指出，在希帕卢以前，阿拉伯人早已在阿拉伯海的航行中利用季风了。更有人把这一"发现"归功于公元前4世纪随马其顿的亚历山大远征归来的一位将军尼耳楚。[18]总之，无论其最初发现者为谁，阿拉伯海上的航海家利用季风离开沿岸曲折的航程而开辟了穿越海上的航路一事，是为时很早的。到了郑和的船队远航到波斯湾口和进入红海的时候，这些海上航路的来往贸易，已经是非常发达的了。

　　这里需要提出的是，另外一个远为值得注意的问题，即在表示郑和航路的地图上（图6-1），从锡兰南端的别罗里（今贝里格姆）或从南印度西岸之古里到非洲东岸卜剌哇（今布拉瓦）或木骨都束（今摩加迪沙）之间的直达航路，究竟是什么时候开辟起来的？我们知道，非洲东岸赤道附近地区和印度以及中国之间的海上交通，也是开始得很早的。例如公元8—9世纪时，中国已经有了关于现在索马里和肯尼亚沿岸的记载。[19]到1071年（宋熙宁四年）非洲东岸的层檀国还曾派使臣沿海岸航行，经过160天才来到中国的广州登陆，1083年（元丰六年）再使中国。宋王朝很重视这一外交关系，曾向使臣赠送了优厚的礼品。[20]按"层檀"是"层拔"二字传写之误，

for *Tsengpa*, which represents a clipped pronunciation of Zanzibar.[21] The two are, however, not strictly identical, as *Tsengtan* in those days embraced the eastern coast of Africa together with the islands off the coast. From the twelfth century on reference to various countries on the eastern coast of Africa occurred with greater frequency in Chinese geographical works.[22] Particularly worthy of notice are the results of recent archaeological excavations on the eastern coast of Africa. These include T'ang and Sung copper coins as well as large quantities of chinawares (fragmentary or otherwise) dating back to the Sung Dynasty, the Yüan Dynasty or a later date. All this is incontrovertible proof that trade relations had long existed between China and the eastern coast of Africa.[23] But the contact (direct or indirect) was exclusively dependent on the route over the Arabian Sea, and remained so up to the middle of the thirteenth century.

It should be recognized that there was a profound difference between the direct route that led from Ceylon or South India across the Indian Ocean to the eastern coast of Africa and the other route over the Arabian Sea. One needed only the monsoon to sail safely along the latter route. In case of the former, however, even with the help of the monsoon, successful voyaging would be extremely difficult, if not impossible, unless one enlisted the additional aid of the compass. Chinese navigators began using the compass in making their voyages in the eleventh or twelfth century.[24] The compass is one of the most significant contributions made by the Chinese labouring people to world civilization. For, with the invention of that instrument, man finally gave up his old way of sailing closely to, or a short distance from, a winding and tortuous seacoast, and launched out boldly for the open ocean. Thus the seemingly unlimited kingdom of billowing waves became another sphere where man could display his power and adventurist spirit.

It has been conjectured that the knowledge and use of the mariner's compass passed from China to Europe via the Arabs.[25] At any rate, European seagoing ships only began using the compass at the end of the twelfth or beginning of the thirteenth century. It is conceivable that the direct route across the Indian Ocean joining Ceylon or South India with the eastern coast of Africa could have been discovered before the beginning of the fifteenth century when Cheng Ho made his voyage. But as far as Chinese maps and documents are concerned, the first unmistakable reference to the route occurred at the time of Cheng Ho's expeditions. The appended sailing chart of Cheng Ho shows clearly that there were two direct routes leading from Ceylon and South India, respectively, to the eastern coast of Africa.

即今桑给巴尔之对音[21]，不过当时叫做层檀的地方，主要指今非洲东部沿岸大陆和沿海岛屿，而不是专指今天的桑给巴尔。12 世纪以后，中国地理书上有了更多的关于非洲东部国家的记载。[22] 尤其值得注意的是，近世纪来，非洲东岸一带还曾掘得中国唐代宋代的铜钱以及宋代元代及其以后的大量瓷器、瓷片，更足以作为中国和非洲东岸很早就有通商贸易的证明。[23] 不过上述中国与东非之间的来往，还都是沿阿拉伯海的航路直接或间接进行的，晚至 13 世纪前半期，仍然如此。

应该认识到从锡兰或南印度到非洲东岸之间的横越印度洋的直达航路，较之穿行阿拉伯海的航路，是有很大差别的。因为后者凭借季风便可安全航行，而前者虽然仍有季风可以利用，但是如果没有航海罗盘的帮助就非常困难，甚至是不可能的了。中国航海家早在 11—12 世纪之间，就已经利用罗盘于海上航行了。[24] 这是中国劳动人民对于世界文明所作出的重要贡献之一。人们一旦掌握了这一工具，就终于离开自古以来沿着海岸或离开海岸不远而行驶的迂回曲折的航路，顺利地驶入了大洋，从而有可能使波涛汹涌、茫无涯际的大洋，开始成为被探险和被征服的人类活动的新领域。有人推测中国关于航海罗盘的使用，首先传给阿拉伯人，然后又经过阿拉伯人传往欧洲。[25] 至于欧洲人开始使用罗盘则已是 12 世纪末到 13 世纪初叶的事了。可以设想，横越印度洋直接联系锡兰或南印度与非洲东岸的航路，在 15 世纪初郑和远航之前，是有可能被发现的。但是在中国图籍里关于这条航路的明确记载，则是从郑和远航时开始的。在所附郑和航海路线的地图上，可以看得很清楚：在锡兰与非洲东岸以及南印度与非洲东岸之间，都是直达航线，

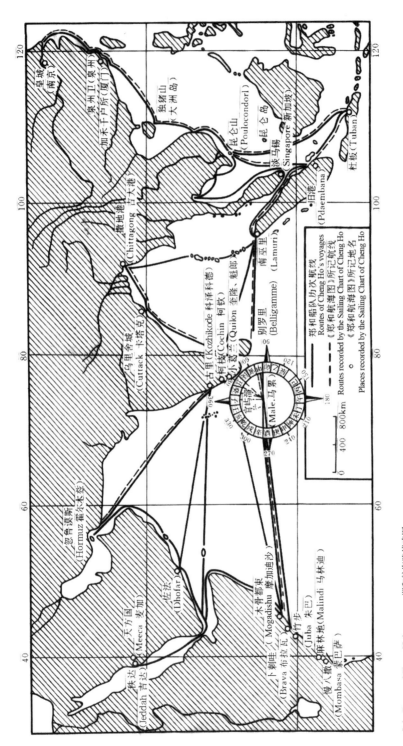

5-1 Routes of Cheng Ho's voyages 郑和航海路线略图

The routes might pass through *Kuanyuliu* (the Island of Male), but it was not necessary. We know for certain that in the seventh voyage, *Kuanyuliu* was used as a midway station. Cheng Ho's original chart contains the following note:

> From *Kuanyuliu*…one arrives at *Mukutushu* (i.e. Mogadishu), following the *Keng-yu* needle.[26]

We shall find, by checking the route against a modern map, that the sailing direction is wonderfully accurate, as what he called the *Keng-yu* needle represents roughly 262° on the compass.

The geographical work of Fei Hsin[27], who accompanied Cheng Ho on four of his voyages, tells us:

> Sailing southward from *Peiloli* (Belligamme) in Ceylon…one may arrive at Brava after twenty-one days and nights.

> With a favourable wind, it is possible to sail from *Hsiaokelan* (Quilon) to *Mukutushu* in twenty days and nights.

可以经过官屿溜（今马累岛，Male），也可以不经过它。至于第七次的航行中，官屿溜则被用作中继站，郑和原图上并有下列文字记注说：

> 官屿溜用庚酉针……收木骨都［束］。[26]

所谓"庚酉针"就是罗盘上的262°左右的方位。按之今图，这一行驶方向是完全正确的。

其次，随从郑和四次出航的费信在所著地理书[27]中也有如下记载：

> 卜剌哇国……自锡兰山别罗［里］南去二十一昼夜可至。

> 木骨都束国……自小葛兰顺风二十昼夜可至。

Here are clearly set forth the two direct routes across the Indian Ocean, one leading from Belligamme in Ceylon to Brava on the eastern coast of Africa, and the other from Quilon to Mogadishu, also on the eastern coast of Africa. However, the direction given is incorrect, and Cheng Ho's chart should be regarded as the final authority. The opening up of the sea route was the joint work of the Asian and African peoples who inhabited those districts. As has been pointed out before, it was by following this route, and by enlisting the guidance of the expert Arabian sailor, Ibn Madjid, that da Gama successfully accomplished his voyage at the end of the fifteenth century.

Cheng Ho's voyages must not be looked on as a fortuitous incident. They were an important extension of the oversea communications and friendly trade relations that had long existed between the Asian and African peoples. Official organization enabled these voyages to be carried out on an unprecedented scale, but it did nothing to change their nature, since there is ample evidence to show that these voyages aimed primarily at enlarging oversea trade. That the Ming court was also eager to hunt down foreign treasures and fancy products need not be denied, but the means adopted remained as always one of peaceful exchange and free bartering. Trade relations built on such a basis naturally fostered diplomatic relations. What is more important, following these voyages, private trade also had considerable development. The immense amount of gold, silver, coins, silken fabrics, chinaware and copper ware with which Cheng Ho's fleet was loaded, was a means to promote private trade, in return for such exotic goods as spiceries, dyes, pearls, precious stones and rare birds and animals (lions, zebras, ostriches, leopards, giraffes, etc.).[28] The fleet also carried foreign messengers and merchants back and forth. All in all, China's private oversea trade greatly expanded during this period.

To sum up, Cheng Ho's voyages were a powerful stimulant to the oversea trade and cultural interflow between China on the one hand and

South Asia and East Africa on the other. The direct route connecting China with East Africa marks, in particular, a new stage in oversea communications.

But ever since da Gama "discovered" this route to the Orient, more and more Westerners followed in his wake. Not satisfied with merely reaching India, they kept pushing farther eastward, and it did not take them long to sail through the Strait of Malacca and enter the South China Sea,

这里所记，也就是从今天锡兰的贝里格姆和印度南部的奎隆分别到达非洲东岸布拉瓦和摩加迪沙的横越印度洋的直达航路。只是所记方向不确，应以郑和航海图为准。在开辟这一航路上，亚非有关地方的人民都作出了自己的贡献。如前所述，15 世纪的末年，达·伽马正是沿着这一航路，再加上伊本·马吉德这位卓越的阿拉伯航海家的领航，这才得以顺利地完成了他的航行。

郑和的远航，不是一个偶然事件，而是长时期以来亚非人民泛海来往和进行友好贸易的重要发展。由于这次远航是官方组织的，因此规模巨大，远远超越前代。但是这并没有改变这次航行的性质，因为事实证明，航行的主要目的就是要开拓海上贸易。无可讳言的是明朝宫廷很想借此猎取海外珍奇，但所采取的手段仍然是和平交易、互通有无。通过这样的贸易关系，也促进了外交关系的发展。值得重视的是随着这种关系所进行的民间贸易。郑和的船队携带大量金银、钱币、丝绸、瓷器、铜器等作为民间交易的媒介，换取回国的则是各地特产如香料、染料、珍珠宝石以及珍禽异兽（如狮子、斑马、鸵鸟、金钱豹、长颈鹿）等等。[28] 随着郑和的船队还有外国使者和商人来往，也就在这时期，中国民间的海外贸易也有了很大发展。

总之，郑和的航行大大促进了中国和亚洲南部以及非洲东部诸国之间的海上贸易和文化交流，而中国和东非的直接通航，更是海上交通的新发展。

但是，自从达·伽马找到了这条到东方来的航路之后，后继者跟踪而至。他们并不以到达印度为满足，而是向东方继续前进，很快地就通过了马六甲海峡，进入中国南海，

arriving eventually in 1516 at Canton, which formed the southern entrance to China on the seaboard. In the van were the Portuguese, while many other nations of Western Europe, such as Spain, Holland, Great Britain and France, showed an equally ardent desire not to be left behind.

Since then a totally different chapter in the history of oversea communications between the East and the West has to be written and here is the proper place for the present study to stop.

1516 年终于来到了中国南方的海上门户——广州。走在最前面的是葡萄牙人，其他西欧国家如西班牙、荷兰、英国、法国等也不甘落后，这是一股汹涌而至的殖民主义的逆流，它冲击着非洲大陆，侵袭着印度洋上以及太平洋西部的众多国家，世代相传友好互惠的亚非人民之间的海上往来，从此被打断，代之而起的却是殖民主义者对财富的掠夺、对土地的征服以及对无辜人民的奴役、贩卖和屠杀。

今天，民族解放运动空前高涨，民族解放革命的胜利不可阻挡。在殖民制度的扩张中被广为传布的所谓新航路的发现这一名词，必须予以纠正。因为这个名词不但歪曲了历史的事实，也抹杀了亚非人民在航海事业中的贡献。

❻ A MODERN INTERPRETATION OF ANCIENT CHINESE GEOGRAPHICAL LITERATURE*

Example I: *A Commentary on the Book of Rivers*

China is now facing a great historical transformation. In order to get rid of the backwardness of her science and technology and to speed up the effort of the realization of her socialist modernization, it is necessary for us, on the one hand, to learn the advanced knowledge and experience of others countries. And, on the other hand, we must also re-estimate the real value of all the things we have inherited from our forefathers: Chinese culture, old traditions and history. We must absorb and utilize all the things that are beneficial to us. It is through such endeavours that we hope to produce a new culture which is typically Chinese and modern. In other words, we need a new culture for the age of socialism. This great historical transformation is in reality a new Renaissance of China.

Since liberation, this Chinese Renaissance has developed rapidly in the different fields of human knowledge. Indeed, there were serious interruptions and damages during the ten years of political turmoil. Nevertheless, all the things that obey the law of historical development will prosper in spite of the will of the reactionary gangs. And this is true to the Chinese Renaissance.

To give a full account of the Renaissance in this short talk is impossible. It is also out of my personal ability to do so. However, it is possible for me to try to use my personal judgment to re-estimate the real value of ancient Chinese culture and traditions from the field of studies with which I am familiar. Let me illustrate my view point by showing two concrete examples. I sincerely wish that by so doing I may offer some help to my friends who want to know something about New China.

I would like to introduce to you two important books of ancient Chinese geography in order to illustrate how we, the modern Chinese students, make use of ancient Chinese literature and bring to light from them new value and inspiration.

The first book was compiled in the 6th century A.D. It is a voluminous manuscript called A *Commentary on the Book of Rivers.*

The other book was written 340 years ago by an outstanding Chinese traveller. It was written in the form of a diary with detailed descriptions of his observation and fieldwork. The title of the book is *Hsü Xia-Ke's Travels,* which is named after the author.

陆 古代中国地理文献的现代解释*

例一：《水经注》

　　中国正在经历着一场伟大的变革，企图摆脱长期落后的局面努力在实现社会主义现代化的宏伟目标下迅速前进。为此我们有必要向外国学习一切先进的东西，这是一个方面，另一方面，我们还必须重新估价自己的历史文化遗产，从中吸取一切有益的东西。只有这样，我们才能创造出真正的、富有自己民族特色和富有生命力的新文化，也就是适应社会主义时代要求的新文化。实际上这也可以称之为一次中国式的"文艺复兴"。

　　解放以来，这个中国式的"文艺复兴"，在知识领域的各个部门里已在蓬勃发展，这中间虽然遭遇到反动势力历时十年的严重摧残和破坏，可是符合历史发展规律的新生事物，不是任何人的意志所能消灭的。

　　现在要想把这个正在发展中的中国式的"文艺复兴"作个全面的介绍是不可能的，更不是我所能胜任的。我所能做的，只是从自己比较熟悉的领域里，根据个人感觉到的从旧的文化遗产中去发现新价值这件事，举出两个具体的例子，略作论明。这样做，或许对愿意了解新中国的朋友们，不无一点帮助。如果能做到这一点，也就是我最大的愿望了。

　　我想以中国古代地理学的两部重要著作为例，来说明：我们在今天是如何从旧的文化遗产中，去发现它们的新价值的。

　　第一部是写成于公元6世纪的一部巨著：《水经注》。

　　第二部是三百四十年前一位卓越的旅行家所留下的一部以日记为体裁的野外考察记录，后人就以这位旅行家的名字，命名这部记录，叫做《徐霞客游记》。

Both of these books were written in very beautiful and fluent prose. Indeed they had been preserved because of their literary style and beauty. It is only in modern times that their importance in scientific terms was recognized.

We shall discuss *A Commentary on the Book of Rivers* first. I would like to introduce to you the life of the author and a brief summary of the contents of the book.

Li Tao-Yuan, the author of *A Commentary on the Book of Rivers* was a native of Tsor-Hsien of the present Hopei Province which is about a hundred kilometers southwest of Beijing. He was born between 465 and 472 A.D. and died in 527 A.D., which is about 1453 years ago.

During the time of Li Tao-Yuan, China was divided into the South and the North. In the South, there were several kingdoms of Han nationality which governed the district one after the other chronologically. In the North, there were different minority nationalities fighting against one another for the sovereignty of the district. And throughout the whole era of the South and the North Dynasties, political hostility existed between the two parts of China. However, in spite of the existence of such political hostility, Li Tao-Yuan kept up his studies and research on the geography of China as a united whole. This idea of unity is most important to us modern students of Chinese Geography. We learn from Li Tao-Yuan that political fragmentation does not mean fragmentation of culture. It is this unity within a developing culture that acts as a motivating force which bound the different nationalities in China steadily. Under such controlling force, they influenced and assimilated one another and a new type of culture with Han nationality as the main stem gradually formed and finally yielded a new culture of special Chinese characteristics. But, at the same time, there still existed in the minority nationalities, their own traditions and culture with their special characteristics. Another point to be noted is that in the process of the development of the Chinese culture, there were the continual absorption and assimilation of foreign civilization and influence. It is an undeniable fact that Chinese culture was enriched by foreign influence.

Li Tao-Yuan's father was a civil officer of a local district. He had to travel on duty to different places in different districts and the young boy Tao-Yuan went with his father on such occasions visiting places. This gave Li Tao-Yuan many chances to travel and thus nurtured his interest in studying geography. When Li Tao-Yuan grew up to be an official himself, he had even more chances to travel and so he visited many more places, which broadened his knowledge and experience.

这两部书都是用极其优美的散文所写成的，首先是以其文学价值流传后世的，只是到了现代，我们才真正认识到它们所包含的极其重要的科学内容。

现在请让我先把《水经注》这部巨著的作者及其主要内容，作个简要的介绍。

《水经注》的作者郦道元，其故乡在今河北省涿县。涿县在北京城西南不到一百公里。他出生的年代在公元 465 与 472 年之间，死在 527 年。去今已有 1453 年。

郦道元的时代，正处在中国的政局南北分裂的时代。当时南方是几个汉族小王朝先后统治的地区，北方则是不同少数民族的统治者互相角逐的场所。同时南北两方又长期处于相互敌对的地位。但是这种分裂的局面，并没有妨碍郦道元对于全国地理作为一个统一的整体来进行研究，这一点是很重要的，足以说明政治上的分裂，并不能破坏文化上的统一。正是这种统一的，而且是在不断发展中的文化，作为一种无形的力量，才把中国的各族人民逐渐维系在一起，互相影响，又互相融合，终于形成了以汉族影响为主的独具特色的中国文化，同时在一些少数民族里也还保存着某种固有的民族文化的特征。其次，在中国文化发展的过程中，也曾不断从外部的文化吸取营养，丰富了自己的内容，这也是无可否认的事实。

郦道元从少年时代起，随着他的父亲离开家乡。他父亲作为一个地方官吏，在任职过程中，到过不少地方，道元随行，从而得到了一个旅游的好机会，并且培养了研究地理的兴趣。他自己年长做官，到过的地方更多了，见闻更广了，研究祖国地理的兴趣也就

And his interest in studying the geography of his motherland increased by leaps and bounds. In addition to his fieldwork observation and practical experience, Li added to his knowledge by reading a lot of books, ancient materials and manuscripts. It must be mentioned that China of that time was a kingdom which had enjoyed a cultural unity for several hundred years through the prosperous dynasties of Qin and Han, and the Chinese culture had developed rapidly. There were many writings concerning national and regional geography, history, folklore and tradition, and some of them were of good quality. According to a study and calculation of the writings of Li Tao-Yuan, we find that the books and writings he used for reference in his work amount to 437. It is a pity that most of these books have been lost. In addition to these references, he also collected a lot of writings from stone tablets and folklore and folk literature for his own reference. During the time of Li Tao-Yuan, there were some geographical literature and writings circulating among the elite circles. To Li, these were far from being satisfactory, some being too simple, some being too dry and insipid, and others being too confusing with no definite system for reference and research. It must be noted that most of these materials of geographical descriptions were little more than the compilation and gathering of raw materials and rough sketches of all sorts of natural phenomena. And there was no standard system of classification for these geographical records.

Li Tao-Yuan decided to set up a standard and unified system of recording the geographical materials of China. He used the *Book of Rivers*, a book written by some scholar before him, as an outline for his studies. The original *Book of Rivers* was completed in the third century A.D. It had the descriptions and records of 137 rivers in China, with reference to their sources, estuaries, tributaries, etc. It had a definite system of recording of its own. The only defect of the book is that there was little or practically no reference to the geographical condition of the land irrigated by each river. Li Tao-Yuan used this book as an outline for his research; he filled up many vacancies and supplemented a lot of materials. The number of rivers he studied and recorded increased to 1252. More important is the fact that he compiled detailed descriptions of each river including the geographical condition of it, the natural phenomena of the district concerned and their changes, with reference to the historical development and influences. Many of the descriptions were facts collected and recorded by Li himself. The completed works of Li Tao-Yuan amounted to three hundred thousand words which is about twenty times more than that of the original *Book of Rivers*.

与日俱增。在实地考察之外，他还涉猎了大量的图书资料。因为当时的中国，已经经历了自秦、汉以来几百年之久的统一时期，文化有了迅速的发展，关于全国以及各地区的地理、历史、风土、传说等各种写作，已经积累有很大的数量，种类也很繁多。据统计，道元在他的著作中直接引过的这类图书，就有437种之多，可惜现在大部分已经失传了。此外，他还搜集了一些碑刻文字，采取了不少的民间传说、故事，以备参考。当时也已经有几种描述全国地理的著作在流传中，可是他看了都不满意，有的太简单，有的太枯燥，有的内容零乱，缺乏系统。应该看到，当时的地理描述，还停在资料堆砌和现象罗列的初步阶段。怎样才能把十分复杂的各种地理现象记录下来，还缺乏很好的办法。

郦道元有志把全国的地理进行统一的描述，他的办法，就是利用前人所写的《水经》一书，作为自己写作的纲领。《水经》一书，大约写成在公元221到279年之间，书中记述了中国的河流共计137条。每条河流都是从上源写到下游，从主流写到支流，脉络相寻，自成体系。可是河流所经各地的地理情况，书中很少叙述。郦道元以这部书为纲领，又大大加以补充，把河流的数目增加到1252条，更重要的是，还把每条河流所经过的地方都作了详细的描述，从一些自然地理现象，一直到地方变化的情况，历史演替的事实，无不包括在内。（许多描述都来源于郦道元搜集和记载的资料。）只就补充的字数来说，就多于原书20倍，约近30万字。

As to the system of compiling his book, Li decided that all the rivers originally recorded in the old book (*Book of Rivers*) should be printed in bold type while all the materials supplemented by Li himself should be printed in small type, as references and footnotes. The name of the new book still preserved the name of the old, i.e. *Book of Rivers*, but the only change was by adding the word "Commentary" and thus the full name of the book became *A Commentary on the Book of Rivers*.

In his life time, Li Tao-Yuan had written many books and essays, but only this book got left. This book was preserved to us because of its beauty in writing style, especially its excellence in describing natural scenery. For example, in his records of the Three Gorges of the Yangtze River, the readers would be deeply attracted by his interesting description of lively actions and meditating quietude, its changing colours and poetic sounds of the magnificent pictures of Mother Nature. It is this passage of the Three Gorges of the Yangtze River that students of later times used to recite and memorize as a model of standard prosaic style and literary form.

Recently the Three Gorges of the Yangtze River was opened to all foreign friends and tourists as one of the sight-seeing spots in Central China. Special launch trips are arranged at scheduled time. Our foreign friends are welcome to come to China to enjoy the trip to the Gorges. I regret that I do not have the ability to translate and bring to life the beautiful prose style and literary achievement of Li Tao-Yuan in his descriptions of the magnificent scenery of the Three Gorges. I must confess that his special literary style and accomplishment are very difficult to interpret and translate. Without understanding, it would be difficult for our foreign friends to appreciate the beauty and essence of Chinese literature and prose form.

To consider Li's book from the point of view of a modern scholar, its beautiful literary style is not the only point of attraction and influence. I would like to point out that the scientific value of his observation and research is even more important. This emphasis is also based on my own personal experience. Let me show my point by telling a short story.

In the summer of 1949, after I concluded my studies in the University of Liverpool, England, I returned to Peking which had just been liberated. The next spring, under the direction of the Municipality of Peking (Beijing), a Committee for City Planning was established. Its duty was to make plans for the reform of old Beijing and the construction of a new Beijing city. I was responsible for the research of the historical geography of Beijing. Actually, I had done some research on this subject during my studies at the University of Liverpool under the guidance and tutorship of Prof. H. C. Darby. But this time the aim of the research was much more concrete: I was

在书的写作格式上：凡是原书所记每条河流都用大形字体来写，补充的部分，则用小形字体作注。全书仍用《水经》原名，只是加了一个"注"字，就叫做《水经注》，意译就是 *A Commentary on the Book of Rivers*。

郦道元生前的著作不只是一部《水经注》，但是流传到现在的，只有这一种。主要原因是这部书的文笔非常优美，描写的自然景物尤为出色。例如，他描写长江三峡壮丽的风景，有动有静，有声有色，不知不觉就把读者吸引到大自然的怀抱中去。因此，这段描写常被选为描写风景的范文，为人所传诵。

现在长江三峡已被开放为外国友人的游览区，有特备的江轮，定期航行，为来自世界各地的游人服务。可惜的是，郦道元描写三峡的优美文字和它特有的风格，很不容易用译文传达出来，供来这里观光的外国朋友，共赏中国散文的精华。

但是现在看来，《水经注》可贵之处还不仅仅在于它的优美的文字，更重要的还在于它所包含的具有科学价值的内容。这一点对我个人来说，也是深有感触的。这里我只能举一个很小的例子来作个说明。

1949 年夏，我结束了在英国利物浦大学的学习，回到了解放后的北京。转年春天，在北京市人民政府的直接领导下，成立了一个城市规划委员会，着手进行改造北京旧城和建设新城的规划工作。在这个委员会里，我分担了北京城市历史地理的研究工作。实际上我在利物浦大学时，在 H.C.Darby 教授的指导下，已经进行过这方面的初步研究。现在在实际任务的要求下，目的更加明确，就是要弄清楚

to make clear the process of the development of the old city of Peking, especially to make clear why the geographical site of the city had experienced many changes. This was not an easy job, because the long history of Beijing is very complicated. Well, from where should I begin? I was inspired by Prof. Darby's theory when I considered this problem. Prof. Darby emphasized that in the long process of the development of geographical environment, we must try to choose from the different periods in the development some historical cross-sections and endeavour to restore them to their original conditions. Then we line up these historical cross-sections chronologically, and study them by means of comparison and discover the process of development of each restored cross-section. Thus we can obtain a deeper understanding of the geographical outlook of the district concerned.

Under the guidance and inspiration of this theory, I looked through Li Tao-Yuan's *A Commentary on the Book of Rivers*, and extracted from its contents the passages concerning the geographical condition of Beijing and its surrounding areas. I succeeded in restoring a map of Beijing and its surrounding districts of more than 1450 years ago. This is the earliest one which is possible to be reconstructed. With the help of this map, we were able to trace out the origin of the city of Beijing. The same map also offered a reliable guide to the study of the changes and development of Beijing and its surrounding areas in later times. The above story shows that because of the needs of the modernization of China, we revived ancient Chinese classics through the use of modern scientific theory and methods. Considering the above incident from such an angle, we may say that this can be considered as an example of Chinese Renaissance.

Concerning the modern estimation of the value of the book *Hsü Hsia-Ke's Travels*, I would like to discuss it in the next lecture.

Example II: *Hsü Xia-Ke's Travels*

In my last lecture, I tried to use a specific example to illustrate how we discover the scientific value of Li Tao-Yuan's book: *A Commentary on the Book of Rivers*, which was famous and well-remembered for its beautiful prose form. Today I would like to introduce to you another famous Chinese book which is also well-remembered by the Chinese people for its excellent literary style and prose form. Through the records of the author's geographical observations and investigations in his book, we discovered its scientific value and also the author's achievements and influence in his time. To us modern students of geography, the latter

北京这个古老城市的发展过程，特别是要确切了解它的城址在历史上多次变迁的原因，为现在的规划工作提供必要的参考。这并不是一件轻而易举的事，因为历史久远，变迁复杂，从何入手呢？在这个问题上，Darby 教授的一个理论，给我以很大的启发，就是要在地理环境长期演变的过程中，尽可能地选择不同时期的历史剖面进行"复原"，然后按着时代的顺序，把这些"复原"了的"剖面"，进行比较研究，找出其前后演变的过程，这样就可以对现在这一地区的地理面貌，获得更为深刻的理解。

正是在这一理论的指导下，我借助于郦道元的《水经注》一书中有关当时北京城及附近地区地理情况的描述，"复原"了一千四百五十多年以前北京及其近郊的一幅地图。根据这幅地图，可以上溯北京城的起源，同时也为研究后来北京城及其郊区的变化，提供了一个可靠的起点。这是一个很小的事例，但是也足以说明：新时代建设事业的要求，借助于现代的科学理论，使古代的经典著作，发射出新的光芒。从这个意义上来说，不是也可以算作中国式的"文艺复兴"的一例吗？

关于《徐霞客游记》的现代评价，下次再进行讨论。

例二：《徐霞客游记》

在上一讲里，我试图用一个具体的例子来说明我们如何从郦道元的《水经注》这部过去以优美散文为人所重视的巨著里，去发现它的科学价值。今天我想用另外一部同样以优美散文而得流传于世的著作来说明：我们如何从这部著作的地理描述中不但去发现它的科学价值，而且从它的作者从事地理考察的事实中，去发现他之所以从事这项

point is more important. The name of the book is *Hsü Xia-Ke's Travels* which I mentioned in my last lecture.

As in Western history, there are also famous travellers in the Chinese history. They also made long and difficult journeys and travels. The records and literature of what they had done broadened our knowledge of geography and also helped to promote the development of human civilization. For instance, in the first half of the second century B.C. (138-126 B.C.) the famous traveller Zhang Qian who by the command of the Central Government of his time, started from Chang-An, the political capital city, travelled westward and crossed the Pamir Plateau and finally reached Central Asia. He made diplomatic contacts with the political sovereignty there. He spent more than ten years in his travels and return journey, conquering numerous difficulties and untold hardship. He became the pathfinder of the famous "Silk Route". Again, for instance, in the last year of the fourth century (399 A.D.), Fa-Xien, a much respected monk, also travelled from Chang-An. After crossing the Pamir Plateau, he turned down south to India. From India, he travelled by boat to Ceylon, then sailed in a big sea-going boat back to China in 412 A.D. Again, in the first half of the seventh century (627 A.D.-645), another famous monk called Shuen-Zhaung, followed a similar route taken by Fa-Xien some two hundred years before. He started from Chang-An, went westward and arrived in India where he stayed for more than ten years. Then he travelled by land back to Chang-An. Without doubt, the achievements of these travellers are never to be neglected. Their achievements helped to broaden the knowledge of the Chinese people. Also, they brought back the influence of other people from abroad. However, to investigate into the aims of their endeavour, we may obtain the conclusion that their achievements were by-products only. To Zhang Qian, his aim was to carry out a political mission; whereas to Fa-Xien or Shuen-Zhaung, it was religious fervour that motivated them to take the travels and stand all the trials of hardship.

Now, the traveller Hsü Xia-Ke born in the late sixteenth century (1587-

1641) is also well known for his daring journeys. Nevertheless, his travels were completely different from that of the people we mentioned above. More than half of his lifetime was spent in travelling. He travelled with neither political assignment nor any religious motives. He travelled because he wanted to seek knowledge and to explore the secrets of Mother Nature. Hsü Xia-Ke was a native of Jiang-Yin Xien in Jiang-Su Province on the southern bank of the Yangtze River. It was at the age of twenty-two, that is, 1607 A.D., that he left his home at the Yangtze Delta and started his planned trips. His aim was to visit the most famous mountains in China. Usually,

科学活动的时代意义。在今天看来，这一点是更为重要的。这就是我在上一讲中已经提到过的那部《徐霞客游记》。

在中国历史上和在西方历史上一样，曾经出现过一些长途跋涉从而大大开拓了人们的视野的大旅行家。他们的活动增加了人类的地理知识，促进了人类文化的发展。例如，公元前第 2 世纪前半（公元前 138—前 126），张骞从当时中国的政治中心长安出发，奉中央政府之命西行，越过帕米尔高原，直到中亚细亚，与那里的统治者进行外交上的联络，往返途中克服了种种困难，经历了十多年的时间，成为开辟有名的"丝绸之路"的先驱。又如，公元 4 世纪末，中国僧人法显，也是从长安出发，越过帕米尔高原后，转往印度。最后又从印度渡海到达现在的锡兰，再从锡兰乘大船返回中国，也用了十多年时间（399—412）。到了 7 世纪前半（627—645），又有一位中国僧人玄奘，大体沿着二百多年前法显西行的道路，从长安出发到达印度，在印度各地逗留了十多年，然后仍从陆路返回长安。这些著名的旅行家，虽然对扩大中国人民的地理知识、吸收外来的影响，作出了很大的贡献，但是这只能称是一种副产，而不是他们长途跋涉的目的。他们的旅行，有的是负有政治使命，如张骞，有的是为了求取佛经，是出于宗教上的要求，如法显、玄奘。

出生于 16 世纪晚期的徐霞客（1587—1641），虽然也是以旅行家见称，但是他的旅行和上述诸人却完全不同。他几乎有半生的岁月都在旅途中度过，既没有任何政治使命，也没有宗教上的动机，完全是为了寻求知识，探索自然的奥秘。他的家乡在扬子江三角洲上的江阴县，靠近扬子江南岸。他从 22 岁那一年，也就是公元 1607 年起，开始离开家乡作有计划的旅行，主要目的是访问名山胜景。一般都是当年

he completed one trip within a year. The mountains he travelled to visit in the North included the Tai-Shan in the Province of Shantung, and the Pan-Shan which is near the northeast of Peking. He also journeyed to the northern part of the Province of Shansi where he visited the Wu-Tai Mountain. Then he went to the Northwest where he explored the magnificent sceneries of Hua-Shan of Shensi Province and the Wu-Dong Shan of Hupei Province. In Central China, he visited the famous mountains of Huang-Shan in the Province of Anhui and the Lu-Shan of the Province of Kiangsi. Then he made a trip down South to the Lo-Fu Shan of Kuangtung Province, and also to the Southeastern coastline where he explored the Yen-Dang Shan of Chekiang Province. In early 1636, he made a long-distance travel to the provinces of Southwest China, reaching the western border of Yunnan Province. It took him nearly four years to complete the trip back and forth. It was the longest journey he had ever made, a distance of about seven thousand kilometers. In all his travels, he made very detailed records and descriptions of his observation, especially that of the provinces of Kuangsi, Kweichow and Yunnan. He wrote down all the geographical phenomena of these places in a detailed way. I would like to point out that if we find in his earlier travels he only enjoyed the beautiful and magnificent sceneries of Nature, then in his latter journeys we find his interest was that of all the natural phenomena. He persisted to walk in all his tours and very seldom he rode or took a boat. Thus, he was able to walk to the farthest corners of the countryside and wilderness and climb to the deepest canyons and the loftiest mountains. He nurtured the habit of writing down immediately everything he had a chance to explore and observe. He made detailed records in the form of a diary of all his trips and activities, with also his own personal opinions and deductions from what he had seen, especially his opinions on natural and geographical phenomena. He had very keen observation power and he was not afraid of the dangers in his journey. Very often, he climbed a high cliff or a deep canyon alone or crept into a deep cave without the company of anybody to explore and investigate. Some writers after him described his activities saying "he climbed high like a monkey and explored caves like a snake". In addition to these, he wrote in an excellent prose style, interesting and attractive, with vivid descriptions of natural sceneries. The way he recorded geographical phenomena was accurate and concise in effect. It was actually because of these special accurate records of his observation and fieldwork that he was much respected and esteemed by the scholars of his time. His writings were copied and read and were considered as the finest literary accomplishment. After his death, his writings were collected and compiled into a volume with the title *Hsü Xia-Ke's Travels*. It was a collection of

外出，当年回来。向北，经过山东的泰山，到达北京附近的盘山和山西北部的五台山。向西北到过陕西华山和湖北武当山，中间还访问过安徽的黄山和江西的庐山。向南，直到广东的罗浮山。在东南沿海地区又访问过浙江的雁荡山和福建的武夷山。最重要的是，从1636年起，他更远游西南各省，直到云南西部边境。往返之间，将近四年，路途跋涉约七千公里，这是他一生中旅行路线最长的一次。沿途作了详细的观察和记录，特别是对广西、贵州和云南三省的一些地理现象，描述得最为详尽。如果说他早期的旅行，还是以欣赏大自然的壮丽风景为主，可是到了后来，他的全部注意力，几乎都为自然地理的各种现象所吸引。他在野外一直坚持徒步跋涉，很少骑马和乘船。这样就便于他深入人迹罕至的穷乡僻壤和深山大野，而且他还养成了随时随地进行观察和随手记录描写的好习惯。他的记录都是以日记的体裁写下来的，十分详细地记载了他每日的行程和观察所得，有时也包括了关于一个地区特点的概括性的论述，或是关于某一地理现象的总结式的评论。他有十分锐敏的观察力，更有不怕一切艰险、只身攀登悬崖峭壁或者潜入洞穴深处进行考察的精神。有人描写说他攀援登高时像一只猴子，探索洞穴时像一条蛇。特别是他还写得一手极好的散文，描写自然景物，逼真生动，富有感染力；记述各种地理现象，又有精确、简明、刻画入微的特点。正是因为这个原因，他的这部野外考察的记录，才受到当时一些人的重视，作为文学读物，争相传抄。他去世之后，又有人把这些记录加以搜集整理，编订成册，

more than four hundred thousand words. It is a pity that some of the contents have been lost during the past years. The present volume is not the original edition.

The book was titled "Travels", but actually it is a classic on geographical research with very important scientific contents. It is important because it opened up a new way in the study of geography in China, using a thoroughly empirical method. Its influence and achievement in the development of Chinese sciences are unique. I must confess that it is out of my ability to convey to you the literary value of Hsü's book. However, it is necessary for me to explain briefly what the author had done in opening up a new way of geographical research.

Even before the time of Hsü Xia-Ke, the study of geography had a long development in China. There were many books which may be classified into the field of Chinese Geography. However, most of these earlier writings and books were nothing more than confusing collections of geographical phenomena. Practically none or very few of them referred to the reasons or factors yielding or influencing such phenomena. Furthermore, most of the writers of this kind of books were "indoor scholars" who did not have any fieldwork experience. All they did was to write books which were based on some legends from some miscellaneous documents. Very few of them were books of serious research and systematic compilation. The rare exception probably is the work of Li Tao-Yuan's *A Commentary on the Book of Rivers* published in the sixth century A.D. The fact is that the oppression of feudalism lasted for so long a time that the level of production was very low, and as a result of this, geographical research and records were also limited. When it came to Hsü's time, he broke away from the old tradition and walked out of the small study of his house and made long outdoor trips with definite purposes and preparations. He made outdoor observations at first hand. With his keen observation he discovered and accumulated the numerous, colourful geographical phenomena and the knowledge of the internal causes of these phenomena. For instance, he looked into the nature and characteristics of rocks, the power of water in erosion, the use and influence of underground water, the shaping and structure of land forms, the changes of temperature and wind on different levels and latitudes and their influences on vegetations, and many other things which he tried to give scientific explanations of their making. More significant was the travels he made in the latter years of his life when he visited the southwestern part of China where he systematically observed the special nature of topography of the great expanse of karstland there, and made classified descriptions of them. His intense interest in the

定名为《徐霞客游记》，共有四十余万字。可惜已有部分散失，后来刻印成书的，已经不是全稿了。

这部书虽以《游记》为名，实际上却是一部地理考察文献，具有十分重要的科学内容，在中国的科学发展史上，为研究地理学开创了一条新道路。在这里来介绍这部书的文学价值，不是我所能胜任的，但是简要说明一下它的作者所开创的地理学研究的新道路，却是必要的。

在徐霞客的时代以前，中国的地理学已有长期发展的历史，可以列为地理这一门类的书籍，为数也很多。但是，这些书籍，几乎都是表面的地理现象的罗列，极少涉及这些地理现象产生的原因和彼此之间的内在联系。而且这些地理书籍的作者，又多半是一些"书斋里的学者"，很少有野外考察的经验。他们只是根据别人的传说，或是把别人一些零散的记录，编写成书。即使这一类的编辑工作，能做到像郦道元写《水经注》那样广收博采，严加考订的，实在也极少。实际上，在长期的封建社会里，由于生产水平的限制，对地理记载的要求，也就是这样。可是到了徐霞客，他却打破了旧传统，走出了小书房，有目的、有计划地到野外作长途旅行，进行实地考察。他热爱大自然，有锐敏的观察力，从丰富多彩的地理现象中，他逐渐认识到造成这些现象的一些内在原因。例如，他对岩石的性质、流水侵蚀的能力、地下水的作用、地形塑造的过程、高山上下温度风力的变化对于植物的影响、不同气候区域之间植物群落的显著差异，如此等等，他都有合乎科学的解释。尤其重要的是，他在晚年的西南之行，使他对广大石灰岩地区的地形特征，有了系统的观察和分门别类的描述。特别是

investigation of the caves in the karstland led him to go into more than one hundred deep caves of which he made very minute observations and detailed records. For example, he went twice to the eastern part of Kweilin in the present Autonomous Region of Kuangxi Zhuang, to explore the famous "Seven Stars Cave". He investigated and recorded the outside and inside details of this great cave in a minute way. The "Seven Star Cave" is one of the most mysterious and complicated caves in the karstland of Southwest China. In 1953, some Chinese geographers surveyed and measured the system of the "Seven Stars Cave" by modern methods and equipment. They drafted the ground plan inside and a rough sketch of the outside environment of the cave. When comparing their survey with the descriptions and records of Hsü Xia-Ke, they were very much amazed by its similarity and accuracy. The conclusion is that we can consider and use Hsü's book and his records as reliable references in the research of these caves and the karstland of China. I would like to emphasize that the distribution of limestone in the provinces of Southwest China is most widespread in areas of limestone topography in the world. And the time Hsü Xia-Ke spent in exploring and investigating this area was also the longest of all his travels. The records of the distribution of limestone topography, the difference of geographical zones, the different types of topography and the causes of their forming were written down by Hsü Xia-Ke in details with also his own explanation. Undoubtedly these records of Hsü's are the earliest documents of its kind concerning such a big area of limestone topography.[1]

The facts mentioned above show clearly that by his life-work in the research and investigation outdoor, Hsü Xia-Ke had paved a new way for the studies of geography in China. As a pioneer in the scientific research in geography Hsü is probably comparable to Alexander von Humboldt who laid the foundation of the studies of geography in Germany. Von Humboldt lived about one hundred and fifty years after Hsü Xia-Ke. Von Humboldt also devoted his life in making long-distance travels and investigations. However, von Humboldt lived in a time when the modern industrialization in Europe had already begun and when the studies of natural sciences in the West had also developed rapidly with inventions and making of new scientific equipment and instruments which were of much help to geographical research and fieldwork. These conditions offered necessary facilities to Western geographers for their research which former geographers had been unable to obtain. Alexander von Humboldt was able to use the new equipment and, furthermore, he had also the opportunity to go by sea to the developing South America for his geographical research. Thus, he was able to offer his achievements to the civilization of the whole world. As to Hsü Xia-Ke, although he

对石灰岩地区特有的溶洞的研究，更引起了他极大的兴趣。他深入考察过的洞穴就有一百多处，并作了十分详细的观察和记录。例如，他曾两次考察过桂林东部有名的七星岩洞穴，并且对洞内和洞外都作了十分详细的观察和记录。这是一处十分复杂的洞穴体系。1953年地理学家用科学手段对这个洞穴体系进行了测量，绘制了内部的平面图和外部的素描图。令人惊异的是，用三百四十年前徐霞客对这个洞穴体系所作的描述，与这些图相对比，竟是如此之相似，以至他的这些描述至今仍可作为对照研究这处洞穴的参考。中国的西南诸省，石灰岩分布面积很广，是世界上最广大的石灰岩地貌区域之一，而徐霞客在这一地区考察的时间又最长，对石灰岩地貌的分布、地区的差异、各种类型及其成因，都有详细的论断和记述。这应该是世界上最早的有关大面积内石灰岩地貌的宝贵文献了。[1]

上述事实足以说明：徐霞客半生的野外考察，确实是为中国地理学的研究，开创了一条新道路。从这个意义上来说，他和一百五十年以后在欧洲历史上通过野外的长途旅行和考察，从而为现代自然地理学奠定了基础的德国地理学家洪堡德是颇有相似之处的。不过洪堡德的时代，西方的自然科学随着近代工业的开始兴起，已经有了很大的发展，特别是各种有助于野外考察的科学仪器，为地理学家提供了前所未有的技术装备。而且，洪堡德还有机会远渡重洋，到正在开发中的南美洲进行考察，因此使他有可能在科学发展史上为全人类的文明作出重大的贡献。徐霞客虽然也曾有扩大他的考察

had the desire and ambition to expand the area of his observation and investigation, and even expressed the wish to go to the countries outside China, owing to the condition of China of his time, he was unable to fulfill his wish. It must be noted also that Chinese society of Hsü Xia-Ke's time had only just began to witness the spirit of capitalism. But due to the oppression of the feudalistic sovereignty, its development was retarded, and consequently the development of natural sciences was very slow, and thus, having any scientific instruments for fieldwork for Hsü was definitely out of the question. All Hsü Xia-Ke could do was to walk with his two feet in his travels and to work with his empty hands in his research and investigation. Indeed, he collected some rocks or plants as specimens for his studies even they were rare, as he had to carry everything for himself with his two hands and on his bare shoulders. Under such an environment, how could Hsü Xia-Ke's work compare with Alexander von Humboldt who could make use of sea transportation and use big boats to carry his great amount of specimens and manuscripts?

The story of Alexander von Humboldt is very different. He spent five years in South America. When he returned to Europe in 1804, he brought with him in the boat thirty large cases of specimens and records for his studies and references. He was able to live in Paris for twenty years to study and analyse his records and to write his thirty volumes of research on the New World. After that, he went back to Berlin. Then, again, he travelled to Central Asia. He spent the latter part of his life in studying and writing. He died at the old age of 90 in 1859.

Hsü Xia-Ke spent more than three years in the southwest of China exploring (1636-1640). When he returned to his native land, he brought back only a few rocks as reference plus an exhausted body. And within a year after his being back home, he died of poverty and illness, with the research and exploration of Chinese geography unfinished. According to an account of his life, even when he was seriously ill in bed, he still had his few rocks by his bedside and continued to study them and fondle them until the last moment of his life. He was only 56 when he died. Except the few hundred thousand words of fieldwork diary and records of observation and a few essays on his studies, he left no other writings.

The main reasons that I try to compare Hsü Xia-Ke of China of 340 years ago to Alexander von Humboldt of Germany of 130 years ago are not only to show the difference of their fate, but also to convey to you by means of emphasizing their important influences to the development of the sciences in the East and in the West, how the studies of sciences had

范围远到中国以外的遥远地区的强烈愿望，只是由于客观条件的限制，未能如愿。尤其是当时的中国，还停留在封建制度的束缚之下，生产的发展受到很大的限制，各种有关的自然科学还没有相应的发展，更谈不到近代科学仪器在野外考察中的应用。徐霞客只是赤手空拳，徒步跋涉，偶尔也采集岩石和植物标本，但是一切采集品都要靠自己背负携带，哪里能和洪堡德那样利用漂洋过海的轮船作为运载的工具相比呢？

洪堡德在中南美洲进行了五年之久的考察旅行，于1804年回到欧洲的时候，他随船带来三十大箱的标本资料，随即在巴黎居住下来，开始进行整理研究工作，一直持续了二十年，写成了三十卷的《1797—1804年新大陆热带区域旅行记》。后来他回到柏林，又曾到中亚考察，晚年仍孜孜不息，勤于著述，一直到90岁的高龄（1859年去世）。

徐霞客在中国西南广大地区进行了三年多的野外考察（1636—1640），于1640年回到家乡江阴县的时候，他随身带回来的，是仅有的一些岩石标本，和一个由于过度劳苦而受到严重损害的身体。结果他回家后不到一年，就在病中含着未竟之志与世长辞。有记载说，在他卧病期间，他还把野外带回来的岩石标本放在病床旁边，进行细心观察，直到生命的最后一息。他享年只有56岁。除去几十万字的野外考察日记和几篇专题论文之外，再没有留下其他著作。

在这里，我把三百四十前中国的徐霞客和一百三十年前欧洲的洪堡德，作个比较，主要目的不仅在于说明他们个人之间命运上的悬殊，更重要的是想以这两位卓越的地理学家的影响为例，来说明

developed into two different ways from times of these two prominent geographers on.

The scientific activities of von Humboldt had a far-reaching influence in Europe. For instance, it was under his influence that the British government sent a boat "The Beagle" in 1831 to the seacoast around South America for a scientific survey and research. On board the ship, a young man brought along with him von Humboldt's books. He read the books enthusiastically and sent letters home asking for more of von Humboldt's new books. The name of this young man is Charles Darwin. With this expedition as his starting point for his scientific research, he finally established the theory of "The Origin of Species". And with Darwin, sciences in the West had a big leap from the starting point of von Humboldt.

To return to our consideration of Hsü Xia-Ke's contributions to sciences in China, we find that in spite of his hard work, he had very little influence in the intellectual circle of his time. Indeed, there were some people who acknowledged his talent as a literary man; there were also some but fewer people who appreciated Hsü's life as an explorer who faced dangers bravely. However, there was practically none who noticed his achievements in geographical research and, after his death, there was no one to follow his footsteps or continue his studies. Even his book of such a mine of geographical wealth was ignored and it was not until recently that its value in geography was discovered. Isn't it most absurd and unreasonable?

I would like to point out that even before the time of Hsü Xia-Ke, science and technology had developed steadily in China. There had been important inventions by the ancient Chinese, such as the compass for sea travelling, the method of printing in block types, etc. These inventions were first used by the Chinese and then they were taken up by the world at large. Their influence on world culture and civilization is great and important. And even in Hsü Xia-Ke's time, there were important scientific writings and literature, such as *Ben Cao Gang Mu*

(*The Principles and Index of Herbs and Minerals for Medicine*) by Li Shi-Zhen (1518-1593). Its influence on botany, mineralogy and pharmacology is undeniably great. There was also the book written by Sung Ying-Sing (born ca. 1600) *Tien Gong Kai Wu* (*Exploitation of the Works of Nature*). We know that its first edition dated to 1637 and it was a very important work on agriculture, textile weaving, pottery, foundry and casting and other contents concerning the making of tools and instruments.[2] These two books and the one written by Hsü Xia-Ke were the forerunners in the scientific research in old China. They opened up new paths for

东西方科学的发展，从这两位科学家的时代开始，各自走上了完全不同的道路。

洪堡德的科学活动，在欧洲产生了巨大的影响。例如，正是在洪堡德的影响下，英国政府于 1831 年派遣了 The Beagle 号船，去南美洲的一些沿海地带，进行考察测量。参加这次考察的一个青年科学工作者，随身携带着洪堡德的一些著作，热情地阅读着，而且寄信给家人，要求把洪堡德新出版的书籍，继续寄给他。这个青年人就是以这次考察的收获为开端，而创立了进化论的达尔文。达尔文的贡献又超过了洪堡德，对西方自然科学的进一步发展，产生了更为深远的影响。

回过头来看看徐霞客一生的科学活动，在中国知识界所产生的影响，真是微乎其微。有人只是欣赏他的卓越的文学才能，有人只是赞叹他探险搜奇、勇于跋涉的精神，而他所开创的地理学研究的新方向，竟然后继无人，甚至他所遗留下来的唯一的一部著作的科学价值，也只是到了现代才被发现，这不是一个很奇怪的现象吗？

应该看到，在徐霞客的时代以前，中国的科学与技术一直在不断的发展中。有些重要的发明和创造，例如用于海上航行的罗盘、用于传布文化知识的活字版印刷术等，都是首先在中国被广泛应用的，从而为人类文化的发展，作出了重要贡献。就是徐霞客同时代的一些重要科学著作，如李时珍（1518—1593）的《本草纲目》在植物学、矿物学、医药学以及宋应星（生于1587年）的《天工开物》（1637年初版）[2] 在农业、纺织、制陶、冶炼以及其他器物制造的研究和应用上，和徐霞客在地理学的考察上所开创的新道路一样，

the people after them. Their achievements were undoubtedly among the most advanced in their age and also in the world. Nevertheless, the development of Chinese scientific research after the time of Hsü Xia-Ke lagged far behind that of the West. Thus, even until recent times, to learn from the advanced science and technology of the West is still our problem which we must acknowledge. How did it happen?

As a student of historical geography I do not have the ability to answer this question in full. However, from the angle of the development of natural sciences, there are some few points which we ought to notice when we look into this problem.

Since we know that as production of social development, natural science and technology also develop accordingly. And as early as the third century B.C. ancient China had already been in the state of feudalism, a feudalistic kingdom of centralisation of states and sovereignty. In China, the authority of the Emperor is supreme and unquestionable. Since then and for a long time of feudalism of more than two thousand years, the society of China had been built on the economy of small-scale farming; then out of this grew the handicraft workshops. In the early part of feudalism in ancient China, such mode of production developed and with it, the field of science and technology yielded new inventions and discoveries. When it came to the latter part of feudalism, productivity in China continued to develop, but management of individual craftsman workshops gradually changed into that of small workshops with hired labourers. This became the soil for the growth of capitalism.

In Hsü Xia-Ke's time, the districts along the middle reaches and the estuary of the Yangtze River, especially the region of its delta, developed greatly in the capacity of production and with this also grew capitalism. With such social background, the progressive intellectuals of that time naturally paid much attention to the research of natural sciences and technology. Their interest was on the investigation and exploration of Nature and also the summarization and propagation of the techniques of production. Such prominent personalities like Li Shi-Zhen, Sung Ying-Sing and Hsü Xia-Ke were leading representatives of the time. But the reactionary forces and backward influences which supported the feudalistic sovereignty went all out to suppress and shatter this new progress in search of truth. Their tactics were to control the governmental examinations. At that time the means of the Emperor and the bureaucrats to select government officials were to give examinations, the contents and subjects of which emphasised loyalty and fidelity of the persons who took the examinations. Natural sciences were not included in the examinations. All those that

都达到了当时世界上的先进水平。可是从徐霞客的时代以后，中国科学技术的发展，开始落在西方的后面，而且是越落越远。直到现在，向西方先进的科学技术学习，仍然是我们所面临的一项重要任务，这究竟是什么原因呢？

我作为一个历史地理的学生，没有能力来答复这个问题。但是从自然科学发展史的角度来看，在探讨这个问题上，还是有值得注意的地方的。

我们知道自然科学和技术是随着社会生产的发展而发展的。早在公元前3世纪时起，中国就已经进入封建社会，开始建立了中央集权的封建国家，在这里，皇帝的权力高于一切。此后在长达两千多年的封建社会里，小农经济是主要的社会基础，手工业也是在这个基础上发展起来的。在封建社会前期，随着生产的发展，在科学技术的领域里，也不断有新的发明和创造。到了封建社会后期，生产力进一步发展，又从原来个体手工业的经营方式中，开始出现了以雇佣劳动为主的作坊工业。在作坊工业里又逐渐出现了资本主义的萌芽。

到了徐霞客的时代，扬子江中下游一带——特别是三角洲地区，社会生产力有了迅速的发展，资本主义的萌芽日益成长。当时知识界的先进人物，更加注意到自然科学与技术的研究，他们把注意力转向了自然界的探索以及生产技术的总结和传布。上述李时珍、宋应星以及徐霞客都是这方面的代表人物。但是社会上维护封建统治的落后势力，则是他们前进的严重障碍。当时的封建皇帝利用考试制度来选拔知识分子，补充政府的官僚机构，从而为巩固封建统治服务。因此在考试科目中，主要是以测验应考者是否效忠封建王朝为唯一标准，自然科学技术的考试科目是没有的。

worked on scientific studies were considered by society as "Laolies" or manual workers and all manual workers or labourers were looked down upon by "Laohsins" or brainworkers. "Brainworkers are the controllers and manual workers are the controlled." This was the social attitude and public opinion of Hsü's time. Thus, the Chinese society was clearly divided into two categories: those who controlled and those who were controlled. And the Chinese term brainworkers means the social group who knows nothing about the ways of production—all they know is using their ink-brushes to play with words. Thus the few people who devoted their time to the research of sciences were also considered as manual workers. And in the eyes of the brainworkers, they were lower in social status, or the outcasts of society, and among this lowly group were the medical men. And for them to take and pass the exams was undoubtedly out of the question. For instance, Li Shi-Zhen was among those of this group who had taken the exams several times but failed each time. As to Hsü Xia-Ke, he despised this corrupt and unfair system of examinations. Even when he was a young man, he showed his hatred of the corruption of the bureaucracy. He decided to devote his life to outdoor fieldwork and explorations, making torturous journeys against all hardships in order to find out the secret of Nature. Here, we see a man against the society of his time, a rebel who broke away from the bound of old traditions and society and did become a pioneer of the new era.

Yet, in the age of the supremacy of imperialistic feudalism, Hsü Xia-Ke was not to live to do what he had wished. Only three years after his death, there began the worst of the feudalistic dynasties in the history of China, that is, the Ching Dynasty, the difficult time under the oppression of the Manchu minority. The intellectuals of the Han society were under strict control of the government. No words or feeling against the Manchus were allowed. Punishment of death was the penalty for all those who wrote anything against the imperial Manchu sovereignty and his relatives. This was called in the Chinese history as the "Criminal Case of the Words", that is, people were put in jail and put to death because of the words they had written. The condition was so bad that many of the intellectuals were driven to hide themselves or to leave their positions. All they could do was to write abstract essays, of no practical use. The beginning or germination of capitalistic thinking and its influence on ideology, that is, the ideas of reacting against the restrictions of feudalism, the efforts to seek freedom and democracy, the new idea of individuality and self-expression, were suppressed and punished. It was the time of the decline of the world of thought in China. There were no more

而且一切从事科学技术研究的人，都被认为是"劳力"的，也就是体力劳动者，而体力劳动者在封建社会里是受鄙视的。因而自古以来，在中国的封建社会里，就是以"劳心者治人，劳力者治于人"作为社会分工的唯一信条。所谓"劳心"者，指的就是不事生产而只会玩弄笔杆、舞文弄墨的人，连搞科学技术，都被认为是"劳力"，因此在"劳心"者看来，都是"下贱"的，是永远不能通过国家考试的。连为人治病的医生，也得不到社会上应有的重视。李时珍、宋应星都是屡次参加地方上的国家考试而未被录取的人。至于徐霞客，从少年时代起，就鄙视这种国家考试，不屑一顾，对于腐朽没落的封建统治，尤其是深恶痛绝。他决心献身于旅行考察事业，不畏一切艰险去探索大自然的奥秘。从这一点来看，他称得上是一个封建社会的叛逆者，是冲破旧社会的束缚，走向新时代的先驱。

但是，专制主义发展到极端的封建王朝，是绝不容忍这样的时代的先驱者。徐霞客去世后三年，中国历史上由一个少数民族——满族所建立的封建王朝——清朝，统治了中国。汉族知识分子身上，又增加了一副新的枷锁，那就是，任何不满于异族统治者的情绪，一旦见于文字，不仅本人可能要遭杀戮，就是亲属也要受到连累，这就叫做"文字狱"——因文字得罪而被关入的监狱。清朝前期因"文字狱"而惨遭杀害的，在知识分子中大有人在。大批知识分子被迫走向脱离生产、脱离实际的道路。资本主义萌芽及其在意识形态领域里的反映——即孕育着反对封建束缚、努力追求自由民主和个性解放的新思潮，更要受到压制甚至查禁。全国的思想界处于萎靡消沉的状态，在

people like Li Shi-Zhen or Sung Ying-Sing or Hsü Xia-Ke in the field of scientific research for over a century. Nevertheless, in the world of literature, there appeared the book by Cao Xue-Chin called *The Dreams of the Red Chamber*, which reflected and echoed the voice of the time. The writer Cao two hundred years ago used his book as a weapon to attack and expose the corruption of the declining feudalism. From this standpoint we may consider Cao's book as a masterpiece of his time.

In China, the age after feudalism is semi-colonial, semi-feudal. Unlike the West, it was not followed by the age of capitalism. We call it "semi-colonialism" because it was the developed capitalist nations that sent troops to China to break down her "closed door policy" and thus put her under the control of the foreign powers. We call it "semi-feudalism" because China still had feudalistic emperors; the only difference was that these feudalistic big heads could no more give orders and be obeyed by the people like former times. Instead, they must rely on the foreign powers to suppress the rebellious people.

In 1911, Dr. Sun Yat-Sen led a revolution successfully against the Manchus and thus ended the imperial dynasties of feudalism which lasted for more than two thousand years. However, it did not end or smash completely the feudalistic forces and their traditional influences. It was in 1919 that the famous "May 4th Movement" broke out; its slogan was: "Anti-imperialism and Anti-feudalism." To us Chinese historians, it means the beginning of the Revolution of Neo-democracy. It was led by the Chinese Communist Party until its final victory in 1949, the liberation of the Chinese People.

In short, from the Opium War in 1840 when the foreign military forces invaded China to the establishment of the People's Republic of China, for a lengthened time of more than one hundred years, the people of China had lived under the yokes of both imperialism and feudalism. They were in most miserable condition, unable to earn their barest living. In such condition, scientist research and technical development were out of the question. The result was the backwardness of China in science and technology.

The birth of New China means the beginning of the age of her socialist reconstruction, which lasts until now for already thirty years. There have been tremendous changes since then through the efforts of her people in the spirit of self-reliance. Nevertheless, because of the backwardness of our science and technology and the weakness of our social foundation,

科学技术领域里，再没有出现像李时珍、宋应星和徐霞客那样的卓越人物。文学艺术毕竟还是反映了时代的最强音的，从这个意义上来说，二百多年前伟大作家曹雪芹的《红楼梦》这部小说，在深入揭露处于崩溃中的腐朽没落的封建社会这一点来说，确实是具有划时代意义的杰作。

但是在中国，真正结束了这个封建社会而相继出现的，和西方的历史进程不一样，不是资本主义社会，而是半殖民地半封建社会。说是"半殖民地"，因为是来自西方已经发达了的资本主义国家的军队打开了中国"闭关自守"的门户，把古老的中国，置于它的强权控制之下；说是"半封建"，因为封建统治者（皇帝）依然存在，只是不能像过去那样独裁一切，发号施令，反而必须借助于外来的势力，以压迫中国人民。

1911 年以孙中山博士为首的革命运动，虽然推翻了统治中国长达两千多年的封建王朝，但是却没有像西方历史上法国大革命那样彻底摧毁封建势力。因此，到了 1919 年，又爆发了有名的"五四运动"，明确提出了反对帝国主义和反对封建主义的双重目标。这也就是在我国所说的新民主主义革命的开始。这场革命在中国共产党的领导下一直继续到 1949 年解放战争的胜利。

总之，从 1840 年鸦片战争中西方武装力量入侵中国，一直到 1949 年中华人民共和国的成立，这一百多年间，中国人民在帝国主义和封建主义的双重压迫下，陷入了极其悲惨的境地，求生存都很困难，科学文化的落后就更不必说了。

新中国诞生之后，开始了社会主义建设的新阶段，到现在已经过了三十个年头了。在这三十年的时间里，经过了全国人民的艰苦奋斗，在自力更生的前提下，国家已经发生了史无前例的变化。但是由于基础薄弱，科学技术落后，我们还是个贫穷的、尚

China is still a poor and developing country, especially after the so-called Cultural Revolution during which we experienced the worst possible damage and interruption, not only in production, but also in practically every field. And it is through the ten years of political turmoil that we begin to realize how the left-over poisonous effects of feudalism and their social influences interfere with our socialist construction, for instance, "The Homologized Court" (that is, everything must be decided by the only one top officer as final); "Tenure System" (that is, once you become the head of a government office, you will always and for the rest time of your life stay as the head of that office); "Personality Cult"; "Isolationist Policy and Self-praising"; "Bureaucracy"; "the social influences and tradition of individual production"; etc. Indeed, these bad points can also be found in capitalist society. However, in China, the destructive effects of such rubbish are much more serious.

Now in New China one of our most important tasks is to restore the spirit of these scientists and scholars, and in geography to rekindle the spirit and method of Hsü Xia-Ke. We have gotten over the bitter experience of the Cultural Revolution. We have brought about greater stability. With the desire to build China into a modern socialist country, we begin the New Long March. But when we raise our heads and look around at the world and the neighbouring countries, we find that their achievements in science and technology have progressed far front before us. We must break away from the former condition of isolation, and learn from our foreign friends their advanced science and technology, so that we can expedite our modernization. Of course, we will still maintain our principle of self-reliance. And by self-reliance we mean that we must also try our very best to discover new value from our ancient civilization. That is to say, we should not simply take everything for granted from the West without any investigations or analyses. Undoubtedly, we shall absorb and utilize everything that is beneficial to our country. But more important is the effort of us to discover the rich hereditary endowments in our history and culture, and to transform them for the use of the modernization of China.

Three hundred and forty years ago, Hsü Xia-Ke had opened up a new way in the seeking of secrets of Nature. Owing to the feudalistic reactionary forces and influences, he had no successor or follower. And now, we the modern Chinese students are determined to sweep

在发展中的国家，特别是经过"文化大革命"前后十年的大动乱，不仅在生产上遭到了极大的破坏，在其他各方面也都受到了极大的摧残。如果说"文化大革命"除去破坏之外还给我们带来了什么值得重视的东西的话，那就是它使我们进一步认识到：残存的封建遗毒还在阻碍着我们在建设社会主义的道路上迅速前进。例如"一言堂"、"终身制"、"个人崇拜"、"固步自封"、"官僚主义"、"小生产的习惯势力"等等，这些弊病有的在资本主义社会里也有，但是在我们这里就显得格外突出。

现在我们在吸取了"文化大革命"的惨痛教训之后，重新收拾残破局面，举国上下团结起来，决心在"新长征"的道路上，奋发前进。但是在现代科学技术突飞猛进的形势下，我们发现自己已经远远落后于西方国家，因此我们必须打破过去那种与世隔绝的局面，向西方学习先进的科学技术，以及先进的管理方法，来促进我们自己的"现代化"的建设。更重要的是我们还必须继续坚持"自力更生"的原则。在中文里"自力更生"这个词，也包括着使自己古老的文明获得新生的意思。有人说"现代化"是不能用金钱买来的，也就说不是能够简单地从外国搬运过来的。我们一方面要吸收西方一切先进的东西，为我所用。我们更需要从自己宝贵的历史文化遗产中汲取精华，发扬光大。

如果说三百四十年前徐霞客在探索自然界的奥秘中所开创的新道路，由于封建势力的阻挠而后继无人，那么今天，在我们坚决扫荡封建遗毒，在现代化的道路上奋发前

away all the rubbish of feudalism, in order to build our New Culture and Civilization. It is because of this determination that I am sure a new age of Renaissance in China will be at hand. We look forward anxiously to its coming, and I am sure that our Western friends will also welcome its appearance.

I thank you.

进的时候，我们一定会创造出自己的新文化，正是在这个意义上，我想，一个中国式的"文艺复兴"的新时代，应该到来了吧！我这样殷切地期待着，我相信我们可尊敬的西方朋友们也会是这样期待着的。

谢谢！

北京大学地理系
一九八〇年九月

❼ THE ANCIENT GREAT WALL IN A NEW ERA*

About one century after the fall of Alexander's empire which extended from Macedonia eastward as far as the Indus River, a great empire began to emerge in the central part of China. It was the Empire of Qin.

The founder of this Qin Empire who came to the throne in 221 B.C., claimed to be the first emperor of China or, in Chinese, Shi Huangdi. It is from the word Qin that the empire was known to the West as China.[1] However, before the Qin Empire China had already had a long period of historical development. The real contribution of Qin Shi Huang is that he was the first ruler in China who created a political system of centralized government by ending the power of the contending feudal states. This marks the beginning of the history of imperial dynasties with absolute power in the hands of a monarch, which lasted for more than 2,000 years until 1911 A.D.

Besides his political achievement, Qin Shi Huang left two material legacies for the present day. One is his tomb with the famous clay army discovered recently. The other is the Great Wall.

Walls were built in China as military fortifications long before Qin Shi Huang's time, but the building of the Great Wall was attributed to Qin Shi Huang. He was the first emperor who mobilized thousands of peasants to connect the walls constructed by three former feudal states along their northern boundaries. In addition, he built new sections both at the east and the west ends. Eventually a great long wall of thousands of miles came into existence; hence the name *Wanli Changcheng* which means a long wall of ten thousand *li*, or simply the Great Wall. Since then the Great Wall was repaired and rebuilt again and again but not entirely along the same line. The last and most well preserved one was built during the Ming Dynasty (1368-1644). Its length is estimated at 12,000 *li*, or 6,000 kilometers with its east end actually making a sheer descent into the Bohai Gulf, symbolizing the dragon's head dipping into the water. Its west end reaches as far as the north edge of the Tibetan-Qinghai Plateau where the famous pass Jia Yu Guan was situated on the ancient Silk Road. The most majestic parts of this Ming Great Wall north of Beijing have become the best vantage points where modern visitors enjoy a spectacular glimpse of this massive but ingenious engineering achievement made by the sheer hands of man.

I do not intend to give you a full picture of the construction of the Great Wall, which is far beyond my ability. There are quite a number of books in the West devoted to the study of the Great Wall. The most comprehensive and readable English language work is probably that by a

柒 新时代的万里长城*

亚历山大大帝从马其顿一直往东绵延到印度河的帝国倾颓后的大约一个世纪，在中国的中原地区开始崛起了一个伟大的帝国。这就是秦帝国。

秦王朝的创始人于公元前221年登基，成为中国第一个皇帝，史称"始皇帝"。正是因为"秦"这个字，这个帝国在西方以China著称。[1]然而，在秦以前中国已经有了悠久的发展历史。秦始皇的真正贡献在于，他是中国历史上第一个结束纷争的封建诸侯国分庭抗礼、建立中央集权的政治制度的统治者。从此开启了国君独掌大权的王朝更迭史，这绵延了两千余年，一直到公元1911年。

除了他在政治上的作为，秦始皇还给后人留下了两件物质遗产，一件是最近发现的埋葬了兵马俑的陵墓，另一件就是长城。

在中国，早在秦始皇之前，就有作为军事工事的防御墙修建，但长城的兴建确是因为秦始皇。作为帝王，他是第一个征用成千上万的农民，将之前三个诸侯国沿北部边界修筑的防御墙连接起来的。此外，他还在东西两端修筑了新墙，最终建成了一条绵延万里的长城，万里长城由此得名，简称长城。此后，长城不断得到修缮和重建，但并不是完全沿原址所建。最新并且保存最完好的长城是明朝（1368—1644）修建的，全长约为12000里（6000公里），东端一头扎进渤海湾，喻示龙头入水，西端直抵青藏高原北缘古丝绸之路上的著名关口嘉峪关。如今，北京城北明长城最雄伟的部分已成为一个绝佳的景点，游人们可以在这里饱览这座人类用双手建成的浩大而精巧的工程。

我无意涵盖长城的整个修建过程，这也远非我力所能及。西方已经有不少专门研究长城的书籍。其中最全面也最易读的英文著作或许就

colleague, Luo Zhewen and his collaborators, Dick Wilson, Jean-Pierre Drege and Hubert Delahaye.

There is one point I would like to emphasize here. This is the tragic human aspect of the construction of the Great Wall in old China. This tragic nature is fully illustrated by the legend of the girl, Meng Jiang, who lived in the reign of Emperor Qin Shi Huang. Her husband, together with thousands of other peasants, was conscripted to build the wall but few came home healthy or even alive. Meng Jiang, being very anxious to see her husband, trudged hundreds of *li* northward to the foot of the Great Wall, only to find white skeletons piled at the foot of the wall. Her wailing and lamentations shook the heavens, and the newly built wall crumbled.[2] The legend of Meng Jiang comes down via one of the classical works of ancient China. There may have been no real Meng Jiang. However, there were indeed thousands of young women having the same fate as Meng Jiang. She has touched deeply the hearts of later generations with her pure and sincere love. Even more important, the symbolism of Meng Jiang's spirit of opposition against persecution has always inspired people under oppression.

As we look back in Chinese history, there has been no need for a long time to rebuild the Great Wall to protect the central part of China. Now, with the birth of New China, under the guidance of the socialist principle that the different nationalities both within and beyond the Great Wall together with those in other parts of China are united as one big family, the old dream of "all men are brothers" has begun to be realized. As the Chinese proverb goes, the march of history has "turned arms into silk and gold". It has likewise changed the former battlefield along the Great Wall into the good earth of the new epoch.

The Great Wall itself, constructed with the sweat and blood, toil and effort of innumerable peasants, has been transformed into a monument symbolizing the renaissance of an ancient civilization. Due to this transformation, in recent years the work of restoring and repairing the

Great Wall at key points has been started with the enthusiastic support and generous contributions of many Chinese people as well as friends in foreign lands.

At the same time, through recent research, some important features of the Great Wall have been revealed for the first time by using modern techniques of infrared light and remote-sensing.[3] For instance, the real length of the Great Wall within the administrative boundary of the Beijing Municipal Government is 629 kilometers, which is far longer than what had been previously known. Furthermore, the wall itself is by no

是我的同事罗哲文与迪克·威尔逊、戴仁、德罗绘合著的《长城》。

有一点我想在这里强调一下。这就是，古代中国修建长城有其悲剧的一面。这通过生活在秦始皇统治下的孟姜女的传说得到了充分的体现。孟姜女的丈夫和数以千计的其他农民一道被征召去修长城，但最后健康甚至活着回家的微乎其微。孟姜女因为急于见到丈夫，向北跋涉了几百里来到长城脚下，结果在那里却只看到累累白骨。她悲恸欲绝，哭声震天，新修的长城也因此倒塌。[2]孟姜女的传说通过古代中国的一部经典著作流传下来。也许历史上并没有真正的孟姜女，但是有成千上万跟孟姜女同样命运的年轻女子。她纯真的爱情深深触动了后人的心。更为重要的是，孟姜女反抗压迫的精神一直鼓舞着后来受压迫的人民。

当我们回首中国历史，有很长一段时期并没有重修长城以保卫中原地区的需要。现在伴随着新中国的诞生，在长城内外的各族同胞和中国各地的其他民族团结一家亲的社会主义原则指导下，"四海之内皆兄弟"的古老梦想已经开始实现。正如中国一句老话说的，历史的行进已经"化干戈为玉帛"，同样也把过去长城两边的战场变成了新时代的沃土。

长城是数不清的劳动人民的血汗辛劳筑成的，它已变成了象征古老文明复兴的标志。由于这一转变，近年来在一些重要地段的修缮工作得到了广大同胞以及外国友人的热烈支持和慷慨贡献。

与此同时，最近的研究借助红外线和遥感等现代技术，首次发现了长城的一些重要特征。[3]例如，长城在北京市行政辖区内的实际长度是629公里，远远超过之前的估计。此外，长城本身绝不是一

means a single but rather a complex defensive system following various topographical features, dotted with different kinds of terraces, fortresses, passes and observation towers. Wherever it was necessary for a garrison, a detour wall was added to the main body. The intricacy of the design has never before been mentioned in any records or discussion. Now a full and accurate picture, essential for the purpose of historical presentation, is revealed to us. Besides the Ming Wall, the ruined foundations of some earlier walls have also been discovered. We hope it will be possible to extend the same kind of study to the whole line of Ming Great Wall.

With the growing interest in the Great Wall, an association has been organized in Beijing to sponsor research and promote education about the Great Wall. Members of this association include those who have made substantial contributions either to the study or the preservation of the Great Wall. The most active members, of course, are the sponsors of this organization. Most of them are prominent figures in public affairs. Honorary memberships will also be offered to foreign friends who meet the same requirement for the Chinese members.

Furthermore, for the sake of the increasing number of visitors at Ba Daling, the spot nearest to Beijing where one can get the best view of the Great Wall, a museum is under construction. By means of essential exhibitions and visual aids visitors, especially those who come from abroad, will be able to get a full picture of the history and a better understanding of this great wonder of the world.

In each age, a country, a society, responds to the conditions prevailing in that period. Ancient society in the central part of China, from before the Qin through the Ming Dynasty, responded to the pressing need for secure defence by building this fortification. Now it is no longer needed. Today China is responding to the modern challenge by honoring and preserving its history, symbolized by the Great Wall, when it is steadily going forward to build a new society for the future.

个单一的，而是结合地形特征的复杂系统，有墙台、敌楼、券门和瞭望塔布设其间。只要驻军有需要，主体墙上还会加筑迂回墙。设计的精妙之前从未被记载或谈及。现在，一个完整而精确的画面终于展现在我们面前，这对于重现历史非常必要。除明长城之外，更古老的长城基址残迹也被发现了。我们希望把同样的研究扩展到明长城全线。

随着对长城兴趣的与日俱增，北京成立了一个支持长城研究、促进长城相关教育的协会。协会的成员包括对长城的研究或保护作出过巨大贡献的同志。最活跃的当然是协会的赞助人，他们大部分是参与公共事务的杰出人物。达到同样入会要求的外国友人也可以成为荣誉会员。

同时，由于游客数量的激增，距离北京最近的长城景点八达岭正在兴建一座博物馆。通过必要的展览和视觉辅助，游客，尤其是来自外国的游客，将能全面地把握它的历史，更好地了解这一世界奇迹。

每个时代，国家和社会都回应着当时的情势。中国中原地区的古代社会，从先秦一直到明朝，都因安全防御的迫切需求修建这一防御工事。如今，已经没有这种需要了。今天的中国正通过尊重和保护以长城为象征的历史，来回应现代的挑战，稳步向前建设一个面向未来的新社会。

邵冬冬　译

8 ANCIENT CITY RUINS IN THE DESERTS OF THE INNER MONGOLIA AUTONOMOUS REGION OF CHINA*

During the first century B.C. the Chinese built cities along the Hexi Corridor to protect the ancient Silk Road from raids by Huns. A Hun ruler reciprocated by founding his own city and later Chinese dynasties repeated the process. Urban populations were fed by cultivating oases and by harnessing melt-water streams to irrigate and reclaim areas of grassland. Where trees fell and cultivation broke surface layers of alluvium and clay, water and wind began to erode and expose underlying beds of sand. Blowing sand encroached upon the cultivated area and eventually drifted across the ruins of former cities. Sites of cities that once housed tens of thousands of people are now being explored scientifically. Research into the recurrent history of desertification throws light on present-day problems faced by one-sixth of the world's population living in arid regions and by one-third of the earth's land surface covered by deserts. By learning from past events we may be able to halt future advances of deserts.

The scenes of my lecture are extremely dreary places, age-old ruins buried, or partly buried, by blown sand for centuries. Nevertheless, these long-forgotten ancient cities have a prosperous past behind them: some have enjoyed great fame in history; others have been visited by travellers of world renown. Now, in today's New China, my young colleagues and I have penetrated into the deserts to investigate these ruins of ancient cities, not to indulge in nostalgic contemplations of the past, nor to revel in the vanished splendours of bygone days. We look back on the past for one purpose only: to make out why such a region that once flourished in history should have turned into a desert. To clarify this point is a matter of great moment. It is for the purpose of creating a better future that we endeavour to understand the past.[1]

Building Cities on the Silk Road

Let us first of all look back on the prosperous stage of this area and start from the world-famous epoch of the Silk Road. As is well known, the historic Silk Road was a most important trade route which spanned the hinterlands of Asia. Its main line started at the east end, from Chang-an, the greatest political centre of ancient China and predecessor of the

捌 内蒙古自治区西部沙漠中几个重要的古城废墟*

主席先生，

女士们、先生们：

在我访问英属哥伦比亚大学这个著名学府的同时，又很荣幸地有此机会为温哥华学会这个富有学术特色和国际联系的团体，介绍一点我个人和我的青年同伴在我国内蒙古自治区西部荒凉的沙漠中徘徊探索的片断见闻，这对我来说是一种不平常的际遇，是我当初进入沙漠时绝对没有想到过的。我只是担心不要把沙漠中那种荒凉的气氛，带到你们这个十分活跃而且丰富多彩的学会生活中来。

今天我所要讲的，在今天看来确实是一些很荒凉的地方，是多少世纪以来已被流沙湮没的古城废墟。但是，这些地方也有自己繁荣的过去。那些已被人遗忘了的古城，有的也曾在历史上享有盛名，有的还曾为举世闻名的旅行家访问过。现在，在新中国，我和我的青年同伴深入沙漠去考察这些地方——这些古城废墟，不是为了单纯地凭吊过去，更不是为了要陶醉在过去的、已经消失了的荣华之中。我们回顾过去，我们试图弄清楚为什么在历史上繁荣一时的地方，而今竟然沦为沙漠。弄清楚这一点是大有意义的。了解过去，正是为了创造未来。[1] 这就是这个新时代所赋予我们的使命。

一

为此，还是让我们先回顾一下过去的繁荣时代吧。这样，我就得从享有国际声誉的"丝绸之路"讲起。众所周知，历史上有名的丝绸之路，是古代横贯亚洲腹地的重要商道。它的主要路线，东起当时中国最大的政治中心长安——也就是现在西安的前身，向西北

present Xi-an, and passed in a northwesterly direction through the Gansu (or Hexi) Corridor where it forked into two routes at Dunhuang, the ancient city which is well known to the world for the art treasures in its caves. These two routes stretched along the southern and northern borders of the Taklamakan Desert in the south part of China's Xinjiang Uygur Autonomous Region. They joined together again at the present Meru in Turkmen Soviet Socialist Republic. Then a single road went on westward to the shores of the Mediterranean Sea where finally it reached the dominions of Rome.

The part of the Silk Road in China was first opened up during the reign of Emperor Wu in the Han Dynasty (140-87 B.C.) when Chang-an was made the capital. Besides being the political centre of the Han Dynasty, Chang-an was also the greatest economic and cultural centre. The Silk Road, with Chang-an as its starting point, was subject to attacks by the Huns from the Mongolian Plateau in the north, at the narrow strip of the Gansu Corridor which was about 1,000 kilometres in length and varying from 10 to 100 kilometres in width. This narrow belt was called the Gansu Corridor because it was situated in Gansu Province; it was also called the Hexi Corridor because it was situated in the westernmost upper reaches of the Yellow River (Fig. 8-1).[2] It ran along the northern foot of the Qilian Mountains at an average elevation of 1,500 metres. The highlands of Qilian were on the northeastern border of the high Tibetan Plateau, the so-called "roof of the world" with an elevation of 4,000 metres in the eastern part, gradually rising to 5,000 metres and more in the west. The mountain tops were covered with snow all the year round and when snow melted, small patches of oases were formed at the foot of the mountains; and it was through these oases that the Silk Road was directed. To the north lay the boundless Gobi and the desert. The narrow belt through which the Silk Road passed ran between the mountains and the desert, hence the name "corridor".

This corridor formed part of the arid area in west China, receiving an average annual rainfall below 100 millimetres in most places and lower than 50 millimetres in its western part. Fortunately, patches of oases scattered here and there were richly endowed with water and grass. The area was then occupied by Huns, a nomadic tribe in the north, who still

通过"甘肃走廊"，从敦煌这个今天以洞窟中人类所创造的世间罕见的艺术宝藏而闻名于世的古城，分为两路，分别沿着我国境内新疆南部塔克拉玛干大沙漠的南北边缘，越过帕米尔高原，在苏联土库曼境内相会，然后继续西行，直到地中海沿岸，最后到达当时的罗马各地。

按时间上来说，在公元前第二世纪以后的一千多年间，大量的中国丝和丝织品，经由此路西运，因此叫做"丝绸之路"。其他商品以及东西方的经济文化交流，也多是通过这条道路。它在历史上促进了欧亚非各国和中国的友好往来，因此也可以说是一条和平友好的道路。

在中国境内，最初打开这条道路，是在汉武帝时期（公元前140—前87年）。汉朝建都长安。长安除去作为汉王朝的政治中心之外，它还是当时全国最大的经济中心和文化中心。以长安为起点的丝绸之路，在穿过甘肃走廊的这一条东西长达1000公里，南北宽自10公里到100公里的狭长地带，最容易受到来自北方蒙古高原上的匈奴人的攻击。这一条狭长地带，叫做"甘肃走廊"，因为它在甘肃省境内，也叫"河西走廊"，因为它在黄河上游之西（图8-1）。[2] 这条地带正当祁连山地的北麓，平均海拔1500米。祁连山地，实际上也就是号称"世界屋顶"的西藏大高原的东北边缘，其东部海拔约4000米，向西升高到5000米以上。山上终年积雪，冰雪溶化之后，沿北边山麓地带形成片片绿洲，丝绸之路就是沿着山麓的这些绿洲开辟起来的。从此山麓地区再往北去，尽是一望无际的戈壁与沙漠。丝绸之路所经过的这一条狭长地带，介于高山与沙漠之间，是唯一便于东西来往的通道，所以叫做"走廊"。

这条走廊上的平均年雨量，大部分都在100mm以下，西部则减少到50mm以下，全部属于干旱区。幸而有片片绿洲散布其间。绿洲上水草丰美，在丝绸之路未曾开辟以前，这里为北方的游牧民

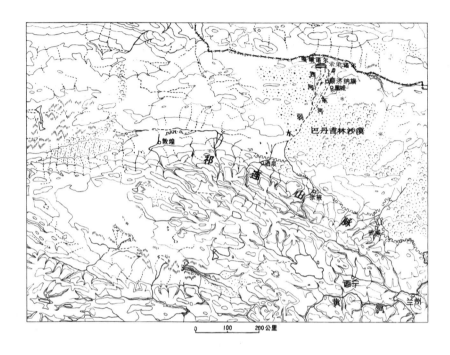

8-1 The physical features of the Hexi Corridor 河西走廊地形略图

Qilian Mountains 祁连山脉	Sogo Nor 索果诺尔	Gaxun Nor 嘎顺诺尔	Ruo-shui 弱水
Ejin Banner 额济纳旗	Black City 黑城	Yellow River 黄河	Dunhuang 敦煌

remained in an uncivilized state and presented a serious threat to the Han Dynasty.

During the reign of Emperor Wu in the Han Dynasty, China, being a powerful country with a flourishing agriculture, industry and commerce as well as increased revenues, was anxious to carry on trade with the world outside. In the decade after 129 B.C. she repeatedly dispatched troops on punitive expeditions against the Huns who fled to the north of the desert. As a result, the Han Dynasty took possession of vast tracts of land in the Hexi Corridor and opened up a trade route leading from Chang-an right to central Asia and Europe, thus bringing an era of prosperity to the Silk Road.

All the while, the Huns who had retreated to the north of the desert were still watching for an opportunity to return south. It was very easy for them to thrust into the middle of the corridor and cut off the Silk Road, for in the central part of the corridor the melted water running down from the north slope of the Qilian Mountains converged into a huge river called the Ruo-shui, now also bearing the name Ejin, which, rising approximately from 40°N latitude, flows north by east and crosses the space between the desert and the Gobi over a span of about 300 kilometres, and finally empties itself by two different channels into Lake Sogo Nor and Lake Gaxun Nor where the elevation drops to 820 metres or so. Thenceforward, the terrain gradually rises again towards the north.

This is the present pattern of surface drainage, but it was not so more than 2,000 years ago when water in the lower reaches of the Ruo-shui emptied itself into a vast lake called Ju-yan situated further to the southeast

族匈奴人所占有。当时匈奴族还处在野蛮时期，全部人口除老弱妇孺外都是战士，习惯于掠夺战争，对汉王朝构成了严重的威胁。

汉武帝时，国力强盛，农业和工商业发展，统治阶级财富增加，也渴望与外部世界通商贸易。从公元前 129 年以后的十年间，屡次出兵征伐匈奴，匈奴远走漠北，汉王朝占有了河西走廊的广大地带，从而打开了从首都长安直通中亚与欧洲的商道，这就是"丝绸之路"上繁荣时代的开始。

但是退走漠北的匈奴，还是经常伺机南下，很容易插入走廊的中部，把丝绸之路从中切断。因为在走廊的中部地区汇集了自祁连山北坡下注的雪水，流成了一条大河叫做弱水，现在也叫额济纳河。这条河流大约从北纬 40° 的地方起，沿着正北偏东的方向，穿过近 300 公里的戈壁与沙漠之间，分道注入索果诺尔与嘎顺诺尔两个湖泊之中，这里的海拔高度已下降到 820 米左右。再往北去，地形又逐渐升高。

以上所叙，是现在的情况，但在两千多年前却不是这样。那时弱水下游注入一个叫做"居延泽"的大湖，其位置还在上述两个湖

of the above-mentioned lakes (Fig. 8-2). The climate at that time was also arid enough, but the Ruo-shui River, running by different channels before it emptied itself into the lake, moistened the land along the way and formed a delta area abounding in water and grass, with dense and luxuriant groves of Euphrates poplars covering its banks. On the way southward, the Huns found it very convenient to assemble at the delta before pushing forward along the Ruo-shui. It provided them with a most ideal route to cross the Gobi and the desert which stretched over hundreds of kilometres from east to west, but it exposed the Silk Road to an extremely serious threat.

To protect the Silk Road, the Han Dynasty had to enclose the banks of the Ruo-shui and the delta of Ju-yan Lake within their military defence line. By stationing garrison troops in the delta, they opened up an important area for reclamation and developed agricultural irrigation. At that time, the Ruo-shui settlement area was mainly composed of the middle and lower parts of the delta and in the year 102 B.C. the famous Ju-yan City was built at the centre of the area. But if you go there today, you will see that everything has changed. What meets your eyes is a vast stretch of sand dunes. With the help of a local guide we were able

的东南方（图 8-2）。这里的气候虽也十分干燥，但是在弱水入湖之前，河道分流，土地湿润，从而形成了一片水草茂密的三角洲，河边上胡杨成林，十分繁茂。匈奴人从漠北南来，最便于集结在这个三角洲上，然后沿弱水长驱直下，这是东西数百公里之间穿越戈壁与沙漠的最理想的通道，因此也就构成了对丝绸之路的最大威胁。

汉王朝为了保卫丝绸之路，不得不把弱水两岸和居延泽上的三角洲，包入军事路线之内，并在三角洲上进行军屯，开辟了一个重要的农垦区，发展了灌溉农业。

当时的垦区，主要在三角洲的中、下部，并于公元前 102 年在这一垦区的中心，建筑了有名的居延城。

可是现在来到这里，一切都变了。沙丘连绵，一望无际。一年半以前，

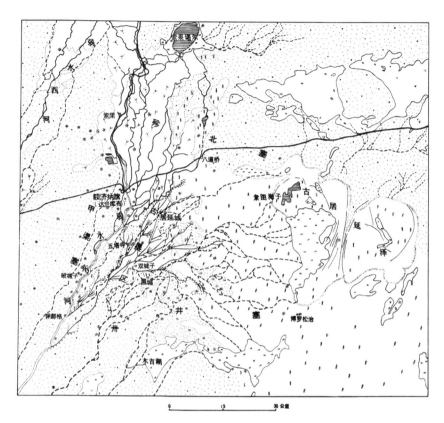

8-2 The ancient delta of the Ruo-shui 弱水下游古代三角洲图

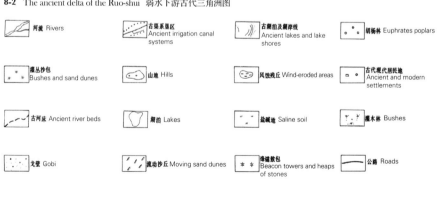

河流 Rivers	古渠系区 Ancient irrigation canal systems	古湖泊及湖岸线 Ancient lakes and lake shores	胡杨林 Euphrates poplars
灌丛沙包 Bushes and sand dunes	山地 Hills	风蚀残丘 Wind-eroded areas	古代现代居民地 Ancient and modern settlements
古河床 Ancient river beds	湖泊 Lakes	盐碱地 Saline soil	灌木林 Bushes
戈壁 Gobi	流动沙丘 Moving sand dunes	峰燧墩包 Beacon towers and heaps of stones	公路 Roads

Sogo Nor 索果诺尔   Ancient Ju-yan lake 古居延泽   Ruo-shui 弱水
Ju-Yan City 居延诚   Ejin Banner 额济纳旗

to penetrate into this area five and a half years ago. We saw nothing but ruins of castles, beacon towers, houses, abandoned fields and irrigation ditches, broken earthenware, wells choked with sand, slightly worn millstones, antique coins, arrowheads and many other artefacts. The ancient Ju-yan Lake had shrunk to a small lake. Amidst the deep sand to the south-west of this little lake, we found the ruins of an ancient city bordering dried up river beds both on the east and south sides. Inside the ruined city walls, the surface was scattered with Chinese tamarisks and sand-sage. Judging from the ruins, we conjectured that it was a city of considerable size and tentatively inferred that it was the site of the city of Ju-yan.

The city of Ju-yan, associated with an irrigated agriculture that flourished in the Han Dynasty, is now yielding a harvest of an entirely different kind. During the last few decades, excavation has brought to light great quantities of historical relics, which are called by archaeologists "the Ju-yan slips of the Han Dynasty". The Han slips discovered here were not made of bamboo as in south China but of wood, on which were recorded documents and archives referring to the Ju-yan area during the Han Dynasty. They were strung together with cords and meant for preservation. More than 30,000 Han slips excavated in this area have been given the name "Ju-yan". Still more are being dug out to add to the growing collection of historical data, rich and detailed in content. It is no exaggeration to call it a bountiful harvest.

Ruins of another ancient city lie some 15 kilometres south by west of the ruins which we have inferred to be the site of the city of Ju-yan. This is the famous Black City, much frequented and more than once excavated by native and foreign investigators. Way back in 1934 when I was a young college student, I read an article in the February issue of the same year's British magazine *The Listener*, written by the distinguished Swedish geographer and explorer Sven Hedin, entitled "The 'Black City' of the Gobi Desert". It immediately attracted my youthful interest, but it was not until

50 years later that I was lucky enough to have a chance to visit the scene and see for myself the ruins of the ancient city. Although quite close to Ju-yan, the Black City, completed in 1035 A.D., was constructed much later than the former. Some 950 years ago, it was a local administrative centre, with the attribute "Black Mountain" preceding the name of the administrative

我们靠了当地的向导，才得深入这一地区。我们所看到的是汉代城堡、烽燧的残迹、居民点的遗址、废弃的田块和渠道，还有房屋的残基、破碎的陶片、被沙填满了的水井、完整的石磨，以及古代的钱币、箭头等等。古居延泽已枯缩成一个小湖了。在小湖西南方的深沙之中，我们找到了一座古城，它的东、南两面都濒临干枯的河床，残破的城墙内部，到处都是柽柳、沙蒿。从残存的遗迹来看，它的规模是相当大的，我们初步推断，这应是居延城的遗址。

如果说居延城的名字在汉代是与繁荣一时的灌溉农业联系在一起的，而现在它却与另外一种完全不同性质的"丰收"联系在一起，这就是近几十年来考古学上所谓"居延汉简"的大量出土。这里的汉简不是写在竹片上而是写在薄木片上的关于汉代居延地区的文书、档案等，木片用绳索穿连着，是有意识地保存起来的，因此是非常可贵的史料，记事的内容也十分丰富。现在从这一地区发掘出来的汉简，统以"居延"为名，已有三万多枚，而且还在陆续出土，说它是考古学上的"丰收"，并不为过。

在我们所推断的居延城故址以南偏西大约十五公里处，有另外一座古城废墟，这是不止一次为中外考察者所访问和发掘过的地方，这就是有名的黑城。

1934 年当我还在大学读书的时候，我以一个偶然的机会，在同年 2 月号英国的《听众》杂志上，读到了瑞典著名地理学者和探险家斯文·赫定的一篇文章，题目是《戈壁滩上的黑城》，引起了我青年时代的极大兴趣。可是经过了整整 45 年，我才有机会来到现场，看看我久已向往的这座古城废墟。

黑城虽然至居延不远，但是它的建筑年代却要晚得多。它建成于公元 1035 年，至今 945 年，是个地方行政中心，但是在这个政区名称的前面，又冠以"黑山"两个字。后来又叫黑城，可能是从黑山演变

division. Later it was shortened to Black City; in the Mongolian language it is called Chara Choto, which bears the same meaning.

This area and the environs of the Hexi Corridor were under the rule of a local regime established by a national minority, known in Chinese history as the West Xia (1038-1227). The West Xia Dynasty was exterminated by the Mongols in 1227, the year when their illustrious chieftain Genghis Khan breathed his last. It was not until Kublai Khan, Genghis Khan's grandson, had unified China and established the Yuan Dynasty that the Black City resumed its position as administrative centre of the region, with a new name Yijinai. The Venetian traveller Marco Polo passed through here in 1272, and by a roundabout route through the Mongolian Plateau, he reached first the city of Shangdu, built by Kublai Khan and later the city of Dadu, predecessor of the present Beijing. Yijinai is now written in Chinese characters as 额济纳 (Ejin), whereas in *Marco Polo's Travels* it is Etsina. Marco Polo stated that he had to acquire stocks of food for forty days there before continuing his journey, which shows that the neighbourhood of the Black City was still an agricultural area at that time.

To reach the Black City today, one has to cross a desolate and unpopulated desert, only a little easier than to approach the ancient city of Ju-yan. The walls of the Black City still stand lofty and magnificent in the desert today. They look as if they were square, but actually the south wall is 425 metres long, 15 metres longer than the north wall; and the east wall is 405 metres long, 48 metres longer than the west wall. On the city walls, we saw stones that had been used as projectiles in ancient times, still piled there as if the garrison had been preparing for a defensive battle. The strange thing is that historically the city was actually taken after a fierce battle. But the stones have remained undisturbed on the city walls ever since, suggesting that the city may have been abandoned as soon as the battle was over. That decisive battle took place in the late 1360s when the emergent Ming Dynasty, having captured Dadu and exterminated the Yuan Dynasty, dispatched a contingent of troops to take the Black City in their advance westward. They stormed into the city and reduced its buildings to ashes. When the expedition was finished, not only was the Black City abandoned, but the middle and lower reaches of the Ruo-shui River were separated from the Hexi Corridor by the newly-built Great Wall. The Ming Dynasty concentrated the energy exclusively on developing the Corridor. The ancient Ju-yan area, protected by an earlier Great Wall, was now given up as "beyond the frontier" and no further effort was spent on its development.

而来的。蒙古语叫做 Chara Choto，也就是黑城的意思。当时统治这一地区和河西走廊一带的，是一个少数民族所建立的地方政权，这就是中国历史上的西夏王朝（1038—1227）。

公元 1227 年，西夏为蒙古族所灭。率领蒙古骑兵西征中亚和东欧的著名首领成吉思汗，也就是在这一年去世的。

到了成吉思汗的孙子忽必烈统一了中国并建立了元朝的时候，这个大城又继续成为这一地区的行政管理中心，只是改名叫做亦集乃城。1272年威尼斯的旅行家马可·波罗正是从这里经过，绕道蒙古高原，先到忽必烈初建的上都城，然后再到大都城的。大都城也就是现在北京城的前身。

"亦集乃"现在汉字写作"额济纳"，在马可·波罗的《游记》中，则写作 Etsina。马可·波罗在他的《游记》中还提到要在亦集乃城准备好 40天的粮食，才能继续前进。这就说明在当时，黑城这一带地方仍然是一个农业区。

现在去黑城，也要穿过荒无人烟的沙漠，只是比进入居延古城要容易一些。现在黑城的城墙依然高大、壮观。看似正方形，实际上南墙长 425米，比北墙长出 15 米；东墙长 405 米，比西墙长出 48 米。在城墙上，我们看到还有在古代作为炮弹用的石块，堆积在那里，好像是为了守城的战斗作好了准备的样子。奇怪的是，黑城确实是在一场激烈的战斗中被攻下了，而堆积在城墙上的石头炮弹，却一直未被清理。这大约是在这次战役之后，城市就被放弃了。这次战役发生在 14 世纪 60 年代末，当时新兴的明王朝，在出兵攻下大都城和灭亡了元朝之后，又继续西征，分兵一支打进了黑城，城内建筑全部为战火所毁。从此以后，不仅是这座城市被放弃了，就是整个弱水的中下游，也都被隔离在明朝新建的长城以外。明朝的统治者只是集中力量开发河西走廊，古居延地区原是包在汉代长城之内的，这时则被看作是"塞外"，再也没有去经营了。

From our investigations, we are of the opinion that the area reclaimed during the Han Dynasty, with the city of Ju-yan at its core, consisted mainly of the middle and lower parts of the ancient Ruo-shui delta. Reclamation by the West Xia and Yuan dynasties, with the Black City at its core, shifted to the upper middle part of the same delta. Certain places were reclaimed on the basis of work done in the Han period; in fact, the Black City itself may have been built upon the ruins of a Han castle. From the Han Dynasty down to the West Xia and Yuan dynasties, the southward shift of the reclamation area was directly related to the drying up of waterways in the delta area. This, however, is a subject undergoing further investigation.

Land Reclamation and Desertification

The ancient Ju-yan area is an outstanding example of desertification occurring in historic times, but many other places in west Inner Mongolia Autonomous Region have suffered a similar fate. During the early years of the Han Dynasty when the Ju-yan area was first reclaimed, another area of importance was also being reclaimed on the south prairie west of the Yin Mountains. Although the average annual rainfall here was higher than in the ancient Ju-yan area, it nevertheless turned into a desert in the end. This area is situated in the north of the present Ulanbuhe Desert. In Mongolian, "ulan" means "red" and "buhe" means "bull", the whole phrase signifying that the scourge of the wind and sand is like an unruly bull. The north part of the Ulanbuhe Desert was originally an alluvial plain formed by the Yellow River, flowing in ancient times north along the west side of the Ordos Plateau, heading straight for the foot of the Yin Mountains (Fig. 8-3). There it turned east and formed the first abrupt turn at the Bend of the Yellow River. As early as the late Pleistocene epoch, the river bed had begun to move eastward long before reaching the Bend. This movement still continues gradually to the present day. During the process of eastward turning, water from the Yellow River frequently overflowed into a lake occupying the deserted old river bed, and occasionally flooded surrounding low-lying country. More than 2,000 years ago, when the Han Dynasty first began to open up this area, a long narrow lake ran from east to west at the foot of the Yin Mountains. It was called Tusheng Lake. During the Han Dynasty land was reclaimed on the alluvial plain to the south of this lake. People were moved here to settle on the land and

经过考察，我们认为以居延城为中心的汉代垦区，主要在古代弱水三角洲的中下部。以黑城为中心的西夏和元朝的垦区，则已移至这同一三角洲的中上部，其间也有部分地区是在汉代开垦的基础上，继续开发起来的。黑城本身也可能就是在一处汉代城堡的遗址上建筑起来的。从汉朝到西夏和元朝，前后垦区自北而南的迁移，和三角洲上水道的变迁直接有关，这是还在继续深入研究的问题，这里就不多谈了。

二

古居延地区是历史时期沙漠化的一个十分明显的例子，这种沙漠化的情况，在内蒙古自治区西部干旱地区的其他地方，也曾出现过。

在汉朝初年开辟居延地区的时候，在阴山西端以南的草原上，也有一个重要的农垦区被开垦起来。这里的平均年雨量，虽然多于古居延地区，但仍然不免变为沙漠，这就是现在叫做乌兰布和沙漠的北部地区。蒙语"乌兰"是红色、"布和"是公牛，全名的含义是说这里风沙为害之烈，有如难驯的红色公牛。

乌兰布和沙漠北部这一带地方，原是黄河的冲积平原。古代的黄河沿着鄂尔多斯高原西侧、从南向北流，直趋阴山之麓（图8-3），然后转而东流，形成了黄河之套的第一个直转弯。从晚更新世以来，这段河道在未转弯之前，就开始向东移动，这种趋势至今还在缓慢地进行中。

在河道东移的过程中，因为河水有时漫溢，就在被遗弃的旧河床及其附近低洼处，积水成湖。两千多年前，当汉王朝最初开辟这一带地方的时候，靠近阴山之麓，还曾有一个东西狭长的大湖，叫做屠申泽。汉代的农垦区就是在这个大湖以南的冲积平原上开辟出来的。

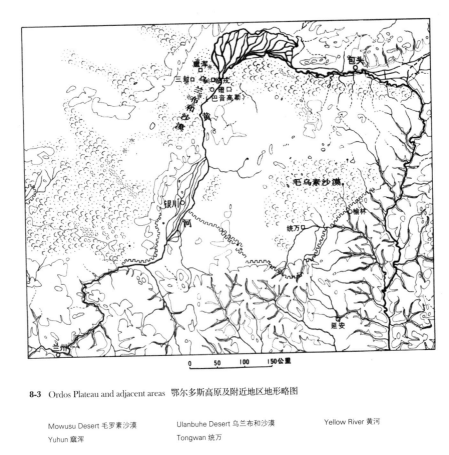

8-3 Ordos Plateau and adjacent areas 鄂尔多斯高原及附近地区地形略图

Mowusu Desert 毛罗素沙漠   Ulanbuhe Desert 乌兰布和沙漠   Yellow River 黄河

Yuhun 窳浑   Tongwan 统万

military fortresses were established to defend the new settlements against invasion and plunder by Huns from the north. During this period, hordes of settlers moved from the hinterlands to the banks of the Yellow River near the southern edge of the Yin Mountains, including the northern part of the present Ulanbuhe Desert and the Ordos Plateau. In 127 B.C. alone no fewer than 100,000 people moved here. The western part of the Yin Mountains and the plains south of Tusheng Lake were particularly important as areas for new settlements. A broad and smooth mountain path to the north-west of Tusheng Lake passed through the gorge of the Yin Mountains and afforded an important pass leading to Hun territory beyond the mountains. To defend the southern entrance to this pass, a small stone fort was built on the steep slope to its west. This fort, the renowned Cock and Deer Fort, has been preserved to this day.

Close to the south-west shore of Tusheng Lake, some 20 kilometres to the south-east of the Cock and Deer Fort, a large city called Yuhun was the city westernmost on the frontier built by the Han Dynasty in this area (Fig. 8-4). It was a place of strategic importance commanding the gorge of the fort, but it was soon reduced to ruins. Remains of city walls are still discernible and sites of blacksmiths' workshops in the city may be identified by fragments of scrap iron, bronze arrowheads and heaps of debris scattered all over the place. Some local shepherds we met told us that there was a huge pit filled with skeletons outside the city, marking the site of an ancient battlefield. Ruins of two other Han cities have been discovered. The first lies some 20 kilometres to the south and the other some 30 kilometres to the south-east of Yuhun. The former was called Sanfeng and the latter Linrong. The space between these two and Yuhun is dotted with groups of Han graves as well as ruins of hamlets and fields, discernible even to

　　汉王朝在这里移民开垦，并建立军事要塞，也是为了防御从北方来的匈奴人的侵扰和劫掠，以保护黄河中上游一带的农业居民。当时傍阴山南麓的黄河两岸、包括现在的乌兰布和沙漠北部和鄂尔多斯高原的北部，曾有大批移民从内地迁来。例如，公元前 127 年一次移民，即达十万人。在这一新的移民区中，阴山西端、屠申泽以南的平原地带，特别重要。因为在屠申泽的西北，有一条穿越阴山的谷道，宽阔平坦，是通往山后匈奴地区的重要孔道。为了守卫这条孔道的南口，就在山口西侧的峭壁般的阶地上，修建了一座小石城。这座小石城还一直保留到今天，这就是古代有名的鸡鹿塞。

　　在鸡鹿塞东南约 20 公里处，傍近屠申泽的西南岸，有一座大城，名叫窳浑城，这是汉王朝在这一地区所建立的最西头的一座县城（图 8-4），是控制鸡鹿塞谷道的军事重镇，现在也已经沦为沙漠中的废墟，但是残存的城墙，还明显可见。城内有大片冶铁遗址，到处可以拣到废铁块、铜箭头，无数的残砖断瓦散布地上。偶然遇到的当地牧民说，这座城外有一处大坑，堆满了尸骨，这是古战场的重要标志。

　　约在窳浑城以南 20 公里和东南 30 公里处，还各有一座汉城废墟。三城之间，有成群的汉墓，散布其间，还有村落、田块的遗址，至今

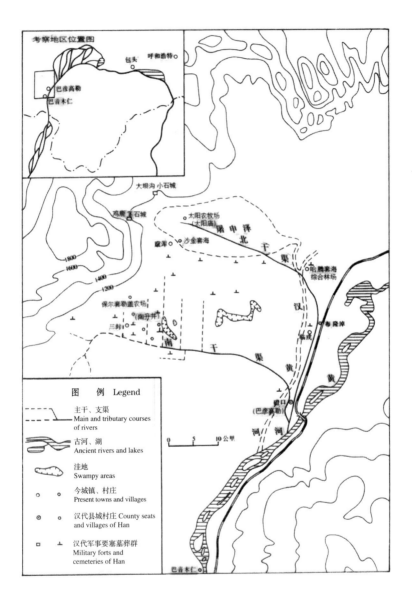

8-4 Sites of ancient cities in the northern Ulanbuhe Desert 乌兰布和沙漠北部汉代遗址与水系分布示意图

Yellow River 黄河   Course of Yellow River in Han 汉黄河   Tusheng Lake 屠申泽

this day. As a result of peaceful co-existence between the Han Dynasty and the Huns, the last 50 years B.C. enjoyed an unprecedented spell of quiet and stability. During this period reclamation extended from the neighbourhoods of the three cities to the southern edge of the Yin Mountains. Historical records indicate that population increased, cows and horses flocked in the fields and that cities which had been securely guarded in the past now shut their gates at a very late hour. It really became a scene of prosperity and abundance.

What does it look like now? The Mongolian term "Ulanbuhe" aptly describes the present state of this area, a region devastated by moving sand. The process started long before modern times. In 981 A.D. a traveller named Wang Yan-de crossed the Yellow River at the Ordos Plateau, passed through here and journeyed westward to the Ju-yan area. He took detailed notes of living conditions in this district, recording: "No food crops ever grew here, except a kind of grass called Denshiang, the seeds of which are gathered for food". According to our investigation, Denshiang is what we now call *shami* (sand seeds or *agriophyllum arenarium*), a kind of pioneering plant growing on sand dunes, the first that

明显可见。在公元前的最后半个多世纪，由于汉王朝与匈奴统治者和平相处的结果，阴山南麓的农垦区，包括上述三城在内的地带，出现了前所未有的和平安定生活，史书描写说这一带人口繁盛，田野里牛马成群，过去防卫森严的城市，现在连城门也都关得很晚了。真是一幅繁饶富庶的景象。

可是现在又是什么情况呢？

"乌兰布和"这一蒙语的意思，说明了这里流沙为害的现状。而这种情况，并不是近代开始的。公元981年，也就是整整一千年前，有一位旅行者叫王延德的，从鄂尔多斯高原渡过黄河，经过这里，西行到居延地区。他详细记录了这一带的情况，说这里已是"沙深三尺，马不能行，皆乘橐驼。"又说沿途"不育五谷，沙中生草曰登相，收之以食。"按登相现在叫做"沙米"，是生长在流动沙丘上的先锋植物，也就是流动沙丘上首先生长的植物。当时能

ever grew on them. The fact that sand seeds could be gathered for food shows that they grew in abundance and yielded large quantities of seeds. It may be inferred that a thousand years ago, this area was still in the early stages of blown sand encroachment and has been entirely desertified in the course of the present millennium.

Near the city of Yuhun, we saw wind-eroded pits of varying sizes, huge pits formed by intense wind erosion. In a natural section at the edge of a wind-eroded pit, we could identify clearly that a horizontally-deposited layer of clay, 70 millimetres thick, had under it nothing but fine sand. It is easy to see that when the surface layer was broken, the fine sand underneath was liable to be blown away by fierce north-west winds. This is the chief source of blown sand in this area. The thickness of the surface layer of clay we saw here varied from place to place, thicker in some places, thinner in others. It was not very difficult to reclaim land where the clay was thick, but where it was thin, if the primeval vegetation was removed and the surface exposed to wind erosion, the place was likely to turn into a sandy tract of its own accord. This is exactly what history has taught us.

The Settlement and Abandonment of Tongwan

Finally, please allow me to touch upon another ancient city in the desert. It is the biggest among the relict sites of ancient cities in the desert of western Inner Mongolia and the most remarkable in architectural engineering I have seen so far. It was built in 413 A.D. as the capital of a short-lived minor Hun kingdom, but its builder, Helianbobo, gave it the extremely pretentious name Tongwan, which means "ruling over all nations". It must be pointed out that the year when the city of Tongwan was founded corresponds to the third year after the West Goths captured Rome and was nearly half a century before Anglo-Saxons entered Britain. It was recorded in history that Helianbobo conscripted 100,000 men to construct this enormous city and that in the operation, thousands of artisans were killed for failing to achieve the desired solidity. Up to the present, this great city, though long abandoned, has preserved a 24-metre high watch-tower standing aloft amidst the rolling sand dunes, reflecting dazzling rays in a scorching sun. It was situated in the south of the Ordos Plateau, close to the north bank of a river called the Red Willow River

采集沙米籽粒为食，说明沙米生长繁茂，结实量大。可以推想一千年前，这一带地方还是流沙初期的阶段，近一千年来，这里已全部沙漠化了。

这里的流沙是从哪里来的呢？

在窳浑城的附近，我们看到了一些大小不等的风蚀坑——由于强烈的风蚀而形成的大坑。在一个风蚀坑的边缘所显示的天然剖面上，可以明显地看到表面是70mm厚的一层水平沉积的黏土层，下面掩埋的则全是细沙。可见表土层被打破之后，细沙就很容易被强烈的西北风吹扬起来，这就是这一地区流沙的主要来源。这里所看到的地表黏土层的厚度，随地而异，有的地方厚，有的地方薄。厚的地方进行开垦，问题不大。薄的地方，如果原始的植被遭受破坏，并继续暴露在强烈的风蚀之下，那就很容易导致就地起沙。历史的教训就是这样。

三

最后，请允许我再讲一个沙漠中的古城。在我所见到的内蒙古西部沙漠中的古城废墟中，这是最大的一个，也是在筑城工程上最值得注意的一个，这是公元413年所修建的一个匈奴族为时短暂的小王朝的都城，但是它的创建者赫连勃勃却为它起了一个大得极不相称的名字，叫做"统万"，意思就是"统治万邦"。

应该指出，统万城创建的这一年，刚刚在西哥特人攻陷罗马城后的第三年（攻陷罗马城在410年），还在盎格鲁撒克逊人进入不列颠以前不到半个世纪。史书记载说，当时赫连勃勃征调了十万人来修建这座大城。在筑城过程中，由于工程没有达到所要求的坚固程度，就有数以千计的工匠被杀死。至今这座大城虽然已久无人居，但还保留有24米高的敌楼，耸立在滚滚流沙中，在强烈的日照下，放射出耀眼的白色光芒。它的位置在鄂尔多斯高原的南部，靠近一条叫做红柳河的

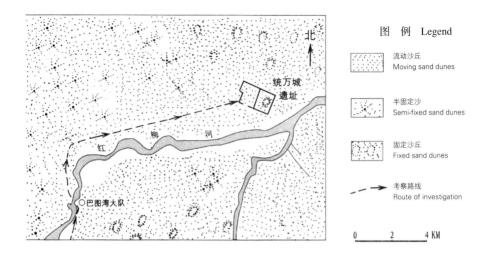

8-5 The site of the ancient city of Tongwan 统万城城址位置图

(Hangliu River) which crossed the south-eastern corner of the Mowusu Desert, carrying vast amounts of sand and clay with it, turning the water turbid. Consequently, it was called the Salawusu River in Mongolian, meaning "yellow water" (Fig. 8-5). The Salawusu River is important in Chinese archaeology because an important late Paleolithic site was discovered here. The people who lived here some 50,000 years ago were called "men of the River Bend", because the site was near the Bend of the Yellow River.

Although deeply buried in the desert, the city of Tongwan has been investigated before, but earlier investigations have been satisfied either with mere descriptions of the ruins or with reporting the discovery of relics. No one appears to have been interested in pursuing inquiries into the relationship between the development of the city and changes in the local environment. In the first instance, was this place a desert when Helianbobo chose the site? How could he have built his capital in a desert? If it was not a desert at the time, when did it turn into one? Where has all that rolling sand come from? As historical geographers, my young colleagues and I visited the historically renowned city of Tongwan with the aim of solving these problems. The visit has left deep impressions on my mind.

It was a summer morning in 1983, the sun had not yet shown its full might. The weather was fine, the sky clear and cloudless. We set out on foot with excitement from our encampment by the Red Willow River towards the city of Tongwan which lay 10 kilometres away. What a splendid tri-coloured picture presented itself to our eyes! Overhead was a spacious, blue sky, arching over the rolling sand which looked like turbulent waves of a vast sea. Suddenly, in the distance between the blue sky and the yellow sand emerged something which looked like an enormous white sail on an ancient seagoing vessel.

北岸。红柳河穿过毛乌素沙漠的东南一角，携带了大量的泥沙，水色浑浊，因此蒙语叫它做"萨拉乌素河"，也就是"黄水"的意思（图8-5）。

萨拉乌素河在中国的考古学上是很有名的，因为沿河上游有重要的旧石器时代晚期的遗址在这里被发现，当时住在这里的人被称为"河套人"，至今大约已有五万年。叫他做"河套人"，因为这里也是属于黄河之套以内的地方。

统万城虽然已深陷沙漠之中，但是也早已被人所考察过。奇怪的是过去的考察者只是满足于对古城足迹的描述或古物的发现，都从来没有人把它和周围环境的变迁联系起来进行探讨。比如说：当赫连勃勃在这里建城的时候，这里是沙漠么？他怎样能在沙漠中建立他的都城呢？如果当时这里不是沙漠，那么从什么时候起开始变成了沙漠呢？这些滚滚流沙又是从哪里来的呢？

作为一个历史地理工作者，我和几位年青的同行，正是带着这些问题，访问了这座历史上赫赫有名的统万城的。这次访问，给我留下了十分深刻的印象。

那是夏季的一个早晨，太阳的威力还没有充分显示出来。天晴气朗，万里无云。我们怀着十分兴奋的心情，从红柳河边的驻地出发，步行向着十公里外的统万城前进。举目所见，那是多么壮观的一幅三色的画面呀！蔚蓝如洗的天空，笼罩在有如大海的波浪那样翻滚着的黄沙上。突然间，我们看到了像古代海船上巨大的白帆一样的东西，

"Look, the White City!" someone cried out. The White City was the name given to Tongwan by shepherds in the neighbourhood. It is a more appropriate name than the latter, because its lofty walls actually shine with dazzling white rays in the sun. On the instant of seeing it, I was affected with an unforgettable poetic sensation, feeling as if I were facing a huge landscape painting. But what is of greater significance is the clear and unequivocal thread it supplies to our investigation of changes in the environment in this area. If it were not for the tall ancient city towering there, people would be inclined to believe that it had been an unpopulated desert from time immemorial. But no, that is not the case. The city of Tongwan was certainly not built in a desert in the beginning. This place was not a desert, but a vast prairie, richly endowed with water and grass.

In the days of Helianbobo, China was in a state of chaos, rent into separate little kingdoms by many contending forces. Besides the Jin Dynasty established by the Han nationality, fifteen minor kingdoms had been set up by national minorities, rising to power one after another. Helianbobo rose on the Ordos Plateau and founded a small kingdom called Xia, occupying the whole plateau and surrounding grasslands. He once stormed into Chang-an. His courtiers advised him to make it his capital, but he insisted on returning to the Ordos Plateau and personally chose a site to build his future capital, Tongwan. It was recorded in a chronicle that when the construction of the city was about to begin, he appeared on the scene himself and mounting a high spot nearby, looked about him and declared with pride: "Among the innumerable places I have seen between the north of the Horse Mountain and the south of the Yellow River, there is no country like this, which is surrounded by vast stretches of grassland and a limpid river." Here, "north of the Horse Mountain" refers to an area on the loess plateau north of the present Liupan Mountain, "south of the Yellow River" refers to an area at the southern edge of the Yin Mountains, "the limpid river" refers to today's Red Willow River, noted for its turbid waters, and "vast stretches of grassland" refer to the present Mowusu Desert.

Unlike the delta area where the ancient city of Ju-yan stood and the alluvial plain near the city of Yuhun, both arid regions receiving very little rainfall, the city of Tongwan enjoyed quite good natural conditions, with an average annual rainfall of nearly 400 millimetres and plentiful

出现在远方的蓝天黄沙之间，"看！白城子！"有人叫起来了。"白城子"就是附近的牧民给统万城起的名字，它比统万城一名更富于写实的意义，因为它那巍峨的城墙在阳光照耀下，确实是发出了耀眼的白光的。

在这初见的一刹那间，我所感受到的那种诗情画意，是永难忘怀的。但更重要的是白城子在探讨这一地区的环境变迁上所提供的确切无疑的线索。如果眼前不是有这样一座巍峨的古城屹立在那里，人们还会认为这一带地方自古以来就是荒无人烟的沙漠呢。

不，不是这样。

统万城最初绝不是建筑在沙漠里的。

这里原来不是沙漠，而是一片水草丰美的大草原。

赫连勃勃的时代，中国的政局，四分五裂，在汉族建立的晋王朝外，还有十五个少数民族建立的小王朝，先后崛起。赫连勃勃兴起于鄂尔多斯的草原上，他所建立的小王朝叫做"夏"，占有整个鄂尔多斯高原及其外围一些地方。他曾领兵打进长安城，当时他的部下劝他建都长安，他却坚持回兵鄂尔多斯，亲自选择了统万城的城址。史书有明文记载说，在建城之前，他曾亲自来到现场，登上附近一处高地，一面瞭望，一面赞叹说："这里草滩广大，河流清澈，我跑过很多地方了，从马岑以北，黄河以南，没有一处地方，比得上这里那么好！"他所说的"马岑以北"指的是现在黄土高原上的六盘山以北，"黄河以南"指的是现在阴山南麓的黄河以南。清澈的河流就是现在以浑浊著称的红柳河，广大的草滩就是现在的毛乌素沙漠。

这里的自然条件本来是不错的，和前面所讲的古居延城所在的三角洲和窳浑城附近的冲积平原不同，那里都是干旱区，降水量都很少，而统万城所在的地方，年平均降水量近400mm，地方上水源

water sources. Why, then, has it also turned into a desert? The city of Tongwan was the largest among the sites of ancient ruined cities partly buried in the sand of the Ordos Plateau. Around it are many other sand-buried ruins of smaller castles and hamlets. It is note-worthy that these relics of ancient settlement were distributed in the desert in such a way that they seemed to move from the north-west towards the south-east in accordance with a progressive sequence through time. For example, the ruins of the Han Dynasty, 2,000 years ago, extended to the furthest limit of the north-western frontier. Moving backward a little to the south-east, are ruins mostly of the Tang and Song dynasties, hundreds of or even a thousand years later than the Han Dynasty. Ruins from the Ming and Qing dynasties of the last 300 to 400 years, are distributed mostly along the innermost south-eastern border of the desert area. This distinctive pattern of distribution is not only closely related to the growth and decline of the power of the Chinese dynasties but also is directly connected with the chronological order of desertification in these areas: the inevitable consequence of unreasonable utilization of land, caused primarily by the reclamation of places unfit for agriculture and secondly by excessive firewood cutting and pasturing. Details of that process await further examination and study.

In short, the Ordos Plateau is one of the most remarkable examples of desertification in Chinese history. The main reason for its desertification lies not in changes of climate or other natural elements but in the activities of man. The area of such "desertified land" accounts for only 9.2% of the total area of deserts in north China, which occupies 1,095,000 square kilometres or 11.4% of the total area of China's territory. The percentage is small, but the cause of desertification is highly significant.

Now in the world, especially in developing countries, desertification remains a serious problem. Deserts and desertified land occupy one-third of the earth's surface and nearly one-sixth of the world's population live in such areas. For this reason, ways of preventing and curing desertification, as important measures of environmental protection, have become questions of world-wide and outstanding interest in the sphere of desert studies today.

丰沛，为什么也会变成了沙漠呢？

统万城是毛乌素沙漠中所淹没的若干古城废墟中最大的一个，此外还有许多较小的城堡和村庄的遗址，也都已被沙淹，值得注意的是这些古代人类活动的遗迹，在沙区内的分布，自西北而东南，有着一定的时代先后的顺序性，例如两千年前汉代的遗址，向西北地区伸展得最远。稍向东南来，则多是比汉代晚了数百年或是上千年的唐、宋时代的遗址。至于近三、四百年明清时代的遗址，大都分布在沙区的东南边缘一带。这一分布的特点，除与中原王朝势力的消长有密切关系外，同时也与沙漠化时期的早晚直接有关。而这一地区的沙漠化，又是不合理的土地利用的必然结果。所谓不合理的土地利用，主要指的是在不宜于农耕的地方进行开垦，其次是过分的樵采和放牧。其具体过程，也有待于更深入的调查和研究。

总之，鄂尔多斯高原是我国历史上沙漠化的发展最显著的地区之一，导致沙漠化的主要原因，是人类本身的活动，而不是气候或其他自然因素的变化。新中国建立以后不久我们注意到这一问题，1963 年后才开始从历史地理的角度上进行有计划的考察。可是 1966 年以后十年间的混乱，中断了这项考察工作的进行。一年半以前，才有可能重新开展这项考察研究工作。我相信，在实现我国社会主义现代化的过程中，这项工作是不可缺少的。

在你们伟大而美丽的国土上，既没有沙漠，也没有遇到沙漠化的问题。但是今天在世界上，特别是在发展中的国家里，沙漠化仍然是个严重的问题。沙漠和沙漠化的土地，占去了地球上陆地面积的 1/3，全世界近 1/6 的人口，生活在这种地方，因此防治沙漠化这一项重要的环境保护的问题，已成为当前国际上关于沙漠研究的一个突出的课题。

Some of the circumstances concerning desertification which developing countries are confronting at present, have repeatedly occurred in our history. To sum up this process scientifically is a task, we may say, of definite relevance to our present and future welfare. In our opinion, it is a task all historical geographers should participate in. I believe the historical geographers of my country will strive to make contributions to this cause which calls for international cooperation.

第 29 届联合国大会通过的 3337 号决议要求采取国家间的联合行动，来同沙漠化进行斗争。贵国的学者，有人在这方面已经作了大量的工作，是值得我们钦佩的。

　　现在一些发展中国家所遇到的沙漠化的问题，有些情况在我国历史上曾经不止一次地出现过。对这一历史的过程，进行科学的总结，在今天应该说是有一定的参考价值的。我们认为这项研究，也是历史地理工作者所应该积极参加的。我相信，我国的历史地理工作者也将会努力工作，为国际的合作，作出自己应有的贡献。

　　谢谢大家耐心地听我的发言，现在我准备答复大家所提出的问题，虽然我不一定都能作出令人满意的答复。

1. Interaction Between the Cultures of East and West and the Trend of the Times

When I came as a first-year freshman to Yenching University, it was the autumn of 1932. At that time almost ten years had passed since construction along a set lay-out had started of the university campus, and it was almost reaching completion.

On the campus the scenery everywhere was very beautiful, overflowing with an ever thriving vitality. This first impression the university had on me when I just arrived, has never left me. Therefore, I will now write down from memory how the very construction of the campus has influenced me. I will discuss this from the following aspects:

1) The campus with its beautiful scenery and classical Chinese architecture.

2) The probe into the campus' history and research on traditional culture.

The recently constructed Yenching University had chosen the north-western outskirts of Peking as its campus location, an area famous historically for its gardens. The main gate faced west, facing in the distance Xishan, the West Mountains. Inside the main gate one crossed a large marble bridge spanning a pool clear as a mirror, and reached the teaching centre. Large buildings in classical Chinese architectural style stood on three sides, with in the centre a wide space with luscious green grass. From the teaching centre one drifted into the campus' hinterland with its winding hills and dense foliage. The main road rose and fell unobstructed by anything ahead, only small footpaths joining it. But suddenly, after going through a section of hills, the ripples of a vast lake stretched out in front, exceeding all one's expectations. The glint of the water had the colour of the sky, the field of vision was open and wide: it was the magnificent Lake Without a Name. A small island adorned the centre of the lake, adding to the boundless view. The buildings of the men's dormitories were lined up one by one on the northern shore of the lake. Tucked away behind hills and a dense forest on the southern shore of the lake was the women's dormitories, in the traditional courtyard style. From the first day of entering the university I was captured by the natural scenery of the campus. I came to know only afterwards that here used to be a famous garden called Shuchun Yuan, the "Garden of the Fair Spring",

玖 我从燕京大学来*

一、中西文化交流与时代趋向

我作为一年级新生进入燕京大学，是在 1932 年的秋天。那时大学校园按着预定的规划设计，经历了前后十年时间，已经基本建设完成。整个校园里，风景佳丽，光彩焕发，洋溢着蓬勃向上的朝气。这是我初入学时的第一个印象，至今难忘。因此在这里先追记一下这座校园建设的本身所给我的影响。先从以下两个方面说起：

1. 风景如画的校园与中国古典式的建筑。

2. 校园历史的探索与传统文化的研究。

新建成的燕京大学校园，选址在北京城的西北近郊，是历史上有名的园林区。校门西向，遥对西山。校门以内，跨过一个波平如镜的池塘上的一座大石桥，就进入了教学中心。中国古典建筑形式的大楼，三面环列，中间场地开阔，绿草如茵。从教学中心深入校园腹地，岗阜逶迤，林木丛茂。大路起伏，畅通无阻。羊肠曲径，经过其间。出人意料的是穿过这一区岗阜，突然展现在眼前的是一片微波荡漾的湖泊，水光天色，视野开阔，这就是享有盛誉的未名湖。湖中有小岛，点缀其间，平添无限景色。男生的宿舍大楼，一座又一座，并列在湖泊的北岸。深在湖泊南岸岗阜密林之后的则是传统庭院式的女生宿舍。从入学的第一天起，我就为这座校园的自然风光所吸引，只是后来我才了解到，这里原是两百多年前与清朝皇室有密切关系的一座名园，叫做淑春园。园中河流湖泊的上游，

closely connected to the Qing imperial court two hundred years ago. The streams filling the rivers and lakes of the garden came from the adjoining Shaoyuan, a famous garden three hundred years ago in the Ming Dynasty already renowned for its streams. When Yenching University opened up its campus in 1921 however, the structures of these two historic gardens had already disappeared without a trace. Yenching University used exactly the spot of these two famous gardens, and after adopting special designs and using the conditions of the natural environment to the full, a very special university campus was built. Even more important, however, was that for the buildings on the campus classical Chinese architectural forms were used, creating an even closer harmony between historical traditions and modern needs.

Furthermore, it has to be pointed out that the principal lay-out of the campus was carried out under the guidance of the American architect Henry K. Murphy, which proved it was in fact a new creation completed under the influence of the cultural exchange between East and West, representing the trend of the times rather well.[1]

At the Yenching University campus there were several other equally picturesque buildings, like a small bell pavilion on a hill under a pine tree, the "Overlooking the Water Cottage" (Linhu Xuan) on the lakeside, the small "Contemplating Merit Pavilion" (Siyi Ting) on the lake's island, and the "Broad Elegant Pagoda" (Boya Ta) towering over the shore, structures which were all rather spectacular. The expression "glimmering lake reflecting pagoda" became the famed proverbial portrayal of the campus' scenery. The Boya Pagoda and the Siyi Pavilion are well worth talking about in more detail.

The name of the Boya Pagoda had much to do with the American professor at that time at the Philosophy Department of Yenching University, Bo Chenguang or Lucius C. Porter. He was influenced deeply by traditional Chinese culture and had been working at the Peking office of the Harvard-Yenching Institute. More importantly, his elders had done a great deal to develop Tongzhou Union University, one of the predecessors to Yenching University. When Yenching University started constructing a water-pagoda to add to the streams inside the campus, in order to commemorate these historical origins, the shape of the famous pagoda of Tongzhou, the Randeng Pagoda ("Sparkling Lamp Pagoda") was adopted, and the name Boya Pagoda was chosen. "BO" refers to the first character in Porter's Chinese name, and "YA" implicates an "elegant scholar". In English the pagoda is simply called "Porter's Pagoda".

来自紧相毗连的勺园。而勺园早在三百多年前的明朝，就已经是一座以水取胜的名园了。可是到了 1921 年燕京大学在这里开始建校的时候，这两处历史名园的建筑，都已荡然无存。燕京大学正是在这两处名园的旧址上，经过独出心裁的规划设计，充分利用其自然条件，建造起一座独具特色的大学校园。还有更重要的一点，即这座校园的建筑物，一律采用了中国古典的建筑形式，这更是历史传统与现代化要求的相互结合。

还须指出，校园的规划设计，乃是在美国建筑师 Henry K. Murphy 的主持下进行的，实际上这也正是在中西文化交流的影响下所完成的足以代表时代趋向的一种新创造。[1]

需要补充说明的是在燕京大学校园里，还有一些类似景点的建筑物，如小山上古松下的钟亭、俯视水面的临湖轩、湖中小岛上的思义亭和湖边上凌空而立的博雅塔，都是十分引人注目的，而"湖光塔影"更成为校园风景中颇负盛名的写照。在这里特别值得一提的是博雅塔和思义亭。

博雅塔的命名和当时燕京大学哲学系的美籍教授博晨光有密切关系。他深受中国传统文化的影响，曾兼任哈佛燕京学社在北平办事处的工作。更重要的是他的前辈曾为燕京大学前身之一的通州协和大学的发展作出过贡献。为了纪念这一历史渊源，燕京大学为供给校园内自来水而建成的水塔，就采取了通州有名的古建筑"燃灯塔"的造型而兴建起来，并且取名博雅塔。"博"字是 Porter 一字第一声的音译，"雅"字有"儒雅学者"的含义。英文就直接叫做 Porter's Pagoda 了。

The name of the Siyi Pavilion has an even more commemorative meaning than the Boya Pagoda's. The "SI" in the name is a diminutive form of "Luce", while "YI" has the meaning of "a magnanimous act undertaken for the public good". In English it is called "Luce Pavilion". It is in commemoration of Henry W. Luce, the first vice-president of Yenching University, who did so much to raise funds to set up Yenching University.[2]

I feel very privileged in arriving at Yenching in the period it had just been completed and being captured by the beauty of its surroundings; I was even more inspired by Professor William Hung's research at that time on the campus' history, which even influenced the direction of my later research.

In the very first beginning, when I had only just enrolled in the university, Professor William Hung's main work on the research of Shaoyuan, "On the Painting and Records of Shaoyuan", had been published smartly by the Yinde Compilation Office of Yenching University Press (the foreword was written on 29 October, 1932). The photo reprint in this book of the hand-drawn "Friends Gathering at Shaoyuan" by the prominent calligrapher Mi Wanzhong, the owner of the garden, drawn in the 45th year of Wanli of the Ming Dynasty (1617 A.D.), makes the scene of three hundred years ago appear vividly before one's eyes. It is said that when Yenching University was established, Professor William Hung had learned from archives that this scroll was still around somewhere, and after painstaking searches he was finally able to purchase it for the Yenching University Library. After the publication of the photo reprint, Professor Hung obtained a poetry text from the late Ming concerning Mi Wanzhong and a description of the lay-out of Shaoyuan, which enabled him furthermore to verify the ancient site of Shaoyuan and its geographical position. At the end of the scroll was added a map of the rivers, lakes and other waterways of the campus and its surroundings, which was extremely valid for reference. Also included was a record stating that the English envoy Lord George Macartney stayed temporarily at the ancient site of Shaoyuan when coming to the Qing court during the reign of the Qianlong emperor.

Thereafter, Hung wrote in English about his research on the Shuchun Yuan, in which he covered important historical circumstances of most of the places inside the Yenching University campus. Furthermore, he gave his special report in English at the "university lecture", which was very well received by both teachers and students.[3]

比起博雅塔更有纪念意义的是思义亭。在这里"思"字是 Luce 一字简化的音译,"义"字有"义举"的含义。英文名称就是 Luce Pavilion。这是为了纪念燕京大学第一任副校长路思义为燕京大学的筹款兴建所作出的贡献。[2]

我深感幸运的不仅是燕京大学校园新落成时就来到了这里而深受其幽美环境的感染,更重要的是当时洪煨莲教授对于校园历史的研究,又使我深受启发,一直影响到我日后的研究方向。

最初,还是在我入学不久的时候,洪煨莲教授关于勺园研究的重要著作《勺园图录考》由燕京大学引得编纂处精印出版(序文写于 1932 年 10 月 29 日)。这部书影印了明万历四十五年(1617)勺园主人、著名书法家米万钟手绘的《勺园修禊图》,使三百多年前校园一隅的景象重现于眼前。按早在燕京大学建校之初,洪煨莲教授从记载中获悉这幅画卷尚流传在人间,遂刻意访求,终为燕京大学图书馆所购得。煨莲师在影印之后,又进一步收录了晚明以来有关米万钟家世以及描述勺园景物的诗文记载,并且进行了勺园故址及其地理位置的考证。卷末还附有校园以及附近地区河湖水系的略图,极有参考价值。其中也包括了清朝乾隆年间英国使臣马戛尔尼勋爵来朝时暂住勺园故址的记述。随后,他又用英文写成了关于淑春园的研究,涉及燕京大学校园中大部分地方的重要历史情况,而且他还用英文在"大学讲演"中做了专题报告,深得师生欢迎。[3]

This historical research by Professor Hung led me to start an actual investigation in the area of the historically famous gardens in the western suburbs of Peking, then extending it to the research of the development of the whole Peking area.

When teaching students in class, Professor Hung was original and demanding, which made me benefit even more from his wisdom. For example, when I was only a second-year student, I attended his class about "Methods on Elementary Historiography". One of the important things was the exercise in writing scientific papers, in which his requirements were very specific. For example, one had to get hold of first-hand material, to annotate the sources of the material, to have new insights or new explanations, and then to write one's paper following a standard form. Only half the time of the term was used for teaching. After that, every student was given a certain topic and asked to go to the library to find material, write everything down on cards divided by subject, and start to sort out the research. The paper for that term made up the academic record. The topic handed out to me at that time was "Who was the most fervent book collector in history?" After browsing through the materials in the library, I found three scholars fit for the description, and I started comparative research on the materials I had found. In class I made oral reports to Professor Hung, and finally I chose one scholar from the Ming Dynasty, and wrote my "term paper": "The most fervent book collector Hu Yinlin". As a result, I was given a remark by Professor Hung in two black characters, written with a calligraphy brush: "Very Fine". This made me feel immensely encouraged, and I kept his calligraphy. Now 62 years have passed, and even though every side of life has changed, I have kept it until today, because it is the first lesson on academic training I had from Yenching University.

Professor Hung's guidance was not only confined to the classroom, he deliberately created some opportunities for me outside the classes, which gave me an even broader job training. This was even more the case when I became his research student. For example, Professor Alice Boring, Dean of the Pre-medical Department of the university, invited me to make a report in English for PAUW on the subject "geographical Peking". The full name of this organisation is Peking Association of University Women, and its members, most of them being graduates of American universities, were naturally good at speaking English. However, as I had never written a lecture in English before, I was of course a bit shy and tried desperately to refuse. Only then professor Boring told me straight on the spot that she

正是煨莲师关于校园历史的研究，引导我进行对于北京西北郊区历史上著名园林区的实地考察，进而又扩大到对整个北京地区开发过程的研究。

在课堂教学上煨莲师的独出心裁和严格要求，更使我深受教益。例如我还在二年级的时候，从他学习"初级史学方法"一课，主要内容之一，是科学论文写作的训练，他的要求十分具体，例如必须掌握第一手资料，必须在写作中注明资料的来源，必须有新的发现或新的说明，然后按照一定的格式写成论文。课堂讲授时间只用了半个学期。然后分配给每一位学生一个问题，要求学生到图书馆去查阅资料，分门别类写成卡片，进行研究整理，写成学期论文，作为学习成绩。当时我所分配到的问题是"历史上最爱藏书的是谁?"经过查阅图书资料，我认为有三位学者符合要求，根据收集所得，进行比较研究，在课堂上向煨莲师作了口头报告，最后选定其中明朝的学者一人，写成我的"学期论文"：《最爱藏书的胡应麟事绩考略》。结果我得到煨莲师两个字的墨笔评语："佳甚"。这使我深受鼓舞，就把这篇写作珍藏起来，整整六十二个年头过去了，虽然历经沧桑，仍得一直保存到今天，这是燕京大学所给我的学术训练的第一课。

煨莲师对我的教导，还不仅限于课业指导，他还有意在课外为我创造条件，使我得到更为广泛的业务训练。在我作为他的研究生之后，更是如此。例如有一次，学校医学预科主任 Alice Boring 教授约我为 PAUW 用英文作一次报告，题目是 Geographical Peking。这个组织的英文全名是 Peking Association of University Women，它的会员自然都是长于说英语的，可是我从来还没有用英语作过讲演，心里有些胆怯，极力推辞。于是 Boring 教授就直截了当地告诉

had originally invited Professor Hung to talk on historical Peking, but he had insisted on recommending me to talk on geographical Peking. After this information I went to see Professor Hung immediately to explain my English was not sufficient to give a talk in public, and to ask him to replace me by somebody else. Professor Hung pointed very solemnly to me and said, "Well, this is an excellent opportunity for you to practise, is it not?" He insisted on me writing out the speech and practising it on him beforehand, before going to the association to do the report. This was a deliberate training for me, and I could not but go along.

Professor Hung had noticed at a very early stage that my academic interest had turned from history to historical geography, so he deliberately arranged for me to go abroad for advanced studies, to get an even better training in the theory of the field. One morning in the autumn of 1938, I was summoned to go to Professor Hung's study at his home, and the first thing he said to me was "there is no school exceeding a master, and there is no master exceeding a famous master". He paused for a while, and then explained, "Harvard is a famous university, but they don't have a department of geography there. The University of Liverpool in England is of course not as famous as Harvard, but they have a famous professor in geography who has also a great knowledge of the geography of China, Professor Percy Maude Roxby. After research by our school it has been decided to send you there next autumn to advance on your historical geography." Professor Hung had close ties with the Harvard-Yenching Institute, and had always sent research students from Yenching's graduate school of history to Harvard for further study, but because of my special interest, he recommended me to go to the University of Liverpool to specialise in historical geography. The following year war broke out in Europe, and I couldn't go. When after the great war had ended I was finally able to go to the University of Liverpool, Professor Roxby had retired, but his successor, Sir Clifford Darby, influenced me deeply. The theories and methods on historical geography initiated by him were introduced by me in China for the first time, and I made my own contribution to the development in the field of Chinese historical geography. When talking now about these matters, I cannot but think of the opportunity Yenching University gave me in the first place.

Just now I have given a few examples of how William Hung guided and trained me, but it was not only Professor Hung who let me share in his knowledge in my years of study at Yenching. There were two other

我说，她原来是要请洪煨莲教授去讲 Historical Peking，而洪教授却一定要推荐我去讲 Geographical Peking。我了解到这一情况后，就立刻去看煨莲师，说明我的英语程度还难以作公开讲演，希望他另外推荐别人。可是煨莲师却十分郑重地指点我说："这正是你练习的好机会嘛！"他一定要我写好稿先面对他试讲，然后再到会上去作报告。这是有意对我进行训练，我也就只好同意了。

煨莲师早已体会到我的学术兴趣已经从历史学转向地理学，就有意为我安排出国深造的机会，便于从学科理论上得到更好的训练。1938 年的秋学期，一天上午，我应命来到煨莲师家中的书房，他开头第一句话就说："择校不如投师，投师要投名师。"随后稍一停顿，他又进一步解释说："美国哈佛大学是有名的大学，可是那里没有地理系。英国的利物浦大学虽然不如哈佛大学那样有名，可是那里却有一位地理学的名师，对中国地理很有研究，他就是 Percy Maude Roxby 教授。现在经过学校研究，已经决定明年秋学期送你到那里去进修历史地理学。"煨莲师和哈佛燕京学社有密切关系，曾派遣燕京大学历史系的研究生到哈佛大学去进修。可是为了我的学术兴趣，他推荐我到利物浦大学去攻历史地理学。只是转年欧战爆发，我未能成行。一直到大战结束后，我前往利物浦大学的时候，Roxby 教授已经退休，而他的继任者 Clifford Darby 教授正是现代历史地理学奠基人之一，我深受 Darby 教授的影响，并把他所倡导的历史地理学的理论与方法，第一次介绍到中国来，并对中国历史地理学的发展作出了自己的贡献。现在讲到这一点，我还是不能不想到当初燕京大学给我提供的机遇。

以上我举出洪煨莲教授如何教导和培养我的一些例子，我在燕大学习期间所深受教益的，不仅是洪煨莲教授一人。当时历史系还

full-time professors at the Department of History: Gu Jiegang and Deng Zhicheng. Both of them were renowned historians, although they were not as good at English as William Hung, who had a thorough knowledge of both Chinese and Western topics. If William Hung's appointment as professor at Yenching had a historical origin, for he was a Christian convert and had close ties to the founding of Yenching, it needs to be pointed out that Gu Jiegang and Deng Zhicheng were not Christian converts nor proficient in English, but because the two of them had made special contributions to the world of Chinese historiography, they were employed by Yenching University. Professor Deng Zhicheng guided me in my research on Chinese historical treatises, and Professor Gu Jiegang deepened my interest in researching Peking's historical geography (I will talk about that later in more detail). Just like Professor Hung, Professor Gu Jiegang had been employed at the Harvard-Yenching Institute's Peking office, where William Hung even had been in charge. I should add that with financial help of the Harvard-Yenching Institute the magazine *Yanjing Xuebao* was edited and published at Yenching, recognised in China and abroad to be one of the leading academic journals on the research of Chinese literature, history and philosophy. Also, there were the publications in volumes of the Yinde collection, about traditional Chinese books and records, esteemed equally in the academic worlds of both China and the West as the *Yanjing Xuebao*. Professor William Hung contributed enormously to the establishing and printing of the Yinde collection. It has to be added here that although after the merging of Yenching University and Peking University in 1952 the above mentioned publications came to a halt, reprints continued to be in circulation. More significantly, the Alumni of Yenching University in Peking and the Second Campus of Peking University started co-operating in 1993 and established the Yanjing Graduate Institute, in order to continue and expand the spirit and stamina of Yenching. At the same time, the academic efforts of mainly the Alumni of Yenching

University were bundled into re-editing and republishing *Yanjing Xuebao*, of which the first "New Issue No.1" was published in August 1995. Moreover, there are plans in progress for continued compilation of the Yinde collection.

It has to be added here that after Yenching University merged with Peking University in 1952 the campus expanded greatly, but the original campus of Yenching University has been fully preserved, the glimmering lake and pagoda reflected thereon are just like in the old days. In 1990, the Municipal Government of Peking decided to have the

有其他两位专任教授，即顾颉刚和邓之诚。他们两位都是著名的历史学家，却不像洪煨莲那样长于英语，学贯中西。如果说洪煨莲来燕大做教授是有历史渊源的，他既是基督教徒，又与燕大的创办有密切关系，可是顾颉刚和邓之诚两位既不是基督教徒，又不谙英语，但在中国史学界都有特殊贡献，因而受聘于燕京大学。邓之诚教授曾指导我研究中国史学专著，顾颉刚教授又进一步启发了我研究北京历史地理的兴趣（详见下文）。顾颉刚教授和洪煨莲教授一样，都受聘于哈佛燕京学社北京办事处，洪煨莲还曾兼任该办事处的负责人。在这里应该顺便提到，由哈佛燕京学社资助，由燕京大学编辑出版的《燕京学报》，被认为是研究中国文学、历史和哲学的最重要的学术刊物之一，传播于海内外。与《燕京学报》同样见重于中外学术界的，还有关于中国古代图书典籍的"引得丛刊"的编纂出版。洪煨莲教授对"引得丛刊"的规划设计以及印刷，贡献最大。在这里还应该附带提到的是，1952 年燕京大学与北京大学合并后，上述两种出版物都停刊了，可是两者的影印本还继续传播于世。更重要的是 1993 年在北京的燕京大学校友会与北京大学分校又进行合作，成立了燕京研究院，为继承和发扬燕京大学的办学精神而努力。同时又组织以燕京校友为主的学术力量，重新编辑出版《燕京学报》，首期复刊即"新一期"已于 1995 年 8 月出版。

还应该附带提到的是 1952 年燕京大学合并于北京大学后，校址范围已经大为扩展，可是原来燕京大学校园，保留如昔，湖光塔影，无异当年。1990 年，北京市人民政府决定将未名湖周围

area around the "Lake Without Name" of the original Yenching campus site put on the municipal cultural heritage list, and had this engraved on a stele to be remembered forever.

2. The Tradition of Patriotism and the Spirit of Devotion

The campus of Yenching University was as pretty as a Chinese landscape painting, but this didn't mean it was a small paradise closed off from the outer world. It was built on the ancient sites of gardens of former times, but the fate of the whole country was still in the midst of restless movement. The first couple of years after the school was set up, the Peking government was controlled continuously by warlords who strived for power by selling out their country, and bureaucracy. The successive national governments in Nanking were facing against Japanese and other foreign aggressions.

It was at this time that the Japanese aggressors staged the "Mukden Incident" of 18 September 1931, to occupy the three provinces in China's Northeast, and the resistance movement against Japan to save the country, initiated by the Chinese people in all kinds of ways, started to develop from this point in time.

The situation as described above was the historical background for my enrollment at Yenching University as a freshman in 1932. At that time, because the Chinese government had moved south, Peking was renamed Beiping, "northern peace", and after Mukden Incident it came day by day closer to the nation's defence front lines.

One day, not long after I became a student, I was strolling on the campus and arrived at the area close to the library full of hills and streams, when suddenly a stone stele, straight as a brush, appeared in front of me, upon which from the top down in large characters one line was inscribed:

"MEMORIAL STELE TO LADY WEI SHIYI"

Followed by an inscription stating lady Wei Shiyi's life story and a short commemorative text. The last three lines, in small characters, stated the persons who erected the stele and the date it had been put up:

Erected in honour by all members of the men's and women's student unions of Yenching University, together with the student union of the Yenching high school for girls, in the 16th Year of the Republic.

So this was the stele erected on the campus to remember the second-year female student Wei Shiyi, who only one year before the erection (1926 in

---

的原燕京大学校园，列为全市文物保护单位，刻石立碑，永作纪念。

二、爱国主义传统与献身精神

燕京大学校园虽然风景如画，却不是"世外桃源"。它虽然是从旧时代的园林废墟上建设起来，可是整个国家的命运还处在动荡不安之中。学校创办的最初几年间，北京政府一直在争权夺利、卖国求荣的军阀与官僚的控制之下。相继而来的南京中央政府，又面临着外患日疾的情况，也就是在这时候，日本侵略者于1931年阴谋制造了"九一八事变"，入侵东北三省，中国人民以不同方式所进行的抗日救亡运动，也就是从这时候进一步发展起来的。

以上情况，就是我在1932年作为一年级新生进入燕京大学时的时代背景。当时，因为中央政府南迁，北京已改称北平，而"九一八"以后的北平，也日渐接近国防的最前线。

在我入学后不久，有一天，我在校园里散步，来到图书馆附近一处溪流环绕的丘岗之间，忽然看到一座笔直的石碑耸立在面前，碑的正面自上而下刻着一行大字：

魏士毅女士纪念碑

碑座上刻着魏士毅女士的小传和纪念她的铭文。最后三行小字刻的是立碑的时间和立碑人如下：

中华民国十六年燕京大学男女两校及女附中学生会全体会员敬立

原来这是为纪念前一年，也就是1926年3月18日在北京青年

fact) on March 18, as a member of the Peking young student patriotism movement, had been killed by the Warlord Regime. This massacre in Peking where so many people were killed and which shocked the whole nation was known as "the March 18 Massacre". My high school was far from Peking when this massacre took place, but I was deeply influenced by the student movement of that time. After coming to Yenching I hadn't expected to experience the profound lesson of that patriotic student movement once again, a lesson which was expressed so well in the inscription on the stele, which reads as follows:

> In the country there are great parasites, the government is without law.
>
> Foxes and rats infest the capital, they vie with each other in unbridled unruliness.
>
> The gates of the government are awash with blood from the killing of our heros.
>
> They slaughtered little me, but in the end there will be a reckoning!
>
> Whether the Dipper stars do not pour wine, or the Sieve conste-llation winnows grain (i.e., whether high officials are aloof or they do care)
>
> The prosperity or decay of the country depends on the support of people!
>
> Please let those who have survived never forget this!

When going over this inscription carefully, I cannot but think that such an stele, so strong in attacking the government and denouncing the warlords, at that time was indeed an important patriotic symbol for the young students of Yenching University, and an indisputable illustration of the protection and development of the young students' patriotic ideals by the Yenching University staff. Thinking back of it now, it must have been the first lesson in patriotism I was taught by Yenching University.

In the four years after I enrolled in Yenching University, the Japanese invaders occupied the three provinces of China's Northeast, and advanced even further to the Great Wall Line in the north. Apart from the normal teaching and studying routine, the staff and students on the campus of

Yenching were incessantly engaged in anti-Japanese activities. Among the professors circulated a publication about promoting resistance against Japan, with big characters "The Torch" in its cover printed; as I remember correctly the calligraphy was by Rong Geng, professor of Chinese literature. Gu Jiegang, professor of history, got everybody in their spare time together to compile propaganda material for resistance against Japan and saving the country, which was published under the

学生的爱国运动中，被军阀政府所枪杀的二年级女同学魏士毅而竖立在校园中的。这次在北京被杀学生多人，是震动全国的大惨案，就叫做"三一八惨案"。惨案发生时我所在的中学虽然远离北京，可是也深受这次学生运动的影响。没有料到，我在进入燕京大学之后，竟然又一次感受到这次爱国运动的深刻教育，这一点，从石碑上所刻的铭文中又充分地反映出来，兹将铭文抄录如下：

国有巨蠹政不纲
城狐社鼠争跳梁
公门喋血歼我良
牺牲小己终取偿
北斗无酒南箕扬
民心向背关兴亡
愿后死者长毋忘

细读这篇铭文，我不禁联想到，如此强烈谴责当时的军阀反动政府的石刻，既是燕京大学青年学生爱国主义的重要标志，又是燕京大学领导维护和发扬青年学生爱国主义思想的无可争辩的说明。如今回想，这应该是我在燕京大学所接受的爱国主义教育的第一课。

在我进入燕京大学本科后的四年间，正是日本侵略者入侵东北三省之后，又进一步向华北的万里长城沿线推进的时候。燕京大学的校园里在正常的教学工作之外，师生的抗日活动也在不断地进行中。教师中曾流传着一个宣传抗日的内部刊物，封面上印着"火把"两个大字，记得是中国文学系教授容庚所题。历史系教授顾颉刚组织大家利用业余时间，编写抗日救国的宣传材料，用"通俗读物编

name "Popular Literature Editing House". The students were constantly busy with activities supporting the army defending the Great Wall Line to resist the Japanese army. Because of the "non-resistance policy" of the central government in Nanking, a patriotic student movement finally broke out on 9 December 1935, which spread gradually to other cities. From the very beginning of the movement the students of Yenching had an important leading role; moreover, they were supported by their teachers, including several foreign teachers. Two of them were quite extraordinary, one was Randolph Sailer, the very popular American professor of psychology, the other one was the American journalist and part-time lecturer at the Department of Journalism at Yenching, Edgar Snow. At that time, the Chinese Communist Party had already established Yan'an as its base to propagate resistance against Japan and form a united front. It was after this student movement of 9 December that Edgar Snow travelled to Yan'an and subsequently wrote his very influential book, *Red Star Over China*. It was also this student movement that increased the admiration of the students for Dr. Sailer, for he showed enormous care and support for students who, though suffering hunger and cold, had walked for miles to join the demonstrations.

Six months after the 9 December demonstrations I graduated from my department at Yenching University. The evening before my graduation Professor Gu Jiegang told me that the university had appointed him as part-time head of the history department from the next term onward, and he hoped I would stay on as his assistant. From September 1936 till June 1937, Professor Gu tried out a new approach with his class "Exercise in Research on Ancient Sites and Ancient Objects". Every fortnight on Saturday afternoon he would take the students to an old building or ancient site which he had chosen beforehand, either inside Peking's city walls or in the surrounding countryside, to make an on-the-spot investigation. He wanted me to make a written report beforehand on the basis of his reference materials and my own inspection results, and hand this out to the students for reference. It was a training very precious for me, which deepened my interest in doing research on Peking's historical geography.

On 7 July 1937 the Japanese aggressors staged the "Marco Polo Bridge Incident" or "July 7 Incident" in the outskirts of Peking, and they attacked and occupied the city, setting off the widespread War of Resistance Against Japan. Professor Gu Jiegang left Peking quickly for the south,

刊社"的名义出版发行。学生中不断发起支援长城沿线抗日将士的活动。但是由于南京中央政府的"不抵抗政策",终于激发了 1935 年 12 月 9 日这一天开始的爱国学生运动,逐渐扩展到其他城市。从运动的一开始,燕京大学的学生就起了重要的领导作用,并且得到教师们的支持,还包括了外籍教师在内,最突出的有两位,一位是在教学上深受欢迎的心理系美籍教授夏仁德,另一位是美籍新闻记者同时又是燕京大学新闻系的兼任讲师 Edgar Snow。那时主张抗日统一战线的中国共产党已经在延安建立了根据地。就是在这次"一二·九学生运动"之后,Edgar Snow 前往延安从而写出了他那部影响广泛的 *Red Star Over China*。也是通过这次学生运动,夏仁德进一步获得了学生们的敬佩,因为他对饥寒交迫中长途奔跑去参加游行的学生们,表示了极大的关怀和支持。

"一二·九学生运动"后的半年,我在燕京大学本科毕业。毕业的前夕,顾颉刚教授告诉我说,学校从下学年起聘他兼任历史系的系主任,要我留校做他的助教。从 1936 年 9 月到 1937 年 6 月,顾颉刚教授别出心裁地开设了一门课,叫做"古迹古物调查实习",每两个星期的星期六下午,要带学生到他所事先选定的古建筑或重要古遗址所在地,或在北京城内,或在城外近郊,进行实地考察。事先他要我先根据他所提供的参考资料和我自己的检阅所得,写成书面材料,印发给同学作参考。这对我是个极为难得的训练,也进一步启发了我对研究北京历史地理的兴趣。

1937 年 7 月 7 日,日本侵略者阴谋制造了北平郊区的"卢沟桥事件"也就是"七七事变",进而攻占北平城,全民抗日战争从此开始。这时顾颉刚教授为避免日寇的逮捕,仓促离开北平南下。

to escape an arrest by the Japanese. Thereafter, I obtained a scholarship by the Harvard-Yenching Institute and became a M.A. research student under the guidance of Professor William Hung. National University had, just as Peking University and Qinghua University, already after the Marco Polo Bridge Incident moved to the south. Although Yenching University was situated in an enemy-occupied area, it could continue to exist because it was run by an American Christian organisation, and Yenching was like a solitary island where the youth in enemy-occupied north China could still pursue their studies. As a research student the first problem I had was what to choose as the field of research and the subject for my thesis. Actually, William Hung had proposed me a subject long ago, when I wrote my graduation paper. Because he knew my interest had moved to historical geography, he hoped I would take the chapter on Shandong province from the work *Tianxia junguo libing shu* (*The Blessings and Ills of All Regions of the Empire*) of the famous late Ming early Qing scholar Gu Yanwu, and then add a compilation from the early Qing to the late Qing and early Republic. The point was to disclose all good and bad aspects of every place inside Shandong province of the past three hundred years, to be of reference when building up the nation, for although we were occupied by the enemy, everyone believed the war would eventually be won, and the nation would be built up again. The choice of Shandong was made because it is my original home, and also because the library of Yenching had the most Local Gazetteers on Shandong province. These Local Gazetteers are characteristic of China, they are books compiled by the authorities on the situation of all districts in all provinces, usually compiled every odd years. Because I had only limited time then, I could not but choose another subject for my thesis with a rather smaller scope. M.A. research students had enough time to do research. It was very important then that I could get a better understanding of the idea of Gu Yanwu's *Tianxia junguo libing shu*. He was born in the late Ming dynasty, and felt great concern for the deteriorating society and politics which caused the people great suffering. Then he compiled his *Tianxia junguo libing shu*. In the foreword to his work, he wrote the following: "I am moved by the many ills that beset all the corners of our land, and thus am ashamed of the lack of skill of the students of the Classics". Then he started propagating his idea of "Use the Classics", attacking the shallow style of study of his contemporaries, and he recommended openly "everybody has a responsibility to protect the world". Thereupon, he called out loudly in distress, saying:

As of today, it is our responsibility (as scholars) to save our people from their state of utter distress and open up an era of peace for ten thousand generations.

其后，我得到哈佛燕京学社的奖学金，在洪煨莲教授的指导下，做硕士研究生。早自"卢沟桥事件"后，北平的国立大学如北京大学和清华大学都已南迁。燕京大学虽然处在沦陷区，因为是美国教会所创办，得以继续存在，犹如一片孤岛，使华北沦陷区的青年还可以升学进修。我自己作为一个研究生，首先遇到的一个问题，就是研究领域和论文题目的选择。实际上，早在大学本科写作论文时，煨莲师就向我建议过一个题目，因为他知道我的兴趣已经转入历史地理，希望我把明末清初著名学者顾炎武《天下郡国利病书》中的山东一省，加以续修，从清朝初年一直续到清朝末年和民国初期。至于选择山东一省，因为我的故乡在山东，而燕京图书馆所藏山东一省的地方志书又最为丰富。更重要的一点是这时我对顾炎武最初编写《天下郡国利病书》的目的，有了进一步的认识。他生在明朝末年，痛感社会政治腐败，人民生活于困苦患难之中。于是他立志编写《天下郡国利病书》。在全书的序文中，就写下了如下两句话：

感四国之多难，耻经生之乏术。

于是他开始提倡"经世致用"之学，痛斥当时读书人的虚浮学风，进而公开提倡"保天下者，匹夫有责"。并且大声疾呼：

今日者，拯斯人于涂炭，为万世开太平，此吾辈之责也。

Even when the Qing armies had entered through the passes and snatched away the ruling power of the Ming Dynasty, he kept resisting Qing Dynasty rule, and refrained from being employed. When my country was in imminent danger, I was able to understand the deeds of his life much better, and I was deeply moved. In the period that the country's crisis deepened after the occupation of Peking, it took me three years to finish my sequel to *The Blessings and Ills of All Regions of the Empire* on Shandong province. William Hung was there to recommend it, and he had my M.A. thesis published as a special edition of the 19th issue of *Yanjing Xuebao*. This work, written under the enemy puppet regime, was full of ideals of saving the country and rebuilding the land, which without Yenching University and the guidance of Professor William Hung would have never seen the light.

However, when in the winter of 1941 this book had just been published, the Japanese invasion army that had recently occupied China meeting with the persistent resistance of the Chinese people, suddenly attacked the American naval base at Pearl Harbour from the air on December 8 (Peking time), setting off the Pacific War. It was very early that day that the Japanese military police surrounded Yenching University quickly and consequently occupied the campus. All students and staff members were expelled from the area, the staff with American nationality were locked up in concentration camps, and a couple of staff and students were arrested and confined in the army barracks of the Japanese military police in Peking, including the university president Leighton Stuart. Eleven people of the staff were arrested in all, among whom I was the youngest. Both my professors, William Hung and Deng Zhicheng, were arrested too.

Here I should go into the reasons of my arrest.

After finishing my M.A. in June 1940, I had decided to stay on at Yenching to teach, and I had already started to prepare classes. Dr. Leighton Stuart the university president, invited me for a talk. He wanted me to be in charge of some student matters part time besides teaching, because there were many problems the students were facing due to the campus' position on occupied territory. Some students had financial problems because of the war, some students couldn't work quietly because of the puppet regime, they all needed to be given care and support. Because I had been a student here for eight years myself, I was rather good in understanding the students. After three meetings, it was decided to set up a Student Welfare Committee, chaired by Professor Sailer

及至清兵入关之后，夺取了明朝的统治权，他却始终反抗清朝的统治，不为所用。我在当时国难当头的情况下，进一步了解他一生的事迹，深受感动。我用了三年时间，在北平沦陷后国难深重的时刻，完成了《天下郡国利病书》山东一省的续编。煨莲师又及时推荐，把这篇硕士论文，作为《燕京学报》专号之十九付印出版，这本书在敌伪统治下包含着挽救祖国、重建家园的思想，如果不是在燕京大学和洪煨莲教授的指导下，是不可能问世的。

可是，就在这本书于 1941 年冬刚刚出版之后，正在入侵中国遭到中国人民坚决抵抗的日本侵略军，又突然于 12 月 8 日（北京时间），空中偷袭美国的珍珠港海军基地，发动了太平洋战争。这天一早，日本宪兵立即包围了燕京大学，继而进侵校园。全体学生与教职员被驱逐出校。美籍教职员被关押到集中营，部分教职员与学生被逮捕，关押在北平日本宪兵队本部，司徒雷登校长也被拘留。被捕的教职员共 11 人，我也在其中，是最年轻的一个。我的老师洪煨莲和邓之诚两位教授，也同遭逮捕。

这里需要说明一下我被捕的原因。

1940 年 6 月我完成硕士学业后，已决定留校任教，并已开始备课。这时司徒校长忽然约我谈话，要我在教课之外还兼管学生工作，因为当时学校处在沦陷区，学生中所遇到的问题很多，有的学生因军事的影响，经济来源困难；有的学生在敌伪统治下不能安心学习等等，都需要给予关心和帮助。因为我在校做学生，已有八年时间，比较了解学生情况。经过三次商谈，最后决定成立一个"学生辅导委员会"，由深受学生钦佩的夏仁德

who was very popular with the students, to facilitate tackling the Japanese if they would come to the university to stir up trouble. I was vice chairman of this committee and acted as a contact with the students. One committee member was chosen among the young and enthusiastic professors of the Colleges of Arts, Natural Sciences and Public Affairs, and the Dean was invited to be secretary of the Committee, to make it easier to communicate with the whole school's various administrative organisations and the university president. On 21 June 1940 President Stuart signed a memo and sent it to everybody appointed. I have kept my personal copy until today, and added it to this paper. Therefore, before I even entered a classroom, I walked into the office of the Student Welfare Committee inside the large office building.

The fact that I had accepted this task had to do with the education I was given by Yenching University as well. The Yenching University motto "Freedom Through Truth for Service" was known by heart by all university students. The understanding of this motto by the students might have been profound or superficial, but there was one thing the students themselves could all feel in a minor or major degree: the spirit of helping others, to be found everywhere on the campus. This spirit of helping was most concrete in the relationship between students and staff, and also most obvious there. The establishing of a Student Welfare Committee by the president of the university is a very concrete example of this spirit. Honouring this university motto became my unshirkable duty.

Student life at Yenching University had, apart from compulsory studying, its special characteristics. Especially when the nation's crisis deepened daily and the students' activities outside the classroom became gradually more and more restricted, one characteristic became obvious, and that was the existence of an organisation called Small Christian Fellowship. As a Christian university, Yenching University had established Colleges of Arts, Natural Sciences and Public Affairs, which were officially registered at the central government in Nanking of that time, but there existed also a College of Religion, which didn't enroll students publicly but attracted students majoring in religion. The College of Religion had its own building, in which was built a small worship hall, where believing and non-believing staff and students could freely attend the Sunday service, although not many people did. There was yet another organisation, called the Christian Fellowship of Yenching University, whose office was inside the building of the College of Religion also. The Fellowship was divided into a number of small fellowships, which were led mainly by student believers. Non-believers could join freely, and some fellowships invited Christian professors to

教授做主席，也便于对付日本人来学校找麻烦。我做副主席，便于和学生联系。从文学院、理学院和法学院的年轻而又热心的教师中各选一人为委员，并特邀教务主任做秘书，便于和全校的教学领导机构，即院长会议进行联系。1940 年 6 月 21 日司徒校长签字发给任命通知书（我个人收到的这份通知书，保存至今）。因此在我尚未走进课堂之前，就先走进了设在办公大楼的学生辅导委员会的办公室了。

　　我接受这项任务，也和燕京大学所给予我的教育有关。燕京大学的校训"因真理，得自由，以服务"是每个燕京学生都熟悉的。对于这个校训的理解，或浅或深可能各有不同，但是有一点却是每个学生都能或多或少亲身感受到的，那就是洋溢在校园中的服务精神。这种服务精神体现在师生关系上最为具体，也最为突出。校长所提出的成立学生辅导委员会的设想，也正是这种服务精神的一种具体体现。遵循校训的要求，对我来说也正是"义不容辞"。

　　从整体来说，燕京大学的学生生活，除去业务学习之外，也自有其特点。特别是国难日深学生的课外活动日益受到限制的时候，这一特点也就格外突出，这就是基督教小团契的组织。燕京大学作为一所由外国教会举办的大学，师生的宗教信仰是自由的。这些小团契主要是由信教的学生带头组织，非教徒的学生可以自由参加，有的小团契还约请教师中的

join as advisors. Every fellowship had its own name, some names had to do with religion, like "Friends of Jesus", or "Shining Salt Group", but not all names were like that. For example, there was a fellowship which from the start was organised by six people, and was therefore called the "Group of Six". These fellowships were full of vigour, because they did not only study the Bible and discuss religious doctrine, but touched upon the problems in daily life, most importantly the discussion about current affairs. If it hadn't been under the name of a fellowship meeting, discussions about current affairs wouldn't have been possible, because it was forbidden explicitly by the puppet regime of that time. Later, the fellowship organisations developed into some small groups specialising in discussions about vocational study. I helped organising a small group on vocational study, whereby everybody came together once every weekend to exchange what one had learned when studying vocationally, called the "Saturday Symposium". Actually these student organisations, given the objective situation at that time, really set off the students' self-education, and brought about the spreading of patriotic ideals. Because the same thing had happened to me when I was a student, I was perfectly happy to share some work in caring for the students through an organisation at school.

At the office of the Student Welfare Committee Dr. Sailer and me took shifts, and started our "spare-time" work for the students. I hadn't attended his classes when I was a student, even though his class on "Mental Hygiene" was universally appraised and received enthusiastically by the students. Now I could see with my own eyes how he gave himself totally for his work, and couldn't help thinking about the Yenching motto about "service", a motto which had clearly been manifested in him. He arranged mainly "Self-Help Work" for the students with urgent financial needs, all kinds of odd jobs being paid for by the hour. Because of the war, the amount of students applying for Self-Help Work increased daily. Sailer's work load increased accordingly, but his attitude towards the students and his work spirit were so admirable that I will never forget.

My main work had to do with the students' problems of quite another nature, problems which were linked with the day-by-day development of the War of Resistance Against Japan. The Japanese invaders were getting crazier every day in "mopping up" the occupied area, so there were a minority of students then who insisted on giving up their personal opportunity to study, and plunged into the struggle to defeat the enemy

基督徒参加为顾问。小团契各有名称，有的与宗教有关，如"耶稣之友"、"光盐"，但并不是都如此。例如有一个小团契，开始是由六个人组成的，就叫做"六人团"。这些小团契富有生命力，因为除去研读《圣经》讨论教义之外，还涉及日常生活中的问题，更重要的是时事讨论。如果不是在小团契聚会的名义下，集体的时事讨论是不可能的，因为这在当时的敌伪统治下是被明令禁止的。后来又从小团契的组织形式，发展成一些专门讨论业务学习的小组。我还参加组织过一个与业务学习有关的小组，在每个周末大家聚到一起，互相介绍自己业务学习的心得，就叫做"星期六座谈会"。实际上这些学生中的组织，在当时的客观情况下，真正起到了学生自我教育的效果，而爱国主义的思想也就因之而得到传播。因为我自己在学生时代是这样走过来的，因此在学校组织上分担一些关心学生的工作，也是心甘情愿的。

在学生辅导委员会的办公室里，我和夏仁德轮流值班，开始了我们"业余"的学生工作。我做学生的时候，没有听过他的课，尽管他的"心理卫生"一课，有口皆碑，是深受学生欢迎的。现在我亲眼看到他在工作中的献身精神，我不由得想到燕京大学校训中所强调的"服务"这一点，在他身上已经具体地体现出来。他主要负责为经济上急需的学生安排各种各样的"自助工作"，因工种的不同，计时付酬。当时由于战火的影响，申请自助工作的学生与日俱增。他工作的负担也就有增无减。可是他对待学生的态度和他的工作精神，却使我永远难忘。

至于我所负责的主要工作，则是学生中所遇到的另一方面的问题，即随着抗日战争的日益发展，日本侵略者在沦陷区的"扫荡"也日益疯狂，这时有少数学生宁愿放弃个人学习的机会，要投身到

and save the country. Students whom I was familiar with came directly to me, and there were also students who went straightaway to university president Leighton Stuart to discuss their plans. The president wanted me to be in charge of these matters, but he also established one principle, being that as long as the students dropped out to join the work for "the United Front Against Japan", no matter if they wanted to go to the hinterland (being the land under Kuomintang rule) or the liberated area (being the area of the Eighth Route Army of the Communist Party), they would have to receive equal treatment: to be given support, including making contacts for their route and helping out with travel costs. If they asked to change their subject of study or asked to leave to go to work, that was a different matter. I started to help the students to leave school on this principle, but as it was best to go unnoticed, I could only operate in the strictest secrecy. At that time, there was an international friend of China, Rewi Alley, who set up an organisation in Sichuan called "Chinese Industrial Cooperation", which got together mainly scattered labour groups in the inner provinces to expand production and support resistance against Japan. A very good friend of his, the English lecturer at Yenching E. Ralph Lapwood, had as early as 1939 left Yenching, and travelled through mountains in the west and the liberated area of the Eighth Route Army towards Sichuan, where he worked for this Industrial Cooperation. There were several students of the school who, influenced by him, wanted to leave and support the same Cooperation. There were also students who actively sought to join the direct struggle against Japan with the liberated area of the Eighth Route Army. In the position of vice-chairman of the Student Welfare Committee in the period of one year since the autumn of 1940, I helped these students to leave university. For a more detailed record of these affairs please read my account "Reminiscences on the Closing Down of Yenching University" in the volume *Peking under the Japanese Puppet Regime*[4]. Unfortunately, some messages written by students who had gone south were intercepted, and I was arrested by the Japanese military police. In June 1942 I was sentenced by a Japanese military court to prison for one year with the execution suspended for three years, and was released on bail, but I had no freedom of migration or travel. When my three-year suspension period was just over, the Japanese invasion army lost the war and surrendered. The university president Stuart was released, and he immediately re-established the university committee, seven people in all, and I was asked to join too, even though I was still quite young.[5] The new university committee set down one strict rule, being that whoever had worked for

抗敌救国的斗争中去。其中有我所熟悉的学生直接找到我，也有学生径直去找校长司徒雷登提出他们的设想。校长就要我具体负责这件事，但是他也确定了一个原则，只要是停学去参加"抗日统一战线"的工作，无论是自愿到大后方（即国民党统治区），或是到解放区（即共产党八路军的抗战区），都应一律对待，给予支持，包括联系路线和给予路费补助。至于要求转学或就业的，不在此例。就是根据这一原则，我开始了帮助学生离校的工作，只是不得公开进行，只能在严格守秘密的情况下，予以帮助。当时有一位国际友人艾黎在四川办起了"中国工业合作社"，主要是把内地分散的手工业组织起来，扩大生产，支援抗日。他的一位好朋友、燕京大学的英籍讲师赖朴吾已应约于 1939 年从燕京大学步行，穿越西山，经过八路军解放区前往四川，支援工业合作社的工作。在他的影响下，有些在校学生自愿前往支援工业合作社。另外也有学生主动要求就近参加八路军解放区的直接抗日斗争。从1940 年秋以后的一年间，我以学生辅导委员会副主席的身份，掩护这些学生分批离校。详细情况见于我所写的《燕京大学被封前后的片断回忆》，收入在公开出版的《日伪统治下的北平》[4]一书中。不幸的是，南下大后方的学生有人走漏了消息，因此我遭日本宪兵逮捕。1942 年 6 月，被日本军事法庭判徒刑一年，缓刑三年，取保开释，但无迁居旅行自由。我的缓刑刚期满，日本侵略军战败投降。校长司徒雷登获释，立即召集成立复校委员会共七人，我虽年轻，也被邀参加。[5]复校委员会做出一项严格规定，即

the enemy when Yenching was closed off by the Japanese bandits, was not allowed to return to university. This rule again proved that Yenching University stuck firmly to its principles, and the rule was resolutely supported by staff and students alike.

Before I end this paper, I should make some additional remarks, being that when I came out of prison and went through my suspension period, in the field of conducting myself in society and the field of studying I received the unremitting guidance and strict demands of William Hung. The couple of letters he wrote to me by hand then are still treasured by me today. Four of these letters I had even photo reprinted, and they will appear in the second issue of the new edition of *Yanjing Xuebao* (*Yenching Journal of Chinese Studies*). This *Yanjing Xuebao*, the magazine that in the past by spreading the splendid Chinese traditional culture became famous at home and abroad, will now, under the enthusiastic support of the Alumni of Yenching University, continue to be published by the Yenching Graduate Institute, keeping its editorial characteristics. How things will develop in the next phase, is a problem I feel should also be considered deeply.

Peking University
March, 1996

凡是在燕京大学被日寇封闭期间，参加了敌伪工作的，一律不得返校复职。这一规定，再一次显示了燕京大学坚持原则的严正立场，得到了全体师生的坚决拥护。

我在燕京学习、工作、生活了近二十年。燕京的一草一木对我是那样的熟悉，燕京的师长和同学对我是那样的难忘。我如今已是八十多岁的老人了，回顾过去，我写了《我从燕京大学来》。

⑩ IN MEMORY OF PROFESSOR P. M. ROXBY

From the School of Geography of the University of Liverpool[*]

A telegram came this morning informing us of the sad news of Professor Roxby's death yesterday in China.

> Thus, Professor Roxby lowered his guiding hand!
> His help to China has stopped!
> May he rest in peace forever!

A great educator of geography, a real scholar in his field and a true friend of China during the hard time of her suffering!

I sincerely believe that when his death is announced in the newspapers, all Chinese geographers, including my senior fellow workers, and especially those who were his pupils, will mourn his untimely death. All those who knew him will remember with grief the loss of a great personality.

I came to the School of Geography at the University of Liverpool drawn by his academic fame and achievements and hoping to further my training under his guidance, in the school established by him. I still remember my Chinese history teacher, Professor William Hung of Yenching University summoning me to say, "It is better to select a teacher than to select a school. But the most happy coincidence is a superior and accomplished teacher in a better school." Professor Roxby was undoubtedly a teacher of utmost accomplishment in the field of geographical education. Unfortunately, by the time I arrived in England, he had already retired from the university and departed for China as a representative of the British Council. In spite of his advanced years, he accepted the responsibility of promoting Sino-British cooperation in science and culture.

Professor Roxby has left behind the School he established and nurtured. He never considered the possibility of dying in the far-off country which he sympathized with, and which he helped so much during her days of suffering. He offered his life to work in and friendship with China.

Early this morning I ran to the School amidst heavy snow taking with me the sad news. I raised my head and looked at the newly painted door of the School. There I saw the golden words inscribed above it: "School of Geography."

拾 悼罗士培教授——寄自罗教授手创之利物浦大学地理学院*

今晨电信传来，散布了罗士培教授于昨日在我国首都逝世的噩耗。

罗士培教授放下了他的手！
罗士培教授停止了他对中国的援助！
罗士培教授永远安息了！

一代地理教育的大师，一个真正的学者，一位患难中的中国伟大的良友！

我相信，当这个噩耗在祖国的报纸上传布出来的时候，国内的地理学家——尤其是得以亲炙其教益的诸前辈——一定要为这个不幸的消息流泪。地理学家以外的，其他真正认识罗士培教授的人，也一定要为这个不幸的消息而同声哀悼！

作者今天来到罗士培教授所手创的利物浦大学地理学院继续受益，原是由于先生的吸引。我还记得当初我的老师洪煨莲教授对我说过这样的话："择校不如投师，投师要投名师。"像罗士培教授这样的学者，也算是地理学界的一位名师了。但是，不幸的很，当我来到英国的时候，罗教授却已经跑到中国去。他这次丢下了他手创的利物浦地理学院，以其退休以后的古稀之年，代表英国的交流协会，来到中国，目的乃是在于促进中英两国科学文化事业的合作。但是没想到他老先生就这样死在了他的工作上，他为他所爱的患难中的友邦，奉献了他自己的生命！

今天早上，我带着这个悲哀的消息，在冰天雪地中跑到学校，抬头看看那所刚刚油漆过的大门，与门额上所写的"利物浦大学地理学院"

Tears filled my eyes. I meditated mournfully: for several decades, hundreds of students of geography had been taught there by the old beloved professor. Now he lay dead in far-off China, my motherland.

I entered the building to seek my tutor, and Professor Roxby's successor, Professor H. C. Darby, intending to inform him of the sad news. I found him in the library reading room. Even before I opened my mouth I noticed his sadness.

"Professor Roxby is dead," I murmured. "Yes, I know," Professor Darby solemnly replied, "Mr. Smith phoned me early this morning. (Mr. W. Smith is a lecturer in Chinese geography whose own specialty is the economic geography of England.) We are waiting for more details. It is a pity indeed. We were to wait for his return in the summer to offer an open-to-all lecture on China." We left the reading room.

Later, I met Mr. F. J. Monkhouse, a young lecturer who taught me cartography. The first few words he said were "As a 'cultural ambassador' to China, Professor Roxby was the best one." I replied, "Undoubtedly. A cultural ambassador is actually an ambassador of friendship. It is not unusual that cultural ambassadors come before any political ambassadors. Such people are pioneers of their age. They are born not made. As a Chinese student of geography my sorrow is twofold. Personally I have lost a respected teacher in my field; as a Chinese student, my country has lost a great friend!" I declared this loudly, standing near the staircase, resembling someone who is making a public speech, but actually it was an expression of my uncontrollable sorrow.

I then went upstairs to the top storey of the building, to the Center for the Study of Chinese Geography. The Center was organized and established by Professor Roxby. Another Chinese fellow-student also came, a Mr. Wu Chuen-Chun from Nanking Central University, who was a lecturer of geography there. We exchanged information concerning Professor Roxby's death. At the end, he suddenly blurted out, "You know, immediately after the Japanese started the war, they tried to buy scrap iron and copper here in England. I don't know how Professor Roxby came to know of this, but anyway, he wrote to the newspapers practically daily, disclosing the facts, and denouncing the Japanese until he finally stopped their plan." Thus even before England declared

的两行金字，不禁潸然泪下。"在这里出入了几十年，栽培了成百成千个地理学生的那位老教授，他死在了我的祖国！"我心里默默的哀悼。

我走进大门去，找我的导师德贝教授（罗士培教授的继任者），预备把这不幸的消息告诉他。找他一直到书画室，还没等我开口，他已经是满面愁容了。他知道我这么早跑进来找他是什么事，他也一定看透了我哭丧的面孔。

"罗士培教授故去了！"我几乎哭出来。

"是的，"他镇静的说，"史密士先生（英国经济地理及中国地理讲师，罗教授的学生与同事）一早就打电话来了，现在我们只在等更详细的消息。真可悲，我还盼望他夏天回来，给我们作关于中国地理的公开讲学呢！"

我从书画室出来，正好遇见教我"制图学"的青年讲师孟先生，他开头一句就说：

"我们没有比罗士培教授更好的人选，作为我们的'文化使节'到中国去了！"

"不错，"我回答说，"'文化使节'是真正的友善的使节，'文化使节'是常常走在'政治使节'的前面的。这样的人，都是时代的先驱，可遇而不可求！在中国学生的立场上，我的悲哀是双重的。在我个人，我丢了一位素所景仰的地理教授；在我的祖国，我们丧失了一位伟大的良友！"我站在楼梯上，好像是对他作公开演讲，实在是发抒我自己不可抑止的悲哀。

于是，我上楼，爬到四层楼顶上残存下来的"中国地理研究室"，中国同学吴传钧兄（南京中央大学地理系讲师）也来了，我们互道罗士培教授逝世的消息。最后，他跳起来说：

"你知道么？卢沟桥战事爆发之后，日本人在这里设法收买废铜烂铁。这事情不知道如何给罗士培教授知道了，他天天在报纸上写文章，大施攻击，一直到把日本人的收买工作完全破坏为止！"

war against Japan, Professor Roxby had already become our comrade in the trench.

Just by chance, I looked back at the wall. There, hanging on it, was a glass frame with Chinese calligraphy by Professor Gu Jie-Gang, who had tutored me in China. It was the full text of "Yu Gong," one of the most ancient classics on Chinese geography, taken from *Shang Shu*, an ancient historical scripture. The frame was a present from two Chinese students of Professor Roxby at the opening of the Center. They are Professor Zhang Yin-Tang of Qinghua University at Peking, and Professor Lin Chao of Central University at Nanking. Looking at the glass frame, I couldn't help but reflect, "Now that Professor Roxby has gone, will this Center continue to function? Will the English geographers keep up their interest in studying China?" True sympathy is rooted in real understanding. Real understanding should be built upon thorough investigation and sound research. Professor Roxby is one person who obtained his real understanding of China through his thorough research. His understanding generated sincere sympathy which he offered whole-heartedly in his help to China. Thus, he was a true friend to China during her age of suffering. And now, Professor Roxby has left us. May we wish him rest in peace forever.

I recently wrote two essays for the Chinese periodical *History and Geography Weekly*. Both concerned Professor Roxby. The first is a Chinese translation of Professor Darby's Inaugural Lecture at the time he succeeded Professor Roxby as Dean of the School of Geography at Liverpool University. It contains the following passage concerning Professor Roxby:

It is customary in an inaugural lecture to render homage to one's predecessors. It is a good custom. But it would be impertinent of me to praise Professor Roxby's 40 years' work here; his own creation, the School of Geography with its long line of devoted students, speaks for itself. Numbered among his students are not only those who have been fortunate enough to study in Liverpool. Others in other universities in Britain are his pupils, and have gained from his idealism and humanity.

Beyond Britain, and particularly in China and Egypt, the same generous influence has been felt. Professor Roxby's work on China has not only enriched our knowledge in the more technical geographic sense, but has deepened our understanding of Chinese civilization.

Professor Roxby has gone, and now it is through words such as those of Professor Darby's that we feel his affection and guidance. I admit that

"这样说起来，在他作'文化使节'之前，在英日还没有宣战之前，他已经作了我们的'战友'了！"

这时，我蓦然回头，看见挂在墙上的大玻璃镜中，顾颉刚师所手写的《尚书·禹贡》全文，这是当"中国地理研究室"成立时，罗士培教授的高足张印堂教授（清华大学）与林超教授（中央大学）所共同赠送的纪念。我心里不禁想道："罗教授去世了，英国研究中国地理的中心，还会在这里继续么？英国的地理学者还会像以前那样对中国研究热心么？"真正的同情，基于真正的了解，真正的了解，基于真正的研究。罗教授是真正由研究而了解，由了解而同情，由同情而援助中国的一位患难中伟大的良友！如今他放下了他的工作，他永久安息了！

在我最近寄给《史地周刊》的两篇文稿中，都会涉及罗士培教授。第一是拙译德贝教授的就任演讲。在那篇演讲中，德贝教授对他的前任罗士培教授曾经说过这样的话：

在就任演讲中，照例是要对前任表示敬意的。但要本人在这里称赞罗士培教授在本校四十年的工作，未免有些鲁莽。罗教授所手创的地理学院，以及其专诚献身的满门桃李，已自昭彰在人耳目。何况，出身在他门墙之下的，还不仅限于幸能身临利物浦以得亲炙教授的人呢！英国其他大学的好多人，也都是他的小学生，并且因他的理想与人性，而深受陶冶。英国之外，特别是在中国与埃及，也同样沾受了他丰厚的赐惠。罗士培教授关于中国的著作，不但在专门的地理学的意义上，增加了我们的知识，并且使我们更进一步了解了中国的文化。

现在，罗教授已经去世了。在他去世之后，我们再重读德贝教授对他的评语，尤觉无限亲切。当我最初翻译这一段的时候，我立刻觉得

when I translated Professor Darby's words I felt he had spoken what I wanted very much to express from my own heart.

Once again I remember the many people who expressed their affection and respect for Professor Roxby since my arrival in England. Here is a letter from a former English student of Professor Roxby, a mother of two children who graduated from the School of Geography at Liverpool:

> I too studied geography at Liverpool many years ago under Professor Roxby, for whom I have great affection and respect. It is a pity that he is not in Liverpool now.

I would like to change the last sentence of her letter to "It is a pity that he is not in this world now." I know she will mourn for him. Her words not only express her own feeling but that of his many friends in England. Professor Roxby was not only a scholar of geography, but a great teacher in geographical education. As a great teacher he not only offered us his knowledge, but also, in Professor Darby's words, nurtured us with his ideals and personality, which is the most important thing.

As an educator, Professor Roxby leaves behind him such a deep impression and influence that he and his achievements will live after him forever. Truly, the spark of his physical life is no more, but his "ideals and personality" will live and be carried on by those who succeed him.

For me, a student who came from far-off China, hoping to be taught by Professor Roxby personally, this hope will now never be realized. Nevertheless, the moment I arrived at the School, I found myself surrounded by his voice, his image and his influences. This is the place where he had worked for forty years. Every corner reflects his image of warm-heartedness and far-sightedness. Recently, for example, a dance party was organized in honour of Mr. and Mrs. Scott (the leader of the Liberal Party). A few hundred people were invited. I was surprised to also get an invitation and found out that they had done so because Professor Roxby had written from China requesting help for me. Even though I knew nothing about dancing, I nevertheless attended. There I met many of Professor Roxby's friends.

德贝教授也说出了我心中所要说的话；同时，我也立刻回想到自从我来到英国之后，有多少人曾当面对我提起了他们对于罗士培教授的亲切爱慕之情。不久之前，我还接到了未曾晤面的一位英国朋友的信，她是早年在利物浦大学地理学院毕业的一位女生，现在已经作了两个孩子的母亲，在她的信里，她曾这样写道：

> ……知道你是来研究地理的，尤为高兴。好多年前，我也是在利物浦大学从罗士培教授读地理的，对于他，我心中怀有无限的爱与敬！真可惜，他现时不在利物浦了！

刻下我找出此信，试译在这里的时候，这最后一句，应该改作："真可惜，他已经不在人世了！"她知道这消息时，一定要痛哭一场！

这位朋友的信，不只代表她个人，在英国，不知道有多少人要对这位老教授说出同样的话来："对于他，我心中怀有无限的爱与敬！"是的，他不但是一位地理学者，他更是一位地理教育的大师。一位大师所能授予人的，不止是他的学问，更重要的乃是他人格的感化，乃是他的"理想与人性"的"陶冶"（德贝教授评语）。世之为人师者，果能予人以如此的影响，果能在人心中留下这样的印象，即遗教在人，虽死犹生！他现在生命的火焰停熄了，但是他的"理想与人性"，却要永远活在后继者的心上！

对罗士培教授，我是一个万里投师而未得亲炙教益的小学生；但是在我来到此处之后，我好像无处不听见他的声音，无处不看见他的容颜。这是他工作了四十年的地方，在这地方的每一个角落里，好像都在反映着这一代大师的和煦慈爱深厚博大的音容。比如前本地自由党的领袖司各特夫妇举行社交跳舞大会，被约请的有数百人，承他们的好意也一定要我去，说是他们的朋友罗士培教授从南京写信给他们，要他们多多关照我。他们认为这是交结社会人士的好机会，所以一定要我去。我虽然不会跳舞，也只好勉强去了。到了那里之后，又遇见了许多罗士培教授的朋友。

All of them talked of him when I was presented to them. I could not help but have the impression that there was an inseparable relationship between every Chinese student here and Professor Roxby. From what these friends told me, I realized what deep affection and consideration the English people have for China, and what influence Professor Roxby has had on his friends. After the party, I wanted to write Professor Roxby a letter, thanking him for his kindness, even though we never got to meet. I have the following draft written in my diary, "Although I had not the opportunity to personally meet you before I left China, I nevertheless still seem to be meeting you everywhere in England." I had intended to write this to him, but later changed my mind, thinking it not so polite to say so, despite its truthfulness. Thus I delayed mailing the letter and it remained undelivered.

In my second essay for the *History and Geography Weekly* titled "A Review of Wartime English Geographers and Their Present State," I mentioned the three volumes on China edited by Professor Roxby. Although this work was completed in collaboration with others, it is chiefly the fruit of his own research on Chinese geography.

Professor Roxby wrote many scholarly papers and theses, but never published a book (with the exception of a booklet). Yet all recent English texts on Chinese geography, without exception, mention his name. In addition to his writings for periodicals, he wrote the section on Chinese geography for the *Encyclopaedia Britannica*. Because he never published a book on Chinese geography, not many people in China know him. His achievements are rooted in the field of teaching geography rather than as an author. Yet his academic achievements in geography cannot be denied. An editorial published in the first issue of the *History and Geography Weekly* contains the following passage:

> Many of us consider history and geography as academic topics only
> for historians and geographers, but not for common people. Such
> a comprehension is incomplete. If not corrected, it will hinder the

development and influence of the study and research of history and geography. Our periodical is preparing to take up the responsibility of media in the popularization of historical and geographical studies. We hope to establish a normal relationship between the research of history and geography and the education of history and geography.

他们看见我，都谈起罗士培教授，好像每一个中国学生都和罗教授有不可分离的关系似的。从他们的谈话中可以知道，罗士培教授实在代表了英国社会人士对中国最高尚最真实最友爱的关切。而此地的人则又似乎无不传染了罗士培教授的影响。当晚回来之后，我想写一封信，谢谢罗教授，因为他虽然知道我来，却是未曾见面，承他如此惦记，实可感激。当时我曾在手册上写下这样两句话："离国之前，未能谒见你，可是来到英国之后，却又无处不遇见你！"但又觉得这样的写法，虽出至诚，然而对于一位年长的前辈，似乎不够尊敬，因此竟然搁置。现在，我再想这样写去时，也没人看了！

其次，在我最近寄给《史地周刊》的第二篇文稿，《战时英国地理学界之回顾及其现状》中，我又提到罗士培教授在"地理丛书"中所主编的《中国地理》三大册，这虽非他独立完成，可是他一生对于中国地理研究的结晶，应当都在这里了。罗教授一生写了不少文章，却没有出版一部书（小册子除外），但是近年以来，凡讨论中国地理的西洋著作，几乎没有一册不提到他。除去在各地理杂志上他所发表的论文之外，早年《大英百科全书》中，关于中国地理的一部分，也是由他执笔的。只因他对中国的研究未出专书，所以国内的一般读者，反而不大知道他。至于他最大的贡献，我觉得与其说是在专门学术上的研究，毋宁说是在地理教育上的推动；与其说他是一位地理学专家，毋宁说他是一位地理教育的大师；自然，他在学术上的贡献也是不可泯灭的。

本刊的编者在第一期的发刊辞上，曾向读者诸君宣告说：

一般人提到史地，马上觉得这是史地学专家的专门学问，普通人不敢也不能问津。这种不健全的现象，若不加以纠正，将使史地研究失掉意义和作用。本刊愿意负责介绍人的责任，作些普及化的工作，使史地研究与史地教育发生正常的关系。

In the eyes of modern geographers, Professor Roxby was the first colleague to accomplish the task of promoting the desired normal relationship between research and education in geography.

On hearing the sad news of Professor Roxby's passing away, I cannot help leaving my daily work undone and planning this short passage to express my feelings about an unforgettable memory. By sending it to this periodical, I hope Professor Roxby's life and work may be an inspiration to all readers. However, do forgive my toughness in writing.

Let us remember Professor Roxby as a great teacher of geography in our time! Let us remember him as our true friend, a friend of China when she was suffering. May we wish that his blessings, ideals and personality be with us, forever!

February 18, 1947. A very cold day.

在现代地理学家中，罗士培教授可以说是作到了"使地理学的研究与地理学的教育发生正常的关系"的第一人！

作者今日得此噩报，痛悼万端，不得不扔下平日的工作，将痛苦抑郁之情，有所抒发，所以信笔写下了这篇追悼的文字。又因为罗教授一生的工作，正是本刊努力的榜样，所以又大胆把这篇私人追悼的文字，寄呈本刊的读者。假如语无伦次，亦是情不自禁，望读者诸君原谅。最后让我们纪念这位当代地理教育的大师！

让我们纪念这位患难中的中国的良友！

愿他的遗泽长存人世！

愿他的"理想"与"人性"继续不朽！

一九四七年二月十八日大寒中

⓫ ADDRESS AT THE COMMENCEMENT OF LIVERPOOL UNIVERSITY[*]

It is a rare honour to speak on behalf of the graduates and honorary graduates to express our gratitude to the University of Liverpool for all we have received from her in training of our minds and increasing our awarenesses.

The young graduates among us will be discovering more and more of this debt as the years pass by.

Others of us must reminisce.

My membership of the University should have begun in 1940 or 1941. In 1939 Yenching University (a private university in Beijing now absorbed into the National Peking University) awarded me the Blue Funnel Scholarship, established by the Alfred Holt Shipping Company. All told the scholarship has been held by six persons working in Physics, Statistics, Economics and Geography.

I remember clearly how one morning in the autumn of 1938, my professor, the distinguished Chinese historian, William Hung, summoned me to his office and said, "Choosing a teacher is more important than choosing a school. The happiest thing is when the good teacher you need is to be found in a good school." While I was wondering what he was talking about, he continued, "We have nominated you for a scholarship for advanced study in the School of Geography of Liverpool University. There you will find a world-renowned teacher of geography in a university of world-wide connections. He is Professor Percy Maude Roxby."

It was not to be, because the Second World War broke out. In 1941, instead of sitting in a Liverpool University lecture hall, I found myself in a Japanese army prison, along with Professor Hung and other colleagues (including Dr. Lin Chia-Tung, an earlier Blue Funneller who studied Statistics here).

The link between Liverpool University and Yenching University survived the war, and in 1946 my dream of coming to Liverpool University was realized, but seven years late. By this time Professor Roxby had retired after 40 years of service. Ironically, he had gone to China as representative of the British Council. Professor H.C. Darby succeeded

拾壹 1984年7月4日在英国利物浦大学毕业典礼上代表应届毕业生及荣誉学位获得者致辞[*]

能够作为毕业生和荣誉毕业生代表发言，以表达对利物浦大学对我们心灵的训练和智识的提升的感激之情，我倍感荣幸。

随着时间的推移，我们中间的年轻毕业生将会越来越多地体会到这份感激。

其他人将会铭记一生。

我跟利物浦大学的联系应该是从 1940 或 1941 年开始的。1939 年燕京大学（北京的一所私立大学，现在已经并入国立北京大学）颁给我阿尔弗雷德·霍特船运公司设立的蓝烟囱奖学金。先后有六位从事物理学、统计学、经济学和地理学研究的学者获此殊荣。

我清楚地记得 1938 年秋的一个早晨，我的老师，著名的中国历史学家洪业教授是怎样把我喊到他的办公室，对我说，"择校不如投师，投师要投名师。"当我还在琢磨他说的是什么的时候，他继续说："我们已经提名你接受去利物浦大学地理学院深造的奖学金了。在这所跟世界广泛联系的大学里，你将会认识一位世界知名的地理学老师。他就是罗士培教授。"

但事情没这么简单。因为第二次世界大战爆发了。1941 年，我非但没有坐在利物浦大学的讲堂里，却和洪教授以及其他同事（包括林嘉通博士，之前在利物浦大学攻读统计学的蓝烟囱奖学金得主）一起被关进了日本军队的监狱。

利物浦大学和燕京大学之间的纽带在战火中幸存了下来，1946 年我来利物浦大学的梦想终于在七年之后实现。这个时候罗士培教授已经服务四十年退休了。而命运弄人，他却作为英国使馆文化教育处的代表去了中国。德贝教授接替他担任地理学院的

him as Head of the School of Geography. His Inaugural Lecture "The Theory and Practice of Geography" made such an impression on me that I translated it into Chinese and it was published in Tientsin in the *History and Geography Weekly*, a supplement of the famous *Yi Shi Newspaper* on March 18, 1947. Alas! that same issue also contained an essay I wrote commemorating Professor Roxby who had just died in China. I have brought a photograph of that issue of the *Weekly* together with an English version of my article, for presentation to the Library of the School of Geography.

The many new ideas on historical geography that Professor Darby developed in his teaching have been influential in China, producing a new school of study that has grown especially fast in the past decade. Just before I came abroad early this year, we established a new Research Centre on Historical Geography along these lines in Peking University.

There is a Chinese proverb 饮水思源: "When drinking water remember the water source." I published a book—a collection of my scientific papers which bear on some aspects of the socialist reconstruction of China. It was natural and proper for me to borrow the title of Professor Darby's Inaugural Lecture, simply adding the word "Historical": "The Theory and Practice of Historical Geography." I am giving a copy of the first edition of this little book to the Harold Cohen Library, which itself is a "water source" so ocean-like that I almost drowned in it nearly 40 years ago.

My key thought for this unforgettable day is pride and gratitude that Liverpool University has been such a bounteous source of the living water of creative thought that flows from people to people and gives us all hope for the future.

Some 40 years ago, just after the Second World War, Professor Darby said it for his particular discipline, ending his Inaugural Lecture with the following words with which I would like to end mine:

As I stand here amid the devastation of war on Brownlow Hill, and in Liverpool, a city with contacts as world-wide as those of any city, I cannot help but think that the point of view of the geographers both abroad and at home is not without some bearing on the New World we hope will be our future.

Thank you.

院长。他的就任演讲"地理学的理论与实践"给我留下了非常深刻的印象，于是我把它译成中文并于 1947 年 3 月 18 号发表在天津著名的《益世报》的副刊《史地周刊》。同一期还发表了我写的缅怀刚刚在中国去世的罗士培教授的文章。这次我带来了这一期周刊的翻拍照片以及我文章的英译本，将呈献给地理学院图书馆。

德贝教授在教学中形成的关于历史地理学的很多新观点已经在中国产生了很大的影响，并催生了一个在过去十年间飞速发展的新学派。就在今年我出国之前，北京大学新设立了一个这方面的历史地理学研究中心。

中国有句成语叫饮水思源——喝水的时候要记得水的源泉。我出版了一本有关中国社会主义重建若干问题的科学论文集。我顺理成章地借用了德贝教授就任演讲的标题，仅仅加上了"历史"这个词——《历史地理学的理论与实践》。我将拙著第一版赠送给哈罗德·科恩图书馆，四十年前正是在这座图书馆徜徉时我几乎被浩瀚的知识海洋所淹没。

这难忘的一天中我最深的感受是欢愉和感激，利物浦大学是创造性思想的宽广丰沛的活水源头，这活水在人们之间流淌着，带给我们所有的人对未来的希望。

大约四十年前，就在二战后，德贝教授就他的学科说了如下这番话，以此结束他的演说，而我正想用它来结束我的发言：

> 当我站在这里，置身布朗洛山的满目疮痍，在利物浦这样一个跟任何其他城市一样与世界紧密联系的城市，我禁不住想到海内外地理学者的观点都不会不涉及一个新的世界，而它正是我们希望的未来。

谢谢。

邵冬冬　译

⑫ HOU RENZHI'S ACCEPTANCE ADDRESS FOR THE GEORGE DAVIDSON MEDAL*

When I was informed that the American Geographical Society was going to award me The George Davidson Medal, I had not thought that in these late years of my life I would receive such a high international honor. This happy news has also brought a considerable and important attention on the part of many of my colleagues in the circle of Chinese geography. I wanted very much to come and to accept this prestigious award personally. Yet, because of my poor health, I cannot but request my good friend, Dr. Diane Obenchain, who is a Visiting Professor at Peking University and who is working with me cooperatively on a project, to represent me. However, if Dr. Murphy or any other member of The Honors Committee of The American Geographical Society has the opportunity to come to China, I ardently hope that we can meet each other at Peking University so that I may in person express my heartfelt gratitude for this award.

What I would like to first explain is that George Babcock Cressey, who, in 1952, was the first to receive The George Davidson Medal, had, in fact, great influence upon me from the very start. Sixty-three years ago, in 1936, the year I graduated from Yenching University, I was fortunate enough to read Cressey's book *China's Geographic Foundations*. This drew my profound interest and is one of the main reasons why I was moved to change from strictly historical studies to research in historical geography. However, because of the eight-year Anti-Japanese War, it was not until the summer of 1946 that I was able to go as planned to Liverpool University in England to specialize in the study of historical geography under the expert guidance of Professor H. C. Darby.

In 1949, Professor G. B. Cressey, as the newly-elected President of the International Geographical Union, was invited to Liverpool University to give a guest lecture entitled "China's Prospects." This occasion remains quite distinct in my memory. The day was April

27th, in the afternoon. A great many people came to hear the lecture, which indicated a tremendous interest in China's future. I also was very moved by the lecture. Professor Darby presided over the lecture and at his request I was invited to give a few words in gratitude on behalf of the audience at the end of the lecture. This was the first time that I had occasion to meet Professor Cressey and it has remained an unforgettable memory for the rest of my life.

拾贰 在美国地理学会荣誉委员会授奖仪式上的发言[*]

　　在我获悉美国地理学会将要授予我乔治·戴维森勋章的时候，我没有想到在我人生的晚年能够获得如此崇高的国际荣誉。这个喜讯，也引起了中国地理界众多好友的高度重视。我极愿意亲自前来接受这一崇高的荣誉，只因健康关系，不能成行，只好拜托在北京大学任教并且和我有合作关系的好朋友欧迪安博士前来代我领奖。但是如果墨菲博士或是美国地理学会荣誉委员会其他负责者，能有机会前来中国，我殷切希望能在北京大学相会，使我得以亲自表示我衷心的感谢。

　　在这里我愿意首先说明的是，早在1952年第一位乔治·戴维森勋章的获得者葛德石，原是对我很有影响的一位学者。六十三年前的1936年，也就是我在大学毕业的那一年，我有幸阅读了他的《中国地理基础》。这本书深深吸引了我，也是促使我从历史学转向历史地理学研究的原因之一。只是随后发生的连续八年的抗日战争，使我直到1946年夏才得以前往英国利物浦大学地理系，在德贝教授的指导下，专攻历史地理学。1949年，葛德石教授作为新当选的国际地理学会的主席，应邀前来利物浦大学作学术讲演，题目是"中国的前途"，非常引人注目，时间是在4月27日下午，当时到会的听众很多，这表明人们十分关切中国的前途。我自己听了很受鼓舞。德贝教授主持了这次演讲会，并要我在讲演完毕后，代表听众致谢辞。这是我和葛德石教授第一次会面，使我终生难忘。

What should be mentioned especially here is that it was only five months and three days after Professor Cressey's lecture that New China was born on October 1st, 1949. And it was just three days before the birth of New China that I returned to Beijing from England.

When New China established the "Beijing City Planning Committee" for reconstruction of the capital, Beijing, I had the honor to be invited as a member of the committee. For research reference and for the purposes of planning construction, my first responsibility was to make geographical investigation of the newly-designated cultural and educational region of the capital. This important region in the northwest suburbs of Beijing city, called the Haidian, was the famous terrain of the summer palaces of the Qing period, and has become today the location of Peking University, Qinghua University, the Chinese Academy of Sciences, Renmin University, the National Library, the Central University of Nationalities, the Agricultural University and several others.

Since the days of those initial tasks on the "Beijing City Planning Committee", fifty years have passed. During these fifty years, except for the few years that I participated in investigations of China's Northwestern desert areas, most of my research work has concentrated upon the historical geography of Beijing city. My intention has been to make a contribution to the planning and construction of the capital.

During the past fifty years, China has undergone enormous changes. Particularly during the last twenty years of reform and opening up to the larger world, cultural exchanges between China and other countries have increased daily. Now, as I look back over the past twenty years, during which I have had the opportunity to visit the United States twelve times, I feel greatly honored to have been invited as a Fulbright Scholar in Residence to give lectures at Illinois University during 1981-1982. I will always remember that significant time.

Following this, I received a letter of invitation from Dr. Alison Casarett, Vice Provost and Dean of the Graduate School of Cornell

University, requesting that I be their Chinese Scholar in Residence during the years 1983-1984 under the Luce Foundation Program for China Studies. In her letter she said, "I note your recent strong interest in the comparative design and layout of the older city portions of Beijing and Washington, D.C." What she said was exactly true. Therefore, her invitation was indeed a precious opportunity for me. Not only did I spend one semester doing in-house research on the campus of Cornell University, which is full of natural beauty, but I also, while on the "Cornell in Washington Program," was able to carry out on-location investigation

现在应该特别指出的是当时葛德石教授演讲的时间，距离 1949 年 10 月 1 日新中国的诞生，只有 5 个月零 3 天，也正是在新中国诞生的前三天，我从英国回到北京。

新中国重新建都北京，成立了"北京市都市计划委员会"，我有幸应邀作为委员。我所承担的第一项任务，就是为首都新定的文化教育区，进行地理考察，作为规划设计的参考。

现在五十年的时间已经过去，在这五十年间，除去有几年的时间我参加了我国西北地区的沙漠考察之外，主要的研究工作，都集中在北京城的历史地理研究上，力求为首都的规划建设，作出贡献。

过去的这五十年，中国发生了巨大的变化，特别是近二十年，在改革开放的新形势下，中外文化的交流，日益增加，现在回顾这二十年来，我曾有十二次来美国访问。其中我深感荣幸的是 1981—1982 年，我曾应邀作为富布莱特驻校学者前往伊利诺伊大学讲学，这是我永远难忘的。

其后，我又接到康奈尔大学副校长兼研究生院院长艾莉森·卡萨特博士的邀请信，约我作为驻校学者受卢斯基金会中国研究计划资助于 1983—1984 学年访问康奈尔大学。信中还特别有如下几句话："我注意到您最近对北京城与华盛顿城城市布局设计对比研究的强烈兴趣。"她讲的确是事实。因此，她的邀请，对我来说，实在是一个难得的机会，结果我不仅在康奈尔大学富有自然之美的校园里度过了一个学期的室内研究，而且还得以按照"康奈尔大学华盛顿研究计划"对华盛顿城的中心部分作了实地考察。我终于完成了

of the central part of the city of Washington, D.C. In the end, I was able to complete my piece for Chinese readers entitled, "From Beijing to Washington, D.C.—Explorations into Thematic Design in City Planning."

To look back on the past is at the same time to look ahead to future developments. This year I am eighty-eight years old. As I look back to that year when G.B. Cressey gave his lecture "China's Prospects," a new picture now unfolds before my eyes. To have this high honor of receiving The George Davidson Medal is truly a great encouragement to me. I will continue to work hard in carrying out research on the historical geography of Beijing. At the same time I join hands and go forward together with the next generation of excellent young scholars. I am very grateful to Professor Diane Obenchain who has represented me in reading my address to you today and extended once again my heartfelt respect and gratitude toward the Council of the American Geographical Society for awarding me this most precious honor. Thank you.

为中国读者写的论文，题目就是"从北京到华盛顿——城市设计主题思想试探"。

现在回顾过去，正是为了展望未来。今年我已88岁，回顾当年葛德石所用过的讲题"中国的前途"，又有新的景象展现在眼前。我能荣获乔治·戴维森勋章，正是对我极大的鼓励，我将在北京历史地理的研究上继续努力，并和后起之秀携手前进。我非常感谢欧迪安教授代我宣读我的讲话稿，并代替我再一次向美国地理学会理事会表示我的敬意和感激之情。谢谢。

NOTES 注释

❶

* 中文稿在《历史地理》（第二辑）发表时，作者曾在本文开头简短作注，现照录如下：
"1980 年春，作者应加拿大不列颠哥伦比亚大学的邀请，前往进行短期讲学，曾作公开讲演三次，现在把有关北京历史地理两讲的中文原稿，略加删改合为一篇，重新标题，发表在这里，请国内读者指正。"本版收录的英文即为作者演讲稿原文，由打印稿转录而来。——编者注

1 中国抗日战争历时十四年。此处八年抗战指从"卢沟桥事变"日本发动全面侵华战争开始，中国人民的八年全面抗日战争。——编者注

2 本书英文部分统用"nationality"指涉中国的民族，此系旧表达，现已弃用。但为保留作品原貌，编者未予改动。——编者注

3 清建国于 1616 年，初称后金，1636 年始改国号为清，1644 年入关。同一问题重复出现不另作说明。各篇文章创作、发表年代不同，人名、地名的拼写、译法或有出入，在单篇文章内保持一致。——编者注

❷

* 中文稿刊于《城市问题》1984 年第 6 辑，作者曾在本文开头简短作注，现照录如下：
"美国芝加哥大学地理系为该系著名地理学家 C. D. 哈瑞斯教授（Chauncy D. Harris）的退休编辑出版了纪念性学术论文集《现代城市变化的世界模式》（*World Patterns of Modern Urban Change*, Michael P. Conzen ed., Chicago: University of Chicago, 1986）。世界各大洲（除南极洲外）都有地理学家应邀撰稿。此文即该论文集 21 篇论文中的一篇，用英文刊出，这是中文原稿。"——编者注

1 Paul Wheatley, *The Pivot of the Four Quarters: A Preliminary Enquiry into the Origins and Character of the Ancient Chinese City.* Chicago: Aldine Publishing Company, 1971, p. 425.

2 Later the name was changed to Jing Shan (Scenic Mountain) and also Mei Shan (Coal Hill).

后来改名景山，俗称煤山。

3 During this period, the canal formerly outside the Royal City's east wall was incorporated into the Royal City, and shipping on the Grand Canal was thus unable to reach Ji-shui Tan. The lower part of Ji-shui Tan was connected with Tai-ye Chi to the south, and the aqueduct which had been specifically created to supply water to Tai-ye Chi was abandoned. Altogether, the city's water system regressed under the Ming Dynasty's management.

这时连同原在皇城东墙之外的运河渠道，也被包入城中，从此大运河的船只，再也不能驶入积水潭，积水潭的下游又恢复了南接太液池的故道，而太液池先前专用的

引水渠也就日渐湮废。因此从河渠水道的调整来说，明北京城较前是退步了。

4 The name "Shan Chuan Tan" was later changed to "Xian-nong Tan" (Altar of the God of Agriculture).

山川坛后来又改称先农坛。

5 During the Ming Dynasty, the Tian-an Men was called the Cheng-tian Men.

明曰承天门。

6 Steen Eiler Rasmussen, *Towns and Buildings*, paperback edition. Cambridge, Mass.: First MIT Press, 1969. Preface, p. v.

7 Edmund N. Bacon, *Design of Cities*, revised edition. London: Penguin Books, 1980, p. 244.

8 The actual work, of course, was not without problems. For instance, in the cases of the demolition of the old city wall and most of the old gates and the filling of the moat, there was serious disagreement in the beginning. From today's point of view, these are simply irretrievably lost.

自然，在实际工作中，也不是全无问题的。例如旧日城墙和大部分城楼的拆除以及部分护城河的填塞，在最初就是有争议的，现在看来已是无可弥补的损失。

9 See *The Beijing Daily* (*Beijing Ribao*), August 3, 1983, and *The Beijing Evening News* (*Beijing Wanbao*), August 4, 1983.

见 1983 年 8 月 3 日《北京日报》和 8 月 4 日《北京晚报》。

❸

* 英文稿原发表于*China City Planning Review* (Sept. 1995)，文前摘要如下："This article has made comments on the three milestones in the construction of Beijing City: the Forbidden City, the Tian'anmen Square and the Public Building Complex outstandingly embodying the new style and features of the capital of the 21st century, along the northern extension line of the middle axis of the whole city. According to this demonstration, the author has further pointed out that the development of the third milestone is in fact the break-through in Beijing's traditional thought of design and demonstrated the origin of this traditional thought of design in accordance with the discovery in archaeology."

中文稿自北京大学院士文库《侯仁之文集》(1998) 选出。——编者注

1 Zhu Wenyi, *Space, Mark, City*, China Building Industry Publishing House, 1993, p. 167.

朱文一：《空间·符号·城市》，中国建筑工业出版社，1993 年，第 167 页。

2 Zhu Wenyi has the narration. Please see "On the Discussion of the Theory of City Sketch" in *Space, Mark, City*, 1993, p. 248.

朱文一同志有记述，参见朱文一：《空间·符号·城市》，中国建筑工业出版社，1993 年，第 248 页。

3 Hou Renzhi, "On the Remolding of the Old Beijing City," in *City Planning Review* (in Chinese), 1983, No. 1, pp. 20-23.

侯仁之：《论北京旧城的改造》，载《城市规划》，1983 年，第 1 期。

4 Hou Renzhi, "The Inheritance and Development of Beijing Forbidden City on Planning and Design," in *National Studies*, 1993, No. 1.

侯仁之：《北京紫禁城在规划设计上的继承与发展》，载《国学研究》，第一卷，1993 年。

5 In accordance with the discovery, there are two palace relics. On the northeast, approximately 150 meters from the No. 1 palace relic, there is No. 2 palace relic, which is smaller in scale but much the same of the model. See Erlitou Work Team, Archaeology Research Institute, Chinese Academy of Science, "Brief Report on the Early Shang Dynasty Palace Ruins Excavation in Yanshi County, Henan Province," *Archaeology*, 1972, No. 4.

中国科学院考古研究所二里头工作队：《河南偃师二里头早商宫殿遗址发掘简报》，载《考古》，1974 年，第 4 期。按该文所载上述发现共有二处宫殿遗址，另有二号宫殿遗址，在一号宫殿遗址东北约 150 米，规模较小而形制略同。

6 China Academy of Architectural Sciences, *Ancient Architecture of China*, China Building Industry Publishing House, 1983.

中国建筑科学研究院：《中国古建筑》，中国建筑工业出版社，1983 年。

7 "Xue Sui Zhai Xuan", *Yu Sui Zhen Jing*, Vol. 19. Block printed at the period of Emperor Jiajing of the Ming Dynasty. Revised version by Li Wentian of the Qing Dynasty.

《玉髓真经》卷十九《穴髓摘玄》，明嘉靖刻，清李文田旧校本。

❹

* 英文稿前原有关于本研究的背景介绍，现照录如下：Comparison between Chinese and foreign municipalities is one of the most important aspects of scientific urban research. Such research has only begun in China. It will help us to improve the process and development of urban construction, to inherit better the wealth of China's culture, to absorb more appropriately the cultural achievements of foreign countries, and thus, to be able to create the kind of Chinese city and urban culture that will bear the special characteristics of the Age of Socialism. Professor Hou's paper "From Beijing to Washington—A Contemplation on the Concept of Municipal Planning" is a persuasive study based on a comparison between Chinese and foreign municipalities. He discusses the subject in the aspects of historical, cultural and chronological differences. He points out the special features of Beijing and Washington and the development of the basic conceptual theme in their designs and plans. He puts forth a detailed comparison between the two cities and offers ingenious suggestions on the future construction and development of Beijing. Professor Hou made a special study in 1984 at the College of Architecture in Cornell University on the subject of the comparison between Beijing and Washington, the choice of the sites of the capitals and their design and plan. This is the first article of his research.

中文原载《城市问题》1987 年第 3 期，本次自北京大学院士文集《侯仁之文集》选出，较前者略有删改。——编者注

1 Steen Eiler Rasmussen, *Towns and Buildings*, paperback edition. Cambridge, Mass.: First MIT Press, 1969. Preface, p. v.

2 Edmund N. Bacon, *Design of Cities*, revised edition. London: Penguin Books, 1980, p. 244.

3 中国建筑工业出版社，1985 年，第 55—56 页。

4 《城市规划》双月刊，1983 年，第 1 期。

5 河南偃师县二里头夏代遗址的上层，发现迄今所见我国最早的大型宫殿遗基两座，距今至少在三千六七百年以前，其中一座的遗址，略成正方形，中部偏北处，有一长方台基，根据基址上柱穴的排列，可以复原为一座殿堂，东西长 30.4 米，南北宽 11.4 米，殿前为广庭，四周为墙基，墙内有廊庑，大门在基址南墙的中间。详见中国科学院考古研究所洛阳发掘队：《河南偃师二里头遗址发掘简报》，载《考古》，1965 年，第 5 期。又湖北黄陂县以盘龙城命名的商代中期都城，距今约三千五百年，城内大型宫殿基址两处，也都是面向正南。详见湖北省博物馆、北京大学考古专业、盘龙城发掘队：《盘龙城一九七四年度田野考古纪要》，载《文物》，1976 年，第 2 期。

6 详见《盘龙城一九七四年度田野考古纪要》。

7 盘龙城平面略呈方形，中轴线方向为北偏东 20 度，城垣至 1954 年仍保存得比较完整。已发现的宫殿基址，在城内东北部，见注 5。又郑州所发现的商城中的宫殿基址，也同样是在略呈方形城垣内的东北部，详见河南省博物馆、郑州博物馆：《郑州商代城遗址发掘报告》，《文物资料丛刊》第 1 辑，文物出版社，1977 年。

8 1776 年，《独立宣言》发表，宣告美国成立。1783 年，英国正式承认美国独立。——编者注

9 朗方设计的城市蓝图的示意图，还镌刻在从白宫到国会大厦的宾夕法尼亚大道中途一个街心广场的石筑台基上，供人鉴赏。1984 年 8 月 6 日，华盛顿市长正式宣布这一天为"朗方日"，以志纪念。当时作者适在华盛顿的康奈尔大会研究中心工作，因此得到机会参加这次纪念会，进一步体会到朗方在今天美国首都人民心目中的地位。

10 《马克思恩格斯全集》第 16 卷，人民出版社，1964 年，第 20 页。

11 1787 年，制宪会议通过《美利坚合众国宪法》。——编者注

12 《马克思恩格斯全集》第 16 卷，人民出版社，1964 年，第 21 页。

13 这是 1982 年应征入选的设计，当时林樱（Maya Lin）尚在耶鲁大学建筑系学习。

❺

* 英文稿曾在 1964 年北京科学讨论会上宣读。中文原载《科学通报》1964 年 11 月刊，本次自《历史地理学的理论与实践》(1979) 选出。——编者注

1 J. N. L. Baker, *A History of Geographical Discovery and Exploration*, London, 1931, pp. 63–70.

2 Herodotus, *The History of Herodotus*, translated by G. Rawlinson, New York, 1946, pp. 216–217.

3 The account of Herodotus has raised much controversy, but of late there has been a tendency to belief. See J. Oliver Thomson, *History of Ancient Geography*, Cambridge, 1948, pp. 71–73. J. N. L. Baker points out that "the geographical conditions do not make such a feat impossible." *Op. cit.*, p. 23.

曾有人对此表示怀疑，却无法加以否定，见 J. N. L. Baker，前引著作，p. 23。Baker 且指出："地理条件使得这样一次航行的完成，并非是不可能的。"关于这一问题讨论的趋势是，越来越认为希罗多德的记述是可信的，详见 J. Oliver Thomson, *History of Ancient Geography*, Cambridge, 1948, pp. 71–73.

4 *Vsemirnaya Istoriya*, TOM. 4, Str. 88, M. M. Smirin (otechestrennyi redaktor), Moskva, 1958.

World History (in Russian), Vol. 4, p. 88, M. M. Smirin (chief editor), Moscow, 1958.

[苏] 斯米林主编：《世界通史》第 4 卷，三联书店，1962 年，上册第 104 页。又 G. Ferrand 引 D. Couto 的考证，谓爪哇人也在很早以前就已远航到非洲大陆的南端，见《昆仑及南海古代航行考》，冯承钧译，中华书局，1957 年，第 66 页。

5 K. G. Jayne, *Vasco da Gama and His Successors: 1460–1580*, London, 1910, p. 48. See also J. N. L. Baker, *op. cit.*, pp. 69–70.

6 With reference to the life and work of Ibn Madjid, see article on Shihab al-Din Ahmad b Madjid in the *Encyclopaedia of Islam*, pp. 362–370, London, 1934.

关于伊本·马吉德的身世、著作以及与达·伽马的关系，见 *Encyclopaedia of Islam*, Vol. IV, pp. 362–370, "Shihab al-Din Ahmad B. Madjid", London, 1934。伊本·马吉德的著作 32 篇原稿现藏巴黎国立图书馆阿拉伯部，编号 2292、2559。

7 *Han Shu* (Dynastic History of Han), *Chüan* 28, *Ti Li Chih* (Book on Geography).

《汉书》卷二八《地理志》。

8 1978年改称斯里兰卡。——编者注

9 For detailed account of Fa Hsien's travel in India and Ceylon, see his own work *Fo Kuo Chi*.

法显于公元 399 年由长安出发，从陆路前往印度，归途泛海，由印度到锡兰，由锡兰回中国，见所著《佛国记》（或称《法显传》）。

10 The Arab Empire is recorded in ancient Chinese works as *Ta Shih*.

11 A distinguished Chinese geographer Chia Tan in the eighth century made a

valuable record on the sea-route from Canton to the Gulf of Iran. See *Hsin T'ang Shu* (New Dynastic History of T'ang), *Chüan* 43, *Ti Li Chih Chi* (Book on Geography, 7).

8 世纪时中国地理学家贾耽 (729–805) 曾经记述了从广州到今波斯湾的航路，见《新唐书》卷四三《地理志七》所转载。

[12] H. Yule and H. Cordier, *The Book of Ser Marco Polo, the Venetian: Concerning the Kingdoms and Marvels of the East*, revised 3rd. ed., pp. 234–235, London, 1903.

[13] Ibn Battuta, *Voyages d'Ibn Batoutah*: Texte Arabe, Accompagne D'une Traduction, Beniamino Raffaello Sanguinetti and Charles Defremery ed. and trans., Vol. 4, Paris, 1922, pp. 268–269.

[14] Situzo Kuwabara has made an extensive study on the life of P'u Shou-keng and his scholarly work has been translated into Chinese by Chen Yü-ch'ing entitled *P'u Shou-keng K'ao* (2nd print, Shanghai, 1954).

日本学者桑原骘藏：《蒲壽庚の事蹟》，东京，1935 年。此书对蒲寿庚身世有详细考证，兼及唐宋时代中国与阿拉伯海上通商的情况。有陈裕菁汉文译本，题《蒲寿庚考》，上海，1954 年。

[15] The dates of the seven voyages of Cheng Ho are as follows:

1. 1405—1407, 2. 1407—1409, 3. 1409—1411, 4. 1413—1415,

5. 1417—1419, 6. 1421—1422, 7. 1430—1433.

During the last ninety years various studies on the life of Cheng Ho have been published by European and American scholars. The French Orientalist P. Pelliot has written a comprehensive dissertation, Les grands voyages maritimes chinois au début du XVe siècle, *Toung Pao*, 1933, pp. 237–452. Owing to the lack of indispensable source materials, mistakes in his conclusions on the dates of the last six voyages of Cheng Ho are unavoidable.

七次航行年代：1405—1407，1407—1409，1409—1411，1413—1415，1417—1419，1421—1422，1430—1433。近百年来，欧美学者研究郑和及其事迹者颇不乏人，著述亦多。书较晚出、影响较大的是法人 P. Pelliot，所著长文：Les grands voyages maritimes chinois au début du XVe siècle，发表于 *Toung Pao*，1933，pp. 237–452。但是由于作者所据的史料不足，对于郑和后六次航行日期的考订，不免有错误。

[16] Chu Yün-ming, *Chien Wen Chi,* article on the voyages of Cheng Ho, *Chi Lu Hui Pien* edition, *Chüan* 202, p. 37.

祝允明：《前闻记》，"下西洋"条，《纪录汇编》卷二〇二，商务印书馆影印明刻本，页三七引。

[17] *Ibid.*, and *Cheng Ho Hang Hai T'u* (The Sailing Chart of Cheng Ho), edited by Hsiang Ta, Peking, 1961.

航海记录见祝允明：《前闻记》，"下西洋"条。航海图原题《自宝船厂开船从龙江关出水直抵外国诸番图》，近经北京大学向达教授加以考订和说明，作为专书，题为《郑和航海图》，于 1961 年由中华书局影印出版。书中还另附郑和远航的略图，图上除去第七次航路外，还表示了前六次所曾经航行过的路线，而且把一些已能确考的现在地名，加注在原地名后面，古今对照，一目了然。这是已发表的有关郑和远航路线图中最好的一幅，本文附图即据此图简化复制。

18 For detailed information, see S. A. Huzayyin, *Arabia and the Far East: Their Commercial Cultural Relations in Graeco-Roman and Irano-Arabian Times*, Cairo, 1942, pp. 112–113, and J. N. L. Baker, *op. cit.*, pp. 19–20.

19 Tu Huan (in *Ching Hsing Chi*) and Tuan Ch'eng-shih (in *Yu Yang Tsa Tsu*) of the T'ang Dynasty gave the earliest information in Chinese records about Molin Kingdom. Tuan's work is easily available, while Tu's work is now preserved in the form of citations in other works. A collection of these citations with commentaries has been published recently by Chang Yi-ch'un under the title *Ching Hsing Chi Chien Chu*, Peking, 1963.

唐朝杜环所著《经行记》一书中，有关于摩邻国的记载，见杜环著，张一纯笺注：《经行记笺注》，中华书局，1963 年，第 20 页。按摩邻国有的学者认为即是麻林（或麻林地）国。又段成式所著《酉阳杂俎》一书中，有关于拨拔力国的记载，见汲古阁刻本，卷四，"异境"条，页四上。《新唐书》卷二二一下《大食传》引用其文。按拨拔力即 Berbera（今译柏培拉）在中国最早之对音。参考冯承钧《诸蕃志校注》，中华书局，1956 年，第 55 页。

20 *Sung Shih* (Dynastic History of Sung), *Chüan* 490, section on *Tsengtan*.

《宋史》卷四〇〇，"层檀"条。

21 Feng Ch'eng-chün, *Chu Fan Chih Chiao Chu*, Shanghai, 1956, pp. 54–55. *Chu Fan Chih* was written by Chau Ju-kua in 1225. It has been translated and annotated by F. Hirth and W. W. Rockhill (*Chau Ju-kua: His Work on the Chinese and Arab Trade in the Twelfth and Thirteenth Centuries, entitled Chu-fan-chi*. St. Petersburg, 1911).

冯承钧：《诸蕃志校注》，第 54—55 页。此书有 F. Hirth 和 W. W. Rockhill 英译本，并加注释，题曰：*Chau Ju-kua: His Work on the Chinese and Arab Trade in the Twelfth and Thirteenth Centuries, Entitled Chu-fan-chi*, St. Petersburg, 1911. 本文所根据的冯承钧校注本采用了 Hirth 与 Rockhill 的注译，并作了订正和补充。又元代汪大渊在 1329—1339 年间，乘海舶远游中国南海及印度洋，就所见闻，著《岛夷志略》一书（约写成于 1349 年），记有层摇罗，即桑给巴尔。

22 See Feng Ch'eng-chün, *op. cit.*, and Wang Ta-yüan, *Tao Yi Chih Lueh*, written about 1349.

例如写成于 1225 年的赵汝适的《诸蕃志》，就有下列各国的记载：勿斯里国（埃及）、中理国（索马里沿岸，包括 Socotra 岛，今译索科特拉岛）、弼琶罗国（Berbera）、层拔国等。

23 Hsia Nai, Porcelain Links in Sino-African History, *Wen Wu Monthly*, Peking, 1963, No. 1, pp. 17–19.

早在 1888 年，桑给巴尔就有宋代中国铜钱和瓷器出土，1898 年索马里的摩加迪沙，也发现宋代中国铜钱和瓷器。近年以来，在索马里和埃塞俄比亚交界处的三个古城废墟，和在坦噶尼喀（Lake Tanganyika）沿岸 40 多处古代遗址，以及松哥玛那拉（Songo Mnara）岛上，都有很多中国瓷器瓷片的发现，其中有宋末元初的龙泉窑青瓷片。在肯尼亚的马林迪附近的给地（Gedi）古城中，还有宋代铜钱出土。此外摩加迪沙还曾有唐代铜钱的发现，详见夏鼐：《作为古代中非交通关系证据的瓷器》，载《文物》1963 年第 1 期。按在 12 世纪时，中国与东非可能已有直接的通商贸易，中国海舶可能已航驶东非。参看张铁生：《从东非史上看中非关系》，载《历史研究》1963 年第 2 期。

24 Chu Yü, *P'ing Chou K'ê T'an*, Shou Shan Kê edition, *Chüan* 2, 1922, p. 3. Hsu Ching, *Hsüan Ho Feng Shih Kao Li T'u Ching*, T'ien Lu Lin Lang edition, *Chüan* 34, p. 12, 1931.

朱彧：《萍洲可谈》卷二，博古斋 1922 年影印守山阁丛书本，页三下；又徐竞：《宣和奉使高丽图经》卷三四，北京故宫博物院 1931 年影印天禄琳琅丛书本，页十二上。

25 Situzo Kuwabara, *A Study of P'u Shou-keng* (in Japanese), Tokyo, 1935, pp. 92‑93.

桑原骘藏：《蒲寿庚の事蹟》，第 92—93 页。

26 Hsiang Ta, *op. cit.*, p. 57.

意即从官屿群岛出发，按庚酉方向（约当 262 度左右）前航到达木骨都束。向达：《郑和航海图》，页五七。

27 Feng Ch'eng-chün, *Hsing Ch'a Sheng Lan Chiao Chu*, Shanghai, 1954, pp. 21, 24. *Hsing Ch'a Sheng Lan* written by Fei Hsin is one of the three important geographical works compiled at the time of Cheng Ho's navigations. The other two works are *Ying Ya Sheng Lan* by Ma Huan and *Hsi Yang Fan Kuo Chih* by Kung Chen. Both Ma and Kung also took part in Cheng Ho's voyages and gave an account of the countries they visited in their works.

费信于郑和远航之第三、四、五、七次随同前往，著《星槎胜览》一书，是从行者所著三部重要的地理著作之一。其余两部是马欢的《瀛涯胜览》和巩珍的《西洋番国志》，后者极为罕见，近来向达教授根据一个抄本加以整理注释，于 1959 年出版。

28 当时交易情况，具见《瀛涯胜览》、《星槎胜览》、《西洋番国志》等书，一般都是在中国船到之时，先以明王朝的名义向有关地方或国家行政当局赠送礼品，然后由该地方或国家行政当局传谕人民，进行交易。

❻

* 1981 年 2 月 11 日作者根据中加文化交流的协议前往加拿大，2 月 11 日—3 月 24 日在英属哥伦比亚大学（University of British Columbia）讲学。本文英文为 1981 年 2 月 13 日演讲稿。本版收录的中英文文本均自作者手稿转录而来，原稿约作于 1980 年。——编者注

¹ Probably it is interesting to know how Professor J. Needham, the distinguished author of the voluminous work *Science and Civilisation in China*, writes about Hsü Xia-Ke, "His notes... read more like those of a 20th-century field surveyor than a 17th-century scholar. He had a wonderful power of analysing topographical detail, and made systematic use of special terms which enlarged the ordinary nomenclature... Everything was noted carefully in feet or *li*, without vague stock phrases." (Vol. 3, London: Cambridge University Press, 1959, p. 524) And it is no wonder that the famous Chinese geologist Prof. Ting Wen-Chiang, who made a great contribution on the study of Hsü's life, once said that Hsü "was essentially a geographical explorer. The spirit of inquiry is so startlingly modern, that it alone would have ranked him as the earliest leader of modern geography in China." (Ting, *The New China Review*, III, 5, Oct. 1921, pp. 325–337.)

² For an English-language edition, see *T'ien-kung K'ai-wu: Chinese Technology in the Seventeenth Century* (University Park: Pennsylvania State University Press, 1966).

❼

* 英文选自《国际古迹遗址理事会第八届全体大会暨"新世界中的古老文化"国际研讨会论文集》第一部。(*Symposium Papers of 8th General Assembly of International Council on Monuments and Sites, and International Symposium "Old Cultures in New Worlds", October 10-15, 1987*, Vol. 1. Washington D. C.: ICOMOS, 1987. Print.) ——编者注

¹ 对 China 一词的起源有多种解释。一种说法认为，China 是在秦的罗马字拼音 Chin 后面加上 -a 表示地域。这一观点在 1986 年出版的《剑桥中国秦汉史》中被肯定。——编者注

² There is another version of the legend saying that a section of the wall crumbled, exposing to Meng Jiang the bones of her husband.

³ Zeng Zhaoming and Gu Wei, *An Investigation on the Present Condition of the Great Wall in the Beijing District*, Remote-sensing Centre of the Ministry of Geology and Mining, 1985.

❽

* 1981 年 11 月 2 日至 1982 年 2 月，作者应美国国际学者交换委员会（Council for International Exchange of Scholars）的邀请，作为富布莱特学者（Fulbright Scholar in Residence）到美国伊利诺伊大学厄巴那 - 香槟分校（University of Illinois at Urbana-Champaign）地理系讲学，公开演讲六次。12 月 9 日演讲 "Outstanding Ancient City Ruins in the Deserts of the Inner Mongolia Autonomous Region of China"（《中国内蒙古自治区沙漠中几个重要的古城废墟》）。英文又于 1985 年发表于《历史地理学刊》（*Journal of Historical Geography*, Vol. 11, No. 3, pp. 241–252），附题注 "This article is a revised version of a lecture presented at several universities in Canada and the United States during recent visits." 本版英文即摘自《历史地理学刊》，中文

自作者手稿转录而来。中英文文本的创作时间均应在 1980—1981 年间，英文再次发表时对文中提及具体事件距当时的时间跨度有相应更改，故与中文有所出入，在本版中保留这几种不对应之处。——编者注

1   A review of major areas of research and recent progress in historical geography in China has been published by the author in English in *Geography in China* (Beijing: Science Press, 1984, pp. 133–146).

2   The help of Mr. Alick Newman at University College London in redrawing the maps is gratefully acknowledged.

❾

*   本文为作者 1996 年在美国克莱蒙·麦肯纳学院（Claremont McKenna College）举行的"燕京大学的经验与中国的高等教育学术研究会"上的发言，演讲为英文。中英文皆为作者所著。——编者注

1   Jeffrey William Cody, *Henry K. Murphy: An American Architect in China, 1914–1935*, Chapter 5 "Old Wine in a New Bottle: Yenching University, 1918-1927." A Dissertation of Cornell University for the Degree of Doctor of Philosophy, Cornell University, 1989.

2   Reference: Hou Renzhi, *Anecdotes about Yanyuan* (in Chinese,《燕园史话》), Beijing: Peking University Press, 1988, pp. 74–75.

Susan Chan Egan, *A Latter-day Confucian, Reminiscences of William Hung (1893-1980)*, Cambridge: Harvard University, 1987, pp. 81–85.

3   Recently, with the aid of some newly discovered finds and new investigations in historical geography, I wrote, with William Hung's research as base, the paper "On Mi Wanzhong's 'Map of the Rebuilt Shaoyuan' ", published in 1993 in Vol. 1 of *Guo Xue Yan Jiu* (National Studies) by the Research Centre of Traditional Chinese Culture of Peking University.

最近，我又借助于一些新发现和历史地理的考察，在煨莲师研究的基础上，写了一篇《记米万钟〈勺园修禊图〉》，刊于北京大学中国传统文化研究中心的《国学研究》第 1 卷，1993 年。

4   See The Research Committee on Historical Materials of the Peking Committee of the Political Consultative Conference of the People's Republic (ed.), *Peking under the Japanese Puppet Regime*, Beijing Publishing House, 1987.

中国人民政治协商会议北京市委员会文史资料研究委员会：《日伪统治下的北平》，北京出版社，1987 年。

5   On 19 August 1945, William Hung wrote to inform me that I had been chosen as one of the members of the Yenching University Committee, and urged me to return to Peking to attend the conference. I have added the original letter here, with a translation in English:

Dr. Leighton Stuart has been released on Friday and we talked for days, which was extremely nice. The new university committee has held its first meeting yesterday. Tomorrow (Monday) early in the morning at nine we will have our second meeting. If you, my young friend, would like to be one of the committee members, you will have to return tonight. I tried to phone you several times but couldn't get through, so had no other way than to ask mister Guo to go to Tientsin to invite you. We will talk later. Hastily I remain, wishing you,... Renzhi, good health.

Written on the 19th.

❿

* 本文中文曾发表于《益世报》副刊《史地周刊》1947 年 3 月 18 日版，英文自作者打印稿转录而来。——编者注

⓫

* 英文为侯仁之于 1984 年 7 月 4 日在英国利物浦大学毕业典礼上的讲话，原文无标题，本版标题为编辑后加。——编者注

⓬

* 中英文均为侯仁之原作。英文于 1999 年 11 月 11 日由欧迪安博士（Dr. Diane Obenchain）代为在纽约美国地理学会上宣读。中文稿中原有少数英文夹杂，已由编辑译为中文。——编者注
1 此为中央民族大学旧称，2008 年已更名为 Minzu University of China。——编者注